MOUNTAINS OF EXPERIENCE:
Interdisciplinary, Intercultural, International

*Journal of the
Appalachian Studies Association*

Edited by
Parks Lanier, Jr.

The Appalachian Consortium was a non-profit educational organization composed of institutions and agencies located in Southern Appalachia. From 1973 to 2004, its members published pioneering works in Appalachian studies documenting the history and cultural heritage of the region. The Appalachian Consortium Press was the first publisher devoted solely to the region and many of the works it published remain seminal in the field to this day.

With funding from the Andrew W. Mellon Foundation and the National Endowment for the Humanities through the Humanities Open Book Program, Appalachian State University has published new paperback and open access digital editions of works from the Appalachian Consortium Press.

www.collections.library.appstate.edu/appconsortiumbooks

This work is licensed under a Creative Commons BY-NC-ND license. To view a copy of the license, visit http://creativecommons.org/licenses.

Original copyright © 1989 by the Appalachian Consortium Press.

ISBN (pbk.: alk. Paper): 978-1-4696-3702-0
ISBN (ebook): 978-1-4696-3704-4

Distributed by the University of North Carolina Press
www.uncpress.org

THE INFLUENCE OF THE SMOOT TANNERY ON THE ECONOMIC DEVELOPMENT OF WILKES COUNTY, N.C. 1897–1940, *Barry Elledge* 105

MOUNTAINS OF EXPERIENCE: INTERNATIONAL

MOUNTAIN FORAGERS IN SOUTHEAST ASIA AND APPALACHIA: CROSS-CULTURAL PERSPECTIVES ON THE "MOUNTAIN MAN" STEREOTYPE, *Benita J. Howell* 114

APPALACHIANISM AND ORIENTALISM: REFLECTIONS ON READING EDWARD SAID, *Rodger Cunningham* 125

LLEWELLYN AND GIARDINA: TWO NOVELS ABOUT COAL MINING, *Laurie Lindberg* 133

TRADITIONAL APPALACHIAN CULTURE AND TRADITIONAL SCOTTISH HIGHLAND CULTURE COMPARED: A PERSONAL PERSPECTIVE, *Clyde H. Ray*...................................... 141

Table of Contents

INTRODUCTION, *Parks Lanier, Jr.* 1

KEYNOTE ADDRESS: APPALACHIANS, PIONEERS
FOR THE NEW AGE, *Marilou Awiakta* 6

MOUNTAINS OF EXPERIENCE: INTERDISCIPLINARY

PREHISTORIC AND HISTORIC HUMAN ADAPTATION IN
APPALACHIA: AN ARCHAEOLOGICAL PERSPECTIVE,
C. Clifford Boyd, Jr.... 15

USED PARTS AND THE POETIC IMPULSE: MACHINES AS
ALTERNATIVE MEANS OF EXPRESSION, *Ricky L. Cox* 28

JANE GENTRY: A SINGER AMONG SINGERS, *Betty Smith* 35

LEGENDARY PLACES: THE LITERATURE OF THE GREAT SMOKY
MOUNTAINS NATIONAL PARK, *James E. Byer* 46

JESSE STUART'S ARCHETYPAL VISION OF APPALACHIAN CULTURE:
THE THREAD STILL RUNS TRUE, *Edgar H. Thompson* 55

ACROSS THE MOUNTAINS: APPALACHIAN LITERATURE AND THE
UNSUSPECTING STUDENT, *Teresa Wheeling*........................ 64

MOUNTAINS OF EXPERIENCE: INTERCULTURAL

AGRICULTURE IN PREINDUSTRIAL APPALACHIA:
SUBSISTENCE FARMING IN BEECH CREEK, 1850–1880,
Paul J. Weingartner, Dwight Billings, Kathleen M. Blee 70

BICULTURALISM: A COMPARISON OF CENTRAL APPALACHIANS
AND THE INUPIAT OF ALASKA, *Nelda Knelson Daley* 81

APPALACHIAN CULTURE AS REACTION TO UNEVEN
DEVELOPMENT: A WORLD SYSTEMS APPROACH TO REGIONALISM,
Roberta McKenzie 93

1988 APPALACHIAN STUDIES ASSOCIATION OFFICERS

Grace Toney Edwards..President
Loyal Jones...Vice President
Parks Lanier, Jr. ....Conference Program Chair
Carl Ross....................................Newsletter Editor/Secretary
Ellen Garrison..........................Treasurer/Membership Secretary

MEMBERS OF THE STEERING COMMITTEE

Grace Toney Edwards, Chair

Pat Beaver
Barry Buxton
Ann Campbell
Ellen Garrison
John Inscoe
Loyal Jones

Helen Lewis
Gordon McKinney
Carl Ross
Jean Speer
Eliot Wigginton

MEMBERS OF THE PROGRAM COMMITTEE

Parks Lanier, Jr., Chair

Doyle Bickers
Woodward Bousquet
Howard Dorgan
Wilburn Hayden

Roberta Herrin
Ronald Lewis
Karen Lohr

MEMBERS OF THE CONFERENCE LOCAL ARRANGEMENTS COMMITTEE

Richard Straw, Chair

Pat Cantrell
William Hrezo
Thomas Shannon
Peggy Shiflett

Melinda Wagner
Ron Willoughby
Douglas Woolley

Introduction

This first issue of the JOURNAL OF THE APPALACHIAN STUDIES ASSOCIATION signals that our organization has come to maturity. Helen Roseberry, in writing her introduction to the 1987 proceedings, spoke of how the goals of the first, the 1978, ASA meeting continue to function "as any good foundation will." Writing in 1986, Carl Ross noted that "we can see that there has long been a reciprocal interaction between the Appalachian region and the larger American society." Anne Campbell noted in 1985 discussions on "international perspectives relating to Appalachia." Sam Gray in 1984 recalled how at the first meeting of what became the Appalachian Studies Association Gurney Norman suggested our region is "intricately connected to distant regions and institutions." It was only natural then, like the maturation of a seed well planted and well tended, that the 1988 Conference take as its theme "Mountains of Experience: Interdisciplinary, Intercultural, International."

As we enter a new decade for the Appalachian Studies Association, we take stock of our trials and tribulations, offer proof of the diversity and dignity of highland life, and anticipate the experiments to come. The decision of the Steering Committee to make a record of our "mountains of experience" a more consistent one by establishing this JOURNAL was timely and judicious. Publication of the proceedings of our annual conferences has been important in binding us together, in making us truly an "association."

This JOURNAL will now make our excellent studies more accessible within the region and far beyond it as well. It will be interesting to see in what far corners of the world our voices will be heard.

The best a JOURNAL like this can hope to be is a representative sampling. The life, the joy, the music, the laughter of the 1988 Appalachian Studies Conference at Radford University cannot all be conveyed here. It was our largest conference, both in members attending and members participating. Many of the best things which occurred cannot be conveyed on paper. Not everything which has been written can be included here. Realizing that, the Steering Committee has recommended that a file of all papers submitted be kept, and that ASA members be able to purchase papers which have not been printed. In this JOURNAL you will find information on how you can obtain that material.

The best thing about our association is that there is plenty of room for all the seedlings which have been nurtured these last eleven years and are coming to harvest.

The 1988 Conference was ample proof not only that we work well but that we work well together. In her keynote address Marilou Awiakta caught our essence: "Appalachians are that kind of people, because we remember how to survive, to abide. Our mountains have taught us."

Parks Lanier, Jr., Chair
1988 Program Committee

THE FOLLOWING PAPERS are on file and available for purchase from the Appalachian Consortium. Following each title is the number of pages, including title page, notes, bibliography, maps, tables, etc.

Anderson, William L. Direction of Current Research on the Cherokees. 11

Asbury, Jo Ann. A Pattern that Endures: Marilou Awiakta's Sense of Place. 11

Askins, Justin. Wendell Berry: The Solace of Dark Spaces. 11

Awiakta, Marilou. Appalachians: Pioneers for the New Age. Keynote Address. 13

Berlowitz, Marvin J. and Arthur Slater. The Negative Influences of Neo-Marxist Radical Social Movement Theorists on the Role of Urban Appalachians in the Struggle for School Desegregation: A Case Study of Cincinnati. 28

Billings, Dwight B. and Kathleen M. Blee. Household Structure in a Preindustrial Appalachian Community: Beech Creek, Kentucky, 1850–1942. 22

———, Kathleen M. Blee, and Paul J. Weingartner. Agriculture in Preindustrial Appalachia: Subsistence Farming in Beech Creek, 1850–1880. 16

Blee, Kathleen M. and Dwight B. Billings. Household Structure in a Preindustrial Appalachian Community: Beech Creek, Kentucky, 1850–1942. 22

———, Dwight B. Billings, and Paul J. Weingartner. Agriculture in Preindustrial Appalachia: Subsistence Farming in Beech Creek, 1850–1880. 16

Blethen, H. Tyler and Curtis W. Wood. The Origins of the Normal School Movement in Western N.C. 21

Borman, Kathryn M. and Elaine Mueninghoff. Expectations for Work Roles and Social Roles in an Urban Appalachian School. 32

Boyd, C. Clifford, Jr. Prehistoric and Historic Human Adaptation in Appalachia: An Archaeological Perspective. 26

Byer, James E. Legendary Places: The Literature of the Great Smoky Mountains National Park. 15

Chadwick, Thomas T. Presidential Voting in Southern Appalachia 1920–1952: The Impact of the New Deal Realignment. 19

Conway, Cece. "The Drunken Hiccups": A Tommy Jarrell Fiddle Song and A Distilled Life Story. 15

Cox, Ricky L. Used Parts and the Poetic Impulse: Machines as Alternative Means of Expression. 15

Crissman, James. Changing Rules of Household Headship in the Rural West Virginia Family. 31

Cunningham, Rodger. Appalachianism and Orientalism: Reflections on Reading Edward Said. 15

Daley, Nelda K. Biculturalism: A Comparison of Central Appalachians and the Inupiat of Alaska. 18

Dickerson, Lynn. Joel B. Lemon 1828–1910: Portrait of a Nineteenth-Century Botetourt (Va.) County Farmer. 11

Elledge, Barry. The Influence of the Smoot Tannery on the Economic Development of Wilkes County, N.C., 1897–1940. 17

Fisher, Steve. National Economic Renewal Programs and Their Implications for Economic Development in Appalachia and the South. 34

Fleming, Dan B. Camelot in Appalachia: JFK in the West Virginia Primary of 1960. 11

Howell, Benita. Mountain Foragers in Southeast Asia and Appalachia: Cross-cultural Perspectives on the "Mountain Man" Stereotype. 14

Hyde, William. A Loss Keenly Felt: High School Consolidation and Community (in northwest N.C.). 15

Inscoe, John C. Olmsted in Appalachia: A Connecticut Yankee Encounters Slavery and Racism in the Southern Highlands. 16

Johnson, Charles W. Walter Biggs' Painting of Mr. and Mrs. Joel B. Lemon. 12

Lang, John. The Shape of Love: The Motif of Sacrifice in Two Novels by John Ehle. 18

Lindberg, Laurie. Llewellyn and Giardina: Two Novels about Coal Mining. 14

Lovingood, Paul E., Jr. and Robert E. Reiman. The Structure of Total Personal Income in the Southern Highlands. 18

McGowan, Thomas. The Blue Ridge Hand-Tied Canopy: Cultural Intervention and Family Tradition. 12

McKenzie, Roberta. Appalachian Ethnicity as Reaction to Uneven Development: A World Systems Approach to Regionalism. 20

Mueninghoff, Elaine and Kathryn M. Borman. Expectations for Work Roles and Social Roles in an Urban Appalachian School. 32

Noe, Kenneth W. Internal Improvements, Slavery, and Secession in Southwest Virginia, 1829–1861: A Preliminary Survey. 20

Rasmussen, Barbara. Clay County, W.Va.: The Social Impact of Concentrated Land Ownership. 18

Ray, Clyde H. Traditional Appalachian Culture and Traditional Scottish Highland Culture Compared: A Personal Experience. 8

Reiman, Robert E. and Paul E. Lovingood, Jr. The Structure of Total Personal Income in the Southern Highlands. 18

Salstrom, Paul. The Subsistence-Barter-and-Borrow System in Southern Appalachia's Traditional Life. 22

Simpkins, Karen Li. What "Community" Does the Arbor Preaching Celebrate?: Comparison and Contrast of St. Mary's Loch, Scotland, and "Timber Trace," West Virginia. 28

Sinclair, Bennie Lee. So Silent a Spring in our Mountains: Defoliation and Burning of the Milliken Forest. 8

Slater, Arthur and Marvin J. Berlowitz. The Negative Influences of Neo-Marxist Radical Social Movement Theorists on the Role of Urban Appalachians in the Struggle for School Desegregation: A Case Study of Cincinnati. 28

Smith, Betty. Jane Gentry: A Singer Among Singers. 12

Spalding, Susan Eike. Old Time Square Dancing as a Reflection of Social and Economic Changes in Upper East Tennessee. 14

Stamm, Henry E., IV. Valle Crucis: An Experiment in Episcopal Monasticism. 13

Stanwitz, Sandra L. Intercultural Factors Affecting Access to Legal Aid: Improving Appalachian Women's Lives. 14

Stevens, Elizabeth C. Appalachian Agriculture in the 1980s: Part-time Christmas Tree Growers in Avery Co., N.C. 11

Thompson, Edgar H. Jesse Stuart's Archetypal Vision of Appalachian Culture: The Thread Still Runs True. 16

Thorn, William H. Technique and Reality: The Jewel Photograph (of Joel and Eliza Lemon). 11

Tribe, Ivan M. "Thar's Gold in Them Hillbillies?": The Six Decade Experience of the Stoneman Family as Commercial Appalachian Musicians. 17

Wallenstein, Peter. Civil War and Appalachia: Union Troops from East Tennessee. 15

Weingartner, Paul J., Dwight Billings, and Kathleen M. Blee. Agriculture in Preindustrial Appalachia: Subsistence Farming in Beech Creek, 1850–1880. 16

Wheeling, Teresa. Across the Mountains: Appalachian Literature and the Unsuspecting Student. 13

Wolz, Lyn. The White Top Folk Festival as an Agent of Change in Traditional Song Repertories. 17

Wood, Curtis W. and H. Tyler Blethen. The Origins of the Normal School Movement in Western North Carolina. 21

West, Mark D. Regional Determination and Public Opinion. 95

Appalachians: Pioneers For The New Age

*Keynote Address
by
Marilou Awiakta*

Before beginning my speech, I should tell you that I already may have committed an unpardonable sin for a Southerner—embarrassed you in public. This afternoon Channel 7 TV interviewed me. I thought the camera was off when the interviewer asked, "What do you think about the stereotyping of Appalachian people?"

His question hit a nerve. I grew up in Oak Ridge, Tennessee, where "outsiders" were in the majority and often said about us natives, "These people don't have any culture. They don't articulate properly. They're non-progressive, lazy, etc." What do I think of such disdain?

I managed to reply calmly. "Appalachians must name ourselves, tell our own stories—define ourselves from the inside out. When stereotypers assume the power to define us, they have control over us."

"And what if the stereotypers won't listen to reason?" I shoved my fist up in the old battle-charge sign and yelled, "Go get 'em!"

The camera was on. If my outburst embarrassed you, I apologize. But if I spoke what you're thinking, I'm glad. At this point in America's history, Appalachians must uphold our values and proceed. Our country needs us. Why that is so, is the subject of my talk.

A New Age is said to be coming—an age of harmony and peace. But it's having a hard time getting here. Consider recent news on television: The Iranian arms scandal. The Wall Street crash. Evangelists Jim Bakker and Jimmy Swaggart preaching against sin in public—and practicing it in private. If the New Age is to come, it needs the help of pioneers of grit and gumption, who know how to connect to the land and to each other. Appalachians are that kind of people, because we remember how to survive, to abide. Our mountains have taught us.

By "Appalachians" I mean the three major ethnic groups: Native Americans, African Americans and European Americans, most of whom have Celtic roots. We are all tribal peoples. Deep in our blood is the memory of the sacred circle of life—the Creator, Mother Earth and all that lives therein. In an age of fragmentation and disintegration, Appalachians remember the ways of connection. We are fit pioneers for the New Age.

You may ask, "How did you come to this conclusion?" I did it the mountain way—by thinking about it for 30 years. During that time I learned that acquired knowledge helps, but when you have your back to the wall, it's heritage that brings you through.

My thought originates in the Native American tradition, which views the Creator, nature and humanity as a circle—a web of life. To speak of "Mother Earth" and of all nature as our "relations"—brother, sister, and so on—is neither romantic nor figurative. It is a literal expression of reality—we are all interconnected. If Mother Earth thrives, all thrive. If she dies..."what goes around, comes around." In this circle, time is a continuum where past, present and future flow as one and where life moves in harmony with the rhythms and cycles of nature. If you're saying to yourself, "But other Appalachians think this way too," then we are of one mind.

The Cherokee advise, "Look at everything three times. Once with the right eye. Once with the left eye. And once from the corners of the eyes, to see the spirit—the essence—of what you're looking at." From here on, let's follow that advice.

With your right and left eyes, look at the people who are here at the conference. There are adults from many states. And for the first time, the youth are convening with us. . . . Or is it the first time? In ages past when decisions of great moment were to be made, our ancestors responded in a traditional way. If we look at this audience from the corners of our eyes, we see an ancient pattern: the gathering of the clans.

Look at the conference program with two eyes only. Once Appalachia was defined primarily in terms of the white European male. But presentations this year include both genders, as well as the three major ethnic groups that inhabit our mountains. Looking at the program from the corners of our eyes, we see a mending of the circle—a reweaving of the web of life.

This conference is historic. I am honored to have been invited to share thoughts about our heritage and the strength it has to see us through. With that power sustaining us, we consider some of the harsh realities of life in 1988.

An overwhelming concern is the threat of nuclear holocaust. I have a sense of *dèjá vu* about it because fear of it was real to me in the late 1940's, when I was growing up in Oak Ridge. The Cold War with the Russians was "hot." Because of its nuclear industry, Oak Ridge was a prime target for attack. At school, scientists warned us about the deathlight, fireball and fall-out. Disaster drills were more frequent than fire drills. In case of early warning, the city had an evacuation plan. I was in my early teens—and terrified I'd never live to grow up.

I asked Mother about it. She said, "Now, Marilou, if the bomb ever drops, it's all over. There're only two major roads out of Oak Ridge. Think of 75,000 panicked people trying to get out! We'd be better off to stay put. If the worst does happen, we have faith that our family will come down on the Other Side and be together again. In the meantime, in case they don't drop the bomb, you'd better go study your French!"

This—not the fatalism stereotypers tout—is the true meaning of Appalachian stoicism. It is the courage to face the world as it is and continue your life with a measure of grace.

I kept studying. In 1956, through the University of Tennessee, one of my dreams came true: a scholarship to the Sorbonne. Another dream collided with it. *The* man, Paul, asked me to marry him instead, promising he would take me to live in France one day. He did. That's how, in 1964, I got to Laon and became an interpreter for the U.S. Air Force during the NATO withdrawal. College courses had prepared me for the French language but not for its use in power politics. Heritage did that. I remembered the mountain philosophy that later became the poem, "Trail Warning," in *Abiding Appalachia:* "Beauty is no threat to the wary/who treat the mountain in its way/the copperhead in its way/and the deer in its way/knowing that nature is the human heart/ made tangible."[1]

My father had always said, "If you treat a bear like a dog, you'll wind up with your face slashed—or worse." And Mother added, "It's the same with people. Learn a person's nature. If you meet a 'copperhead,' give him a wide berth. If you have to go in close, take a hoe!"

These and other Appalachian teachings stood me in good stead. As years passed my conviction grew that the fusion of my Cherokee/mountain heritage with the experience of growing up on the atomic frontier was, in truth, a practical and inspiring heritage. In 1978, the fruits of my thought were published in my first book, *Abiding Appalachia: Where Mountain and Atom Meet.* The title poem is the crux of the book:

> Ancient haze lies on the mountain
> smoke-blue, strange and still
> a presence that eludes the mind and
> moves through a deeper kind of knowing.
> It is nature's breath and more—
> an aura from the great I Am
> that gathers to its own
> spirits that have gone before.
>
> Deep below the valley waters
> eerie and hid from view
> the atom splits without a sound
> its only trace a fine blue glow rising from the fissioned
> whole and at its core
> power that commands the will
> quiet that strike the soul,
> "Be still and know . . . I Am . . ."[2]

Lifting our eyes to the hills has always been the primary source of help for Appalachian people. But we have come to the point in history where even the mountains themselves are in jeopardy. The following three recent poems deal with greed as a destroyer of our Mother Earth and our people, with stereotyping as a killer of the human spirit, and with what many Native Americans still call "the other world"—a world that forces us to cram the roundness of our lives into squares. Coping with these disintegrating forces will require the energies of both elders and youth:

DYING BACK[3]

On the mountain
the standing people are dying back—
hemlock, spruce and pine
turn brown in the head.
The hardwood shrivels in new leaf.
Unnatural death
from acid greed
that takes the form of rain
and fog and cloud.

In the valley
the walking people are blank-eyed.
Elders mouth vacant thought.
Youth grow spindly, wan
from sap too drugged to rise.
Pushers drain it off—
sap is gold to them.
The walking people are dying back
as all species do
that kill their own seed.

WHAT THE CHOCTAW WOMAN SAID[4]

My husband is an alcoholic.
He went to the VA and he told them,
"My spirit is sick. I am dying."
They said, "You need tests. Go to the lab."
He came home.

The last time he went they
sent him to a psychiatrist.
When my husband told him, "My spirit is
sick. I am dying," the psychiatrist
said, "What do you mean by spirit?"

My husband came home. He'll never go back.
My only hope is to get him to a medicine man
but the great ones are in the West.
I don't have the money to take him.

The trouble is, most people look down on
us and our culture. It's harder on a man.
It kills his pride. For a woman it's not
as bad. We have to make sure the children
survive, no matter what.

If I stay with my husband, the children will
get sick in their spirits. They may die.
I have to leave him.

SQUARED

TIME SQUARED to the clock. LIFE SQUARED to television/credit card/truck/car/train/jet—to cubicles piled in high rude rectangles. FILL IN THE SQUARE: name/address/telephone/sex/age/race/occupation. STAY IN THE LINES . KEEP TO TIME SLOTS: work/play/eat/sleep/love. Box 'em, label'em, stack 'em up. COMPETE! Slash to the top of the pyramid. COMPUTE! Compute! Compute! ("No, you can't have your veteran's benefits. The computer shows you 'dead.'") GET HERESY UNDER CONTROL. The creation is clear-cut: God is God; nature is "the other." Choose your side. WOMEN, SQUARE your shoulders, starve your bodies straight. Curves are out. MEN, SQUARE your hearts. Produce! Produce! Feelings don't raise the GNP. The shuttle's SEALS are at RISK . . . ? LAUNCH it! Seven people smeared across the sky translate to the TV monitor, "OBVIOUSLY WE HAVE A MAJOR MALFUNCTION."——OBVIOUSLY.

Via television millions saw *Challenger* and its astronauts explode and scrawl a fiery hieroglyphic on the curved wall of space. A warning. "*Humans have lost connection—with ourselves and each other, with nature and the Creator.*" We do have a major malfunction. We've felt something seriously amiss for a long time. Now, in the blood of seven—a number sacred to the Cherokee and mystic to many of the world's peoples—we have clear warning. To survive, we must set ourselves right and reconnect.

Some people continue to ignore the warning. Others join a growing movement toward the whole, exploring new ways of healing the deep slashes that sever us from relationship and hope. One way is to go back to our homeground and find within it our deepest roots. In that spirit, the clans have gathered at Radford this weekend—in the heart of the mountains that unite Appalachians of all ethnic backgrounds, mountains that have taught generation after generation to face reality and abide in their own souls.

The onslaught of industrialization is slashing "all our relations." We love our land. We don't want to be separated from it. But we have to earn a living. If we don't adapt enough to the square world to survive, we will die. If we adapt too much, we will not survive. What many of us want most is to find somehow a way to live in the round, despite the strictures of contemporary society.

Outsiders who look with two eyes only have stereotyped Appalachians as "primitive, backward, non-progressive, Bible-toting and, sometimes, crazy as loons." We have become too prone to ignore—or at the very worst, to accept—stereotypers' definitions. If we view their words from the corners of our eyes, in the light of our own interpretations, they describe exactly the qualities needed to cope with the dilemma of disconnection. Pioneers of the New Age of harmony and peace have to be independent, sturdy, tenacious, ingenious, spiritually centered—and audacious. One might even say, *"bodacious!"* Are we Appalachians perfectly suited for the task? Our mountains tell us that we are. They also tell us that no individual or ethnic group can mend the circle and reweave the web of life alone.

A great sign of hope comes from the Cherokee. Since April, 1984, the vibrations of it have been traveling from Red Clay, Tennessee, through the root systems of the ancient forests of Appalachia. It is the song of a people who have kept faith with their traditional values and who have reunited their nation at last.

With an ear to the ground, we listen. From the corners of our eyes we see an ancient image emerging: Awi Usdi, Little Deer. A spirit messenger from the sacred circle, a spirit of reverence and justice.

From the heart of the mountain he comes, with his head held high in the wind/Like the spirit of light, he comes—the small white chief of the deer.

> When one of his own is slain
> he instantly draws near
> and finding clotted blood on the leaves

he bends low over the stain—
"Have you heard . . .
Has the hunter prayed words of pardon
for the life you gave for his own?"
If the answer be "No" then Little Deer
goes—invisible, fleet as the wind—
and tracks the blood to the hunter's home
where he swiftly pains and cripples his bones
so he never can hunt again.[5]

"From the heart of the mountain he comes" . . . to assure us that the circle of blessing, like the circle of destruction, is eternal.

It did not seem so when the seven mother clans of the Cherokee met in 1837 at Red Clay for the last council meeting. Within a year the people were walking the Trail of Tears. Of the 17,000 removed to Oklahoma, 4,000 died along the way. Their nation and their web of life were in shreds. In the dominant culture predictions abounded that in 200 years, there would be no more Cherokee.

Tribal elders looked at the damage three times: "In the seventh generation," they said, "the Cherokee will rise again." As generations struggled to reweave the web, these words were passed along. During the fall of 1986, the message went out: "The Eastern and Western councils will reunite at the Red Clay Historical Area (near Cleveland, Tennessee), April 6–7, 1984."

What happened next cannot be scientifically explained. It can only be evoked in terms of the spirit. The Cherokee consider Red Clay sacred ground, hallowed ground. And there, from the heart of Mother Earth, a magnetic energy began to emmanate. In the Four Directions of America north, south, east and west—families prepared for the journey. Early in April they set out for the gathering of the clans.

"We don't know what will happen," said Carol Allison, assistant to Ross Swimmer, principal chief of the Cherokee Nation of Oklahoma. "We've told everybody—the media, the public—that this reunion is to be dignified, an historic council meeting, not a 'drums and feathers' event. But the more we tell them that, the more they want to come. It's still winter in East Tennessee. What if people swamp the motels and others are left milling around in the cold? We're estimating 20,000 people now, about a third of them Cherokee."

What was pulling the non-Indians to Red Clay? Curiosity for some. But for most it seemed to be what a man from Wisconsin said, "The Cherokee have made it through this old world and managed to stay who they are. My wife and I want to see it. We want our children to see it. Because if the Cherokee can make it, we can too."

On the eve of the reunion Paul, our son Andrew, and I stood on the balcony of our motel in Cleveland. Although the driving rain had abated, the mountains seemed frozen, their trees bare-limbed against dark clouds. About five miles away were the council grounds. We knew that medicine men had already come in private to perform the ancient ceremonies—songs and dances to bless Mother Earth and call up her regenerative energies. The sacred ground was ready. But what would happen tomorrow?

The reunion will forever be in the present tense. From the beginning, the sun is radiant. A benevolent and steadily rising wind carries the scent of pine and new green. Among the knolls and planes of the council ground, people flow around the traditional pattern of the web: the open-sided council house in the center; the formal platform and receptacle for the sacred fire on a nearby knoll; at some distance a circle of food and craft tables and beyond that small meadows where children romp. There is a feeling of connection and peace among the people and a murmur that is lively and content. Good humor but no rowdiness. At the same time, there is a look on the faces of many, the expression of those who listen inwardly to another dimension and find it good.

At the ampitheater in the lee of one hill, all is quiet. On the grass stage where the council is in session, Chief Robert Youngdeer of the Eastern Band raises his arms toward the surrounding woods, where trees are tipped with fluttering new leaves. He says, "When we came to Red Clay the trees were closed and cold. See in one day how the leaves have unfurled..."

Looking upward, we in the audience feel his meaning:

See how Mother Earth has renewed herself
how the Cherokee have endured
how hope unfurls ... invincibly!
We shall renew our strength
and mount up with wings ...

Something extraordinary is moving among us. Governor Alexander calls it "electricity." A reporter says, "An aura." Many who know the legend say, "*Awi Usdi* walks among us ..."

I gather Little Deer's image, a healing medicine for bleak seasons I know will come again, and weave it into the last great ceremony of the reunion: the return of the sacred fire.

Signifying the presence of the Creator,/sun/spirit of the people, the sacred fire has been kept burning since the beginning of Cherokee history. On the Trail of Tears it was secretly transported to Oklahoma. In 1951, an ember was returned to the Eastern Band in North Carolina. It, circling back to Red Clay, is in the hands of the youth—the seventh generation. Ten young men, bearing torches, have run in relay the 130 miles from Qualla,

N.C. As word passes of their approach, young women in traditional ribbon dresses clear a way for them among the crowd gathered on the West Knoll. Then they stand as honor guards along the path, where spring grass ripples verdant and sweet in the wind.

The crowd is silent as the men run slowly toward the crest of the knoll. There the torches are joined together and passed around to the council members before coming back to the chiefs for the ceremonial lighting. The chiefs invoke the fire's ancient meanings and Youngdeer extends its light to include the present when he says, "The flame stands for freedom and friendship between the whites and Indians. We hold neither hatred nor malice in our hearts. We remember the past but look to the future."

A powerful presence sweeps through the crowd. Because we have gathered here with reverence and love, *Awi Usdi* is walking among us. A peaceful power assuring all people that if justice and reverence prevail, in the fullness of time, sorrow may be eased, wounds may be healed. And within whatever morass we find ourselves, there is always a green path that leads to the top of the hill, where the sacred fire burns for us all.

A New age *is* a-borning.
Appalachians can help it thrive.
We are one people.

Notes

1. Marilou Awiakta. *Abiding Appalachia: Where Mountain and Atom Meet* (Memphis, 1978). p. 37.
2. Ibid, p. 89.
3. Marilou Awiakta. *Tennessee Conservationist* (Jan./Feb. 1987). p. 12.
4. Marilou Awiakta. *Now and Then*. (Autumn, 1986). p. 23.
5. Marilou Awiakta. *Abiding Appalachia*, p. 18.

Prehistoric and Historic Human Adaptation in Appalachia: An Archaeological Perspective

by
C. Clifford Boyd, Jr.

Abstract

Through the past millenia, a variety of cultures have entered the Appalachians and have adapted to their rich and varied environment. These cultures include prehistoric Native Americans who directly used the raw materials of this region to produce their tools, and who subsisted on a wide variety of native plants and animals still seen today. The early European settlers added new layers of cultural complexity to the human fabric of the Appalachians. Their language, metal tools, economic and political systems profoundly and permanently transformed the contemporary Native American cultures, and formed the basis for the modern cultural adaptations to these mountains.

Archaeological analysis can provide a unique perspective on these cultural transformations through its study of material culture and past settlement-subsistence patterns. In this paper, the contributions of archaeology to the study of cultural adaptations in the Appalachians are outlined. Examples of archaeological research on Native American and Anglo-American settlement and subsistence patterns in East Tennessee, western North Carolina and southwest Virginia are also discussed.

Introduction

For the past 11,500 years, humans have adapted to the environment of the Appalachians. This process of adaptation has taken many different forms at different times, and has involved the use of a variety of natural resources. The young science of archaeology, through its emphasis on the recovery, analysis and interpretation of the material culture remains of past peoples, can provide a unique perspective on the problem of human adaptation. This perspective *is* unique because it can address *both* the synchronic (i.e., observations of a culture at a single moment in time) and the diachronic study (i.e., observation of changes in cultures over time) of human cultures.

In this paper, both perspectives are used to examine change and continuity in the use of space and of natural resources in upper East Tennessee, southwest Virginia and western North Carolina (Figure 1). Specifically, the Tennessee component of this tri-state study area encompasses that portion of the upper Tennessee Valley north and east of the Little Tennessee River. This includes portions of the Blue Ridge and Ridge and Valley physiographic provinces of upper East Tennessee, and the Pigeon, French Broad, Nolichucky, Clinch, Powell, Holston, and Watauga, as well as the Little Tennessee River drainages. The North Carolina component includes the Appalachian Summit area of the western portion of the state, and primarily sites along the Watauga and New River drainages. The Virginia component also primarily encompasses the Blue Ridge and Ridge and Valley or Appalachian Valley physiographic provinces, and the upper Powell, Clinch, Holston, New and Dan River drainages.

Since the measure of time is an important consideration for any archaeologist, I will begin this examination with a brief discussion of the cultural and temporal periods represented in the archaeological record of this study area. Then, I will embark on a more detailed discussion of human adaptation and transformations in settlement patterns and material culture through time.

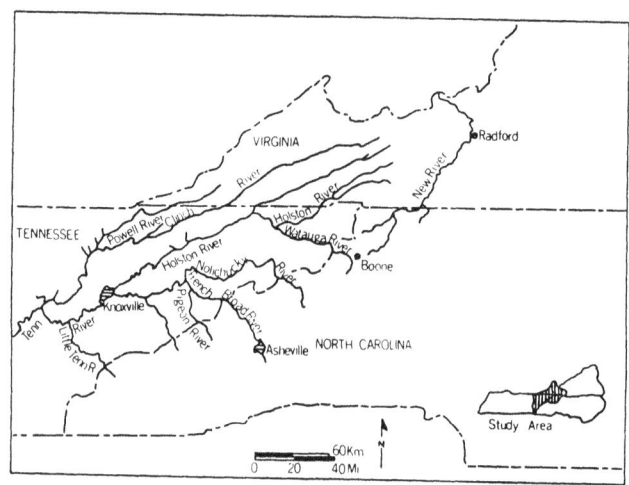

Figure 1. Location of the Study Area.

Temporal Periods

The temporal periods represented in the archaeological record of the study area, along with their corresponding dates, are depicted in Table 1. While the Archaic and Woodland periods as presented here can certainly be divided into early, middle and late periods manifesting distinctive artifact styles and other characteristics, this paper emphasizes changes in material culture as these relate to adaptation to the environment, rather than the historical nature of stylistic change.

Evidence for the first human occupation and use of the study area occurred during the Paleoindian period (Purrington 1983; Turner 1984). These earliest Native Americans lived in small, nomadic bands, hunted late Pleistocene megafauna (such as the mastodon) and foraged wild plant foods. The characteristic tools of the Paleoindians were large stone spear points with concave or "fluted" midsections. Paleoindian occupations are almost exclusively identified by the archaeological recovery of these distinctive points.

The following Archaic period represented a long period of human adaptation to an essentially modern post-Pleistocene environment. The Ice Age megafauna disappeared, and Native American groups began to exploit modern wild animals (such as white-tailed deer, bear and rabbits) wild seeds, and the nut harvest from deciduous trees like the oak, walnut and hickory (Chapman 1975, 1977, 1981). Although the initial domestication of some plants occurred by the late Archaic (Smith and Cowan 1987; Yarnell and Black 1985), dependence was still focused on wild food resources.

Some major technological changes occurred in this area during the *Woodland* period. These included the widespread manufacture and use of clay pottery, the development of the bow and arrow (during the late middle Woodland), and the introduction of maize as a domesticated food plant (Boyd 1986; Chapman 1973; Chapman and Crites 1987). There is also evidence for population growth *and* more complex social organization. For example, mound construction, which began during the latter portion of this period (Keel 1976), certainly was the result of an organized, community effort on the part of the builders.

The Late Prehistoric period was a time of increasing cultural complexity and diversity in this region. As defined here, this period included cultures that some would still define as "Woodland" (Hoffman and Foss 1980), and other societies with more elaborate sociopolitical systems which in the southeastern United States have been called "Mississippian" (Griffin 1967; Smith 1986). These latter Native American cultures developed their complex sociopolitical organizations through long distance trade and a greater dependence on maize. Examples of such cultures include the Pisgah of the Appalachian Summit of North Carolina (Dickens 1976) and Dallas in East Tennessee (Polhemus 1987). These groups showed an emphasis on religious ceremonialism in the form of mound building and the production of specialized artworks, such as shell gorgets engraved with rattlesnakes, sun discs, and other symbols. Increased intercultural conflict is evidenced by the identification of wooden palisades and other defensive features around villages.

In other areas (like southwestern Virginia) Native American cultures selectively expressed certain traits, such as a greater reliance on domesticated plants and the construction of palisaded villages. However, the absence of mound building and extreme status differentiation in their populations suggests a less complex social organization (Egloff 1987). Variety and diversity in ceramic decoration and form also increased significantly during this period (Boyd 1987).

The *Protohistoric* period began with the earliest contacts between Native Americans and the Spanish explorers Hernando de Soto and Juan Pardo (Hudson et. al. 1984, 1985). During the subsequent two centuries, many Native American cultures suffered extinction as a result of European-introduced diseases and warfare. Many Native American groups also quickly became dependent on European traders for firearms and other goods as a result of the European-stimulated trade in deerskins (Peebles 1983). Native American cultures competed with one another for these lucrative trade contacts, and this competition often led to intertribal warfare. Dramatic population migrations, abandonment of previously occupied areas, disruption of social organization, and the amalgamation of previously distinct tribal groups were common events. Thus, the most distinctive characteristic of this period was the process of acculturation all Native American populations were forced to undergo as a result of European contact.

Finally, with the *Historic* Period, European settlements and settlers dominated areas formerly occupied and abandoned by Native American cultures. While Native Americans (primarily the Cherokee) still lived in the area, their continued survival was largely under the control of the British (and later, American) economic, legal and military systems. In this study area, European settlers introduced many elements of material culture from their native Britain, and continued to receive British ceramics and other items from the colonial trade network.

TABLE 1. Suggested Chronology for the Study Area.

Temporal Period	Dates
Historic	A.D. 1750 - present
Protohistoric	A.D. 1540 - 1750
Late Prehistoric	A.D. 1000 - 1540
Woodland	1200 B.C. - A.D. 1000
Archaic	8000 - 1200 B.C.
Paleoindian	9500 - 8000 B.C.

Cultures existing during the major periods briefly reviewed above each used and affected the natural resources of the Southern Appalachians in different ways. Archaeologists can study the artifacts, structures, storage pits, wells and other features these earlier cultures left behind and learn something about their adaptive use of space within the context of the resources of the study area. In the second part of this paper, I will discuss both inter- and intrasite settlement patterns as reflected in the material culture remains from these temporal periods.

Settlement Pattern Variation Through Time

The study of settlement patterns is the study of how humans use space. Archaeologists study this aspect of human cultures by locating and analyzing archaeological sites and looking for patterns in their spatial distribution. An archaeological site is a location which contains the remains of past human activity. It is important to realize that a site may or may *not* be the actual place where these past activities occurred (Ammerman 1981; Whyte 1984)—erosion, flooding and other natural forces can remove and redeposit artifacts and bones together, forming sites which are *natural* and not *cultural* in origin. However, for the many archaeological sites which *were* actual loci of past human activity, we can study the organization of space within the site (intrasite settlement patterns) and the organization of space between sites of the same cultural group (intersite settlement patterns) starting with the Paleoindian period.

Paleoindian settlement in the study area is poorly documented and understood for a number of reasons. First, most of the recovered Paleoindian artifacts (the characteristic fluted points discussed above) are found on the surface with no other materials in association with them. This severely limits our ability to fully understand the use of space by these people, particularly when we acknowledge that these artifacts have likely been moved and redeposited from their original locations by natural forces over the millennia, or remain deeply buried in river sediments (see Turner 1984). Second, the scarcity of these artifacts, particularly in the Appalachian Mountains (Purrington 1983; Turner 1984), suggests that major portions of the study area were only rarely utilized by these early human groups.

In order to more fully understand the Paleoindian settlement pattern in the region, researchers recommend a focus on the investigation of resource areas known to have been exploited by Paleoindian populations in this and other regions. These include high quality cryptocrystalline stone resources which provided raw materials for the production of stone tools, and "locations having high potential for exploitable fauna and flora . . ." (Turner 1984:213) (such as salt licks, water holes and springs, and gaps or narrow valleys) which likely served as animal migration routes (Gardner 1980, 1983).

Evidence for exploitation of the study area in the subsequent Archaic period is much more complete. Early Archaic sites are more numerous than Paleoindian sites (Turner 1984) and indicate efficient exploitation of upland zones in the upper Watauga Valley of North Carolina and the Great Smoky Mountains (Bass 1977; Purrington 1983), *and* the use of floodplain zones and local stone resources in the Little Tennessee River valley (Chapman 1975, 1977, 1978). A wide range of habitats with diverse food resources continued to be exploited throughout the Archaic period in the Appalachian Mountains (Purrington 1983). In some areas, however, late Archaic sites were primarily located in the main river valleys and floodplains (Baden 1985; Bass 1977). The increased use of floodplain zones in the late Archaic has been noted in western North Carolina, southwest Virginia and East Tennessee, as well as other parts of Virginia and Delaware (Catlin et. al. 1982). This change has been interpreted either as an intensive concentration on the exploration of riverine resources *or* as an emphasis on the exploitation of quartzite outcrops and gravel bars for stone for the production of large bifacial spear points (Bass 1977). For the lower Little Tennessee River valley, Baden (1985) suggests that increased exploitation of river terraces may be related to the expanding use of cultigens and early horticulture.

The frequency of late Archaic sites in the uplands of the Blue Ridge in Virginia also increases over that of the earlier Archaic and Paleoindian periods. These sites are found in all environmental zones (hollows, saddles, ridges, upland basins, gaps, slopes and foothills) (Barber and Tolley 1984; Hoffman and Foss 1980). Hoffman and Foss (1980: 194–204) call the late Archaic and the subsequent early portion of the Woodland period in the Blue Ridge the "period of primary forest efficiency." They equate this "florescence of occupation" to Joseph Caldwell's (1958) concept of the development of an efficient, stable occupation of the woodlands of eastern North America based on hunting, gathering and fishing.

By middle Woodland times (beginning about the time of Christ), Native Americans in the study area began to live in more sedentary villages, and there was an increase in the exploitation of floodplain areas (Bass 1977; Ferguson 1986; Purrington 1984). Although specialized exploitation of the uplands for hunting continued, the increasing frequency of the floodplain sites certainly reflects a growing emphasis on the cultivation of domesticated plants. Such plants as squash and gourd were already being cultivated and maize was introduced by A.D. 200 (albeit in small quantities) (Chapman and Crites 1987).

During the subsequent Late Prehistoric period in the Appalachian Summit region of North Carolina, there was an increasing "nucleation of communities on fertile soils in broad river valleys and the emergence of a hierarchy of communities" (Purrington 1983: 147), particularly between A.D. 1300–1500 (Dickens 1986). This emphasis on the construction of large, palisaded villages on or near lands with prime agricultural soils is also seen in East Tennessee and southwest Virginia (Baden 1985; Hoffman and Foss 1980). Because of the scarcity of extensive floodplain soils along portions of the New River and other areas of southwest Virginia, some sedentary villages were located on less agriculturally productive marginal zones (Custer 1984: 81–82). Although the uplands were less extensively exploited for resources than in the earlier Archaic and Woodland periods, as hunting territories for these sedentary populations, they still had an important, specialized role in the total settlement system.

Changes in settlement patterns, particularly in western North Carolina and East Tennessee, are noted during the Protohistoric period (Dickens 1986; Schroedl 1986b). The nucleated settlements and complex sociopolitical organizations of the Late Prehistoric cultures in these areas started to disintegrate, leading to a more dispersed settlement pattern and less social stratification in the early Qualla and Overhill Cherokee in these areas. These changes were possibly stimulated by European contact, environmental instability, or both (Dickens 1986: 85); however, this social collapse was less severe in the Appalachian Summit region of North Carolina because agriculture was not as important as in areas with more extensive floodplains. This flexibility in resource exploitation (i.e., dependence on both wild and domesticated foods) was, in the long run, more adaptively advantageous during this stress-filled period (Dickens 1986: 87).

The settlement pattern of the sociopolitically less complex tribal societies of southwest Virginia apparently did not change as drastically in the Protohistoric period as in East Tennessee and western North Carolina. However, abandonment of settled villages certainly occurred during the last century of this period. Early historic accounts of the last half of the 18th Century by European settlers only mention contact with Cherokee or Shawnee hunting parties (Egloff 1987).

As indicated by abandonment of previously settled areas, change in Native American societies as a result of European contact was sometimes quite dramatic. In western North Carolina, the Qualla Cherokee population moved . . ."from the northern and eastern portion of the Appalachians toward the western and southern portions (Dickens 1986: 84)." Trade contacts with Europeans led not only to changes in Native American economic systems and resource exploitation, but to technological and sociopolitical change (Peebles 1983; Riggs 1987; Schroedl 1986a). Extreme factionalism developed within many Native American societies such as the Cherokee, wherein certain "progressive" or "Anglo-Cherokee" (Riggs 1987) groups attempted to acculturate themselves into Anglo-American culture by adopting Anglo-American names, behavior and material culture. Other more "traditional" elements tried to maintain their aboriginal social and settlement patterns. However, with the forced removal in the 1830s of most of the Cherokees and other "civilized tribes" to the western territories, Anglo-American material culture and settlement patterns became dominant in the study area.

Criteria for site location in the early Historic Period by the earliest Anglo-American settlers were comparable to those used by Native American agriculturalists. Based on a survey of early Historic Period sites in Rockbridge County, Virginia, Adams and McDaniel (1984: 227–228) note that many eighteenth century settlements were on floodplains. Many of these sites also contained evidence for prehistoric Native American occupation (Adams and McDaniel 1984; Boyd and Riggs 1986). In the 1820s or 1830s, movement of occupations into hollows began to occur, with hollows being intensively occupied in the last half of the nineteenth century (Adams and McDaniel 1984: 227). Access to water sources, as well as access to agricultural land was certainly an important determinant in site location.

Building construction by the earliest Anglo-American settlers was also adopted by some of the early Historic Native Americans. Log cabin construction by the Historic Cherokee, for example, is well documented in the enthnohistoric records of East Tennessee and western North Carolina (Riggs 1987; Schroedl 1986a).

Finally, the use of space around eighteenth and nineteenth century historic sites was similar to that of previous Native American groups. Prehistoric Native American villages are often identified by the occurrence of trash (or midden) deposits around structures, or in a ring around a central plaza area (Ward 1986). These deposits often contain broken pottery, stone tools and flakes, animal bone, charred wood, nuts and seeds, and other debris. Often, large pits or features (which were dug for use in food storage) were subsequently filled with debris after their intended use. Similar "kitchen middens" and refuse dumps have been archaeologically identified around Historic Anglo-American structures. Many historical archaeologists have discovered that by excavating these middens, one may learn a great deal about foods eaten, dinnerware and glassware used, and even methods of food preparation of Anglo-Americans of varying socioeconomic status (Boyd and Riggs 1986).

Stanley South (1977) has identified several Anglo-American disposal patterns of the eighteenth and nineteenth centuries. The *Brunswick Pattern* is one in which the inhabitants discarded their refuse adjacent to their homes. This deposit occurs usually at the back, but also at the front door. This pattern is so distinctive that one can locate building entrances simply on the basis of concentrations of refuse discovered during excavation. In addition, the frequencies of artifacts recovered from these deposits can suggest something about the activities performed by the inhabitants of the structure. The *Carolina Artifact Pattern* is one in which the higher frequencies of kitchen artifacts (ceramics, cooking utensils, glassware) and bone indicate domestic food processing and consumption. This pattern is most common around kitchens or at the rear of a house. The *Frontier Artifact Pattern* is one with a higher frequency of architectural items (such as nails), indicating a non-kitchen area or, as the name implies, a more isolated frontier habitation with reduced access to stores, trading posts, and associated amenities. As with Native American features which have ceased to fulfill their original function, historic cisterns, privies and cellar holes were subsequently used as artifact dumps, and as with Native American contexts, these features can tell us a great deal about the material culture of the people who produced, used and discarded these items.

Summary

In conclusion, the study area is environmentally and topographically extremely diverse. There are a number of river systems with varying amounts of floodplain, and sometimes extreme uplands containing mineral and faunal resources. Preagricultural Native American peoples exploited all these environments for edible seeds and nuts, deer and other wild game, and for raw materials such as quartz, quartzite and chert with which to make stone tools. Later Native American cultures using agriculture in the mountainous portions of the study area were not as dependent on this means of subsistence as were other groups living in areas with broader floodplains more suitable for crop production. Still, larger village sites and more intensive utilization of available floodplains occurred in the Woodland through Protohistoric periods.

Exploration and settlement of the study area by Europeans introduced new socioeconomic, political and technological systems which profoundly altered the course of human occupation of the Appalachians. However, early Anglo-American settlers, dependent on an agricultural subsistence base, utilized space in ways similar to those of preceding Native American agriculturalists. They, too, selected floodplains and prime agricultural soils as initial habitation sites and stored foods and deposited refuse in similar patterns. Early Historic Native Americans, in turn, adopted the log cabin structure by the mid 1700's.

This brief review of the prehistoric and historic culture history and adaptation of human groups to a portion of the Southern Appalachians illustrates several important points. First, archaeological investigations of this region (through surface survey and identification of sites and more detailed excavations of some of these sites) can uniquely document culture change and continuity over millennia in cultures for which there are no written records. Archaeology's reliance on the study of the material culture of past peoples also enables the archaeologists to specifically identify and interpret changes in the use of natural resources and the exploitation of space (settlement-subsistence patterns). Finally, the comparison of Native American and Anglo-American adapative patterns can suggest some interesting continuties between these groups that may not be evident from historical documentation.

Acknowledgements

The author sincerely thanks Dr. Melinda Wagner, Dr. Gerald Schroedl and Donna Boyd for reviewing an earlier draft of this paper, and for providing useful comments which greatly improved the quality of the final product. Sheila Swart drafted the figure, and Carolyn Sutphin typed the manuscript. As always, any errors or omissions are the responsibility of the author.

References Cited

Adams, James T., Jr., and John McDaniel
    1984 A Research Design for Archaeological Interpretations of Upland Historic Sites: The Opportunities and Challenges. In *Upland Archaeology In the East: Symposium 2*, edited by M. B. Barber, pp. 220–230. Cultural Resources Report No. 5. U.S. Department of Agriculture, U.S. Forest Service-Southern Region.

Ammerman, Albert J.
    1981 Surveys and Archaeological Research. *Annual Reviews in Anthropology* 10:63–88.

Baden, William W.
    1985 Evidence of Changing Settlement Patterns In the Little Tennessee River Valley of East Tennessee. In *Exploring Tennessee Prehistory: A Dedication to Alfred K. Guthe*, edited by T. R. Whyte, C. C. Boyd, Jr., and B. H. Riggs, pp. 135–156. Report of Investigations No. 42. Department of Anthropology, University of Tennessee, Knoxville.

Barber, Michael B., and George A. Tolley
    1984 The Savannah River Broadspear: A View from the Blue Ridge. In *Upland Archaeology in the East: Symposium 2*, edited by M. B. Barber, pp. 25–43. Cultural Resources Report No. 5. U. S. Department of Agriculture, U. S. Forest Service—Southern Region.

Bass, Quentin R., II
    1977 *Prehistoric Settlement and Subsistence Patterns in the Great Smoky Mountains*. Unpublished M. A. thesis, Department of Anthropology, University of Tennessee, Knoxville.

Boyd, C. Clifford, Jr.
    1986 *Archaeological Investigations in the Watauga Reservoir, Carter and Johnson Counties, Tennessee*. Report of Investigations No. 44 Department of Anthropology, University of Tennessee, Knoxville.

    1987 Cultural Selectionism and the Prehistory of Upper East Tennessee and Adjacent Regions. Paper presented at the 52nd annual meeting of the Society for American Archaeology, Toronto.

Boyd, C. Clifford, Jr., and Brett H. Riggs
 1986 *The 1986 Archaeological Investigations at the Tipton-Haynes Historical Farm.* Draft report submitted to the Center for Appalachian Studies and Services, East Tennessee State University, Johnson City Tennessee.

Caldwell, Joseph L.
 1958 Trend and Tradition in the Prehistory of the Eastern United States. *American Anthropological Association, Memoir No. 88.*

Catlin, Mark, Jay F. Custer, and R. Michael Stewart
 1982 Late Archaic Culture Change in Virginia: A Reconsideration of Exchange, Population Growth, and Migrations. *Quarterly Bulletin: Archaeological Society of Virginia* 37(3):123–140.

Chapman, Jefferson
 1973 *The Icehouse Bottom Site, 40MR23.* Report of Investigations No. 13. Department of Anthropology, University of Tennessee, Knoxville.

 1975 *The Rose Island Site and the Bifurcate Point Tradition* Report of Investigations No. 14. Department of Anthropology, University of Tennessee, Knoxville.

 1977 *Archaic Period Research in the Little Tennessee River Valley—1975: Icehouse Bottom, Harrison Branch, Thirty Acre Island, Calloway Island.* Report of Investigations No. 18. Department of Anthropology, University of Tennessee, Knoxville.

 1978 *The Bacon Farm Site and a Buried Site Reconnaissance.* Report of Investigations No. 23. Department of Anthropology, University of Tennessee, Knoxville.

 1981 *The Bacon Bend and Iddins Sites: The Late Archaic Period in the Lower Little Tennessee River Valley.* Report of Investigations No. 31. Department of Anthropology, University of Tennessee, Knoxville.

Chapman, Jefferson, and Gary D. Crites
 1987 Evidence for Early Maize (Zea Mays) from the Icehouse Bottom Site, Tennessee. *American Antiquity* 52:352–354.

Custer, Jay F.
 1984 A Controlled Comparison of Late Woodland Settlement Patterns in the Appalachian Highlands. In *Upland Archaeology in the East: Symposium 2,* edited by M. B. Barber, pp. 75–101. Cultural Resources Report No. 5. U. S. Department of Agriculture, U. S. Forest Service-Southern Region.

Dickens, Roy S., Jr.
 1976 *Cherokee Prehistory.* University of Tennessee Press, Knoxville.

 1986 An Evolutionary - Ecological Interpretation of Cherokee Cultural Development. In *The Conference on Cherokee Prehistory,* assembled by D. G. Moore, pp. 81–94. Warren Wilson College, Swannanoa, North Carolina.

Egloff, Keith T.
1987 *Ceramic Study of Woodland Occupation Along the Clinch and Powell Rivers in Southwest Virginia*. Research Report Series No. 3. Department of Conservation and Historic Resources, Division of Historic Landmarks, Richmond, Virginia.

Ferguson, Leland
1986 Indians of the Southern Appalachians Before DeSoto. In *The Conference on Cherokee Prehistory*, assembled by D. G. Moore, pp. 1–6. Warren Wilson College, Swannanoa, North Carolina.

Gardner, William M.
1980 Settlement-Subsistence Strategies in the Middle and South Atlantic Portions of the Eastern United States during the Late Pleistocene and Early Holocene. Paper presented at the American Anthropological Association 1980 annual meeting.

1983 What Goes Up Most Come Down: Transhumance in the Mountain Zones of the Middle Atlantic. In *Upland Archaeology in the East: A Symposium* edited by C. R. Geier, M. B. Barber, G. A. Tolley, pp. 2–42. Cultural Resources Report No. 2. U. S. Department of Agriculture, U. S. Forest Service-Southern Region.

Griffin, James B.
1967 Eastern North American Archaeology: A Summary. *Science* 156:175–191.

Hoffman, Michael A., and Robert W. Foss
1980 Blue Ridge Prehistory: A General Perspective. *Quarterly Bulletin: Archaeological Society of Virginia* 34(4):185–210.

Hudson, Charles, Marvin T. Smith, and Chester B. DePratter
1984 The Hernando DeSoto Expedition: From Apalachee to Chiaha. *Southeastern Archaeology* 3:65–77.

Hudson, Charles, Marvin T. Smith, David Hally, Richard Polhemus, and Chester B. DePratter
1985 Coosa: A Chiefdom in the Sixteenth-Century Southeastern United States. *American Antiquity* 50:723–737.

Keel, Bennie C.
1976 *Cherokee Archaeology*. University of Tennessee Press, Knoxville.

Peebles, Christopher S.
1983 Paradise Lost, Strayed and Stolen: Prehistoric Social Devolution in the Southeast. Paper prepared for the Southern Anthropological Society Meeting, Baton Rouge, Louisiana.

Polhemus, Richard R.
1987 *The Toqua Site—40Mr6: A Late Mississippian Dallas Phase Town* (2 vols.) Report of Investigations No. 41. Department of Anthropology, University of Tennessee, Knoxville.

Purrington, Burton L.
1983 Ancient Mountaineers: An Overview of the Prehistoric Archaeology of North Carolina's Western Mountain Region. In *The Prehistory of North Carolina: An Archaeological Symposium*, edited by M. A. Mathis and J. J. Crow, pp. 83–160. North Carolina Division of Archives and History, Raleigh.

Riggs, Brett H.
 1987 *Socioeconomic Variability in Federal Period Overhill Cherokee Archaeological Assemblages.* Unpublished M. A. Thesis, Department of Anthropology, University of Tennessee, Knoxville.

Schroedl, Gerald F. (editor)
 1986a *Overhill Cherokee Archaeology at Chota-Tanasee.* Report of Investigations No. 38. Department of Anthropology, University of Tennessee, Knoxville.

 1986b Toward an Explanation of Cherokee Origins in East Tennessee. In *The Conference on Cherokee Prehistory*, assembled by D. G. Moore, pp. 73–80. Warren Wilson College, Swannanoa, North Carolina.

Smith, Bruce D.
 1986 The Archaeology of the Southeastern United States: From Dalton to DeSoto, 10,500 B.P. In *Advances in World Archaeology*, vol. 5, edited by F. Wendorf and A. E. Close, pp. 1–92. Academic Press, Orlando.

Smith, Bruce D., and C. Wesley Cowan
 1987 Domesticated Chenopodium in Prehistoric Eastern North America: New Accelerator Dates from Eastern Kentucky. *American Antiquity* 52:355–357.

South, Stanley
 1977 *Method and Theory in Historical Archaeology.* Academic Press, New York.

Turner, E. Randolph
 1984 A Synthesis of Paleo-Indian Studies for the Appalachian Mountain Province of Virginia. In *Upland Archaeology in the East: Symposium 2*, edited by M. B. Barker, pp. 205–219. Cultural Resources Report No. 5. U. S. Department of Agriculture, U. S. Forest Service-Southern Region.

Ward, H. Trawick
 1986 Intra-site Spatial Patterns at the Warren Wilson Site. In *The Conference on Cherokee Prehistory*, assembled by D. G. Moore, pp. 7–19. Warren Wilson College, Swannanoa, North Carolina.

Whyte, Thomas R.
 1984 The Watauga Impact: 35 Years of Lacustrine Influence on Archaeological Sites in Northeast Tennessee. In *Upland Archaeology in the East: Symposium 2*, edited by M. B. Barber, pp. 192–204. Cultural Resources Report No. 5. U. S. Department of Agriculture, U. S. Forest Service-Southern Region.

Yarnell, Richard A., and M. Jean Black
 1985 Temporal Trends Indicated by a Survey of Archaic and Woodland Plant Food Remains from Southeastern North America. *Southeastern Archaeology* 4:93–106.

Used Parts and the Poetic Impulse: Machines as Alternative Means of Expression

by
Ricky L. Cox

Before I was old enough to drive, I dreamed often of driving a black pickup truck up one of the hills that surrounded my home. It was always the same truck, a '66 Ford with a short bed and Twin-I-Beam emblems on the front fenders. Though I haven't dreamed that dream in many years, the magic carpet feeling of gliding effortlessly over those confining hills has stayed with me and long outlasted my desire for a black pickup. The magic carpet was mine also in waking hours, for the world of books was opening ever wider before my eyes. These pleasures did not seem incompatible then, but I see now a gulf between them, and though it is not of my own making, I feel ever more strongly its presence as I move from one world, that of engines and machines, to the other, that of literature. I seem not quite to belong to either as long as I am associated with the other. But, maybe the needs these things fulfill are similar in some not easily discerned way. Certainly, they are not the same, but as a means of exploring ourselves and the worlds we live in, they have between them curious parallels which suggest that in this context, the difference between them is more one of form than of function.

Machines are not unique in this parallel relationship with literature, but I have singled them out for two reasons. First, machines have been, literally, vehicles of change in the Southern Mountains during the last century, arguably more so than in most other parts of the country. Their use in tapping natural resources in certain regions of Appalachia has made of them unwitting accomplices to a terrible crime, while in other areas, they have provided people with a means of sharing the benefits of industrial society without giving up physical ties to home and to the relative self-sufficiency this has traditionally afforded. Second, I wish to reconcile my fascination with machinery with my passion for words. As long as I see the needs each of these fulfill as essentially different, I can not help but compare them one against the other and choose one, and the world to which it belongs, as the more worthwhile. My best option, then, is to prove to myself that these interests are sprung from a single seed and that their juxtaposition is in fact a balance rather than a conflict.

In their broadest usage, both machinery and written language are tools, forged and hammered out by countless hands and minds, honed and refined to further the countless pursuits of mankind. Used strictly in this sense, they offer limitless possibilities to the development of society, but little to the growth of the inner man. In this use they have value only to the extent they serve the purpose at hand and as yet, have no spark or breath to give them life of their own. They begin to assume an intrinsic value, only after they are turned to purposes not purely practical, the most popular being diversion and entertainment. Herein lies the connection between my dreamed of truck and *Tom Sawyer*. Both could carry me away, and although the linkage is stretched when the automobile becomes real and Tom and Huck remain bound between the covers of a book, both continue to fill a need for adventure.

While the images conjured up by a literary craftsman are much more universal, and certainly safer, they may be no more satisfying to the reader than are racing engines to those conversant with the language of V-8s and 4–barrel carburetors. On summer nights, when I was a teenager, I would sometimes hear the local hotrodders out ripping around in their cars, running at top speed, or perhaps autographing the hardtop in smoking rubber. The noise they made, rising and falling as they passed through hollows and screamed down long ridges, was a signal to my mother to see that her children were not near the road. To my father, it may have been a reminder of some foolishness he had outgrown. But to me, and others who heard as I did, it was Grendel stalking the moors, daring me out to chase him, and twist not his arm, but a four-speed gearshift. It was a modern Minotaur, demanding a sacrifice. Having no wine-dark seas on the shores of the Blue Ridge we live out our Odysseys on two-lane highways in weekly episodes. A poem by Parks Lanier, Jr., entitled "Hephaestus," marks this connection:

> Smear the marble torso with axle grease
> And stick it deep beneath some jacked-up car
> On a Saturday morning when the sun
> Is warm enough for him to stretch shirtless
> And shoeless on the ground. Then you will see
> How the mountain heirs of Phidias work,
> Not in ivory or stone but in gears
> And piston rings, the true lords of metal
> Who comprehend a car with artist's eyes.
> No assembly lines for them; they work alone
> Or two or three at most to share their craft
> And later test their strength on some straight road
> That valleys out between ridge and river,
> Perfect acropolis marked out by signs

> That say Prepare to Meet thy God, and there
> In smoke and dust on wings of steel they do. (Lanier 26)

How well the need to escape our ordinary lives and become a vicarious or self-styled hero is met by fast cars or epic poetry depends upon many variables in both the person and the chosen medium. Epic poems don't need gas and excessive enjoyment of them won't cause your insurance to go up, but neither can they be driven to work on Monday morning. The important thing is that both may satisfy the need each of us has to visit from time to time the borders of our safe existence.

A psychologist might tell us that the need to escape reality stems, in part, from a feeling of ineptitude in the face of an increasingly complex existence. This psychologist might also suggest that the mastery of some reasonably difficult activity may provide a needed identity along with a familiar source of analogy and metaphor useful in assimilating experiences outside the selected activity.

So it is that the writer finds pleasure in manipulating words and phrases. A lifetime is not long enough to exhaust the possibilities for improvement. The search for the ideal voice and style is as futile as it is alluring, for there are always two elements to the equation, both ever-changing. The man who lays aside his pen is no longer he who sat down to write and the reader who is moved in the least must also be transformed in some minute way.

Absorbed in his quest for perfection, the writer is unaware of his counterpart in the basement garage next door. But are they not alike? Is the mechanic not also intimate with the tools of his trade? He chooses a camshaft as carefully as the poet chooses an adjective, knowing that it will alter the music of his finished piece. Of each component part he knows the individual qualities and function. They are to him as the parts of speech to the writer for they give voice and tone to the completed machine, urging from it fire and thunder or a smooth, silky hum. Pistons become guttural verbs. Their solo voices are harsh, discordant explosions, but when multiplied by four, or six, or eight, or even sweet sixteen, their cadence quickened to four-thousand RPM, they sing a siren song that even Jim Wayne Miller's Brier could not help hearing. He tells how

> his mind throbbed and hummed
> like pistons under the hood of a good truck
> hauling his thoughts over a long open highway,
>   (23–25, Miller 35)

The power of this song is no accident, for the pieces of the ensemble are chosen carefully, just as words and phrases are sifted laboriously by the writer seeking the perfect balance. Indeed, these things may be siblings, for they wear each other's metaphors with style. Economy is important to the poet. He must squeeze a lot of mileage out of his words. The writer of short fiction depends on quick acceleration and can haul but little unnecessary luggage. The novelist is permitted to turn on the cruise control from time to time and has room for the neighbors and the in-laws.

From the writer's point of view, it may sound as if I am making a case for machines as metaphor instead of medium. In one sense, I am, but my point is that the abundance of appropriate metaphor between the two points to a parallel relationship which is more than coincidental. Which element of a metaphor is to be familiar and concrete, and which to be imaginative depends upon the experience of the user. Metaphors should not be thought of as one-way glass. Images, and the illumination they bring with them, should move freely in both directions.

The automobile, as seen in the last paragraph, lends itself to such interchange because it is a major element of popular culture and familiar to everyone. But it is by no means the only subject upon which the inventive hand and mind may turn themselves. In our factories we have machines of infinite variety. They weave fine, beautiful things and stamp out thousand upon thousand of ugly, practical paraphernalia of industrial society, and in everything they do, building and tearing down, molding and crushing, they are but incarnations of the nature of man and every aspect they present is but a face of mankind. And though the builder may not be conscious of such grand notions, he takes pleasure in his small fulfillment of man's age old desire to make his physical ability to do, equal to his mind's ability to conceive. The finished product is almost incidental, for it is the making and doing, looking always for ways to do better that are so attractive.

Machines serve to express a need for adventure and a desire to master the physical world with mechanical extensions of ourselves. These things are in some sense poetic, yet they are inferior to written expression in an important way. Because these things are immediate and firsthand, their expression is inseparable from the actual event. To express, in this direct way, a lifetime of creating things of iron and steel, I must spend a lifetime. And though you stood beside me through all those years, if you did not speak the language of gears and wheels, you might never have heard my song at all. Without the writer's ability to compress long spans of time, this means of expression is too impossibly long to share.

It is also impossibly short. Some say that the true fascination of speed and power is that it provides an avenue to approach death and then snatch oneself back at the last instant. Faster and faster we round the curve, edging ever nearer to the sudden and awful knowledge that we have gone too far. Without the writer's ability to stretch that tiny point in time and examine it at length, we are compelled to live it over and over, staring wide-eyed at an instant, until satiated or dead, and in neither instance does anyone else benefit.

Without a universal language, or the key elements of it, I am bound to barter with hours and minutes and raw emotion. If you cannot pay in kind we are separated forever. Written language provides a wonderful fluid currency through which we may translate our separate experiences into a common tongue. This is accomplished through symbolic representation after the manner of stocks and bonds or commodities. You don't have to drive your hogs through New York City, nor must I route my corn through there on the way to North Carolina, yet there is free exchange between us.

The poet-mechanic has no such medium of free, universal exchange. His language is exclusive at best, and at worst is unique to him. Without a broader means of communication, a need may be expressed only by satisfying it. What is wanted is a means to express *recognition* of the need without having to repeat over and over the actions that fulfill it. The missing ingredients, of course, are symbols. To the writer, this presents no problem as the elements of his medium, words, have no function apart from their use as symbols. Machines, on the other hand, have definite intended functions which complicate their use as symbols and necessitate the imposition of certain conditions.

Before a symbol may appeal to the broadest possible audience, the bonds of time and space, which are essential to firsthand expression of the poetic impulse, must be cast off. Otherwise, the object would have symbolic meaning only to the few who chanced to observe a particular event at a particular place and time. The thing which most firmly binds a machine to a specific place and time is the function it was originally intended to perform. It is required, then, that a distance be somehow achieved between the machine and its original function. One way to do this is to select as symbols machinery which no longer has a function to perform, whether it has succumbed to, or outlived, the purpose for which it was intended. The common name for these marvelous metallic metaphors is junk.

Once the distracting clutter of regular practical function has been raked away by time or accident, machines are free to reveal the countless secrets entrusted to them by our next door neighbors and by nameless, faceless people now buried in Chicago or Des Moines or Detroit. Embedded in the caked grease and faded paint are bits and pieces of people's lives, for machines, like few other objects in American life, are repositories of dreams.

The details are mostly gone, erased by time and distance, but the outline of a grand story remains. There was once a man, or several men, who wanted to build a machine to do more and better, a machine to make farm work easier or transportation more accessible to the common people.

Perhaps he wanted to get rich, too, but that is beside the point. After many setbacks and disappointments, the dream becomes reality, and if the first one is the only one, or the first of ten million, it and each successor will carry with them a little of the mind and spirit that gave them substance. Emerson wrote of good books: "They impress us with the conviction that one nature wrote and the same reads" (57). May it not be the same with a truck, in whose proud lines and sturdy frame we perceive a mind that moves as our own?

Most of these pioneers set their names to their work so that the hills are now dotted with monuments to J.I. Case, John Deere, and Henry Ford. Yet the great majority of the hands that made reality of grand visions belonged to men now nameless, even then faceless, and the dream is theirs also. A factory is built and men come to work to find or finance their own dreams. At a county seat freight depot hundreds of miles away another dreamer waits, able at last to buy a piece of equipment he thinks will help him finally get ahead. Their individual stories are lost, but some hint of them clings to objects once so much a part of their lives. We might search and question and fill in many of the gaps, but with no more than stands before us we know that all these countless people lived and hoped and worked for something better. Here is the proof, a rusted hunk of dreams.

The dreams, perhaps, are visible only to another dreamer, but the long days between are written plainly. There are dents and welded places that tell of bad luck and sledgehammer persuasion. Cracked water jackets and radiators remember some cold winter night and makeshift repairs bespeak a flat broke native genius.

History is often most interesting as a backdrop to personal experience. The stories we cling most tightly to are about ourselves and those dear to us. It is probable, then, that the most popular function of junk as symbol, is junk as journal. Among the wealth of used parts found in discarded machinery is a long life battery which can jump start a hundred memories in an instant. In a culture described as oral, we must make use of unconventional recording devices, things that bring to mind good friends and good times, triumphs and tragedies, and a multitude of other associations attached to things once a regular part of our immediate environment.

As symbols, machines lack the universality and clarity of words, yet they enjoy an advantage in that they appeal directly to the physical senses. The visual impact is obvious, as is the tactile, and usually a variety of identifiable aromas may be stirred up by removing appropriate parts or covers. You may learn, even, how old cars taste if you lay under one long enough. The single missing stimulus is sound, and it may be the one hardest to do without. Even though they may be eloquently mute, machines denied their voices are estranged from their primitive native tongue. I believe that the restorer of machines is keenly, though perhaps not consciously, aware of this silence, and that as a poet at heart he sounds his own voice by resurrecting one thought to be stilled forever. Able to speak again, the machine tells anew the dreams once attached to it and adds a new verse to its song, that of the latest dreamer who would hear it sing once more. And for as long as it is able to speak, the reborn machine will tell their many names over and over, though it be in a strange tongue all men have hearkened to but none may fully comprehend.

It has been my intention here to present an aesthetic, as opposed to cultural, perspective on discarded machines, but I feel compelled to make an observation about the Appalachian affinity for broken, obsolete, or worn out things. Certainly this may be construed as frugality, but I believe that it represents also a wholeness in perspective that may be generally lacking in this country. To say that junk is ugly because it is not pretty indicates a difference of opinion, but to say that it is not pretty because it is old indicates a basic difference in philosophy. A culture which hides from itself the concept of growing old and can see no intrinsic value in inanimate things which are no longer productive has blinded itself to the cyclical nature of all things, manmade or otherwise. When we create a facade of perpetual newness by banishing old machines from the landspace are we not exercising the same rationale that banishes our old people to nursing homes? They can not work; let us put them aside.

One day last fall, a friend of mine, James Bowman, was telling of having just seen the film *Deliverance* for the first time. Early in the film, in a scene set in a junkyard, one of the characters says something like, "I always wondered where everything ended up." It occurred to Mr. Bowman that, among all the coming and going and hustle and bustle of modern life, it is good to know, now and then, where something ends up. I think so too, and wonder if a poet might like that idea. If you see one today, tell him about it.

References Cited

Bowman, James. Conversation with the author. Willis, Virginia, 1987.
   Deliverance, John Boorman, Director; Warner Brothers, 1972.

Emerson, Ralph Waldo. "The American Scholar." *The Portable Emerson*. New Edition. Ed. Carl Bode. New York: Penguin Books, 1981.

Lanier, Parks Jr. "Hephaestus." *Appalachian Georgics*. Radford, Virginia: Unighorn Books, 1983.

Miller, Jim Wayne. "On the Wings of a Dove." *The Mountains Have Come Closer*. Boone, North Carolina: Appalachian Consortium Press, 1980.

Jane Gentry: A Singer Among Singers
A Biographical Sketch

by
Betty Smith

On October 6, 1987 an historical marker was erected by the State of North Carolina in front of a house called "Sunnybank" in Hot Springs. It read:

BALLADRY

English folklorist Cecil Sharp in 1916 collected ballads in the "Laurel Country." Jane Gentry who supplied many of the songs lived here.

From Jane Gentry Cecil Sharp collected sixty four songs and ballads, more than from any other person in this country. "Sunnybank" is a lovely old house, now known as "The Inn at Hot Springs," which Mrs. Gentry ran as a boarding house. The "Laurel Country," so named because of the abundance of rhododendron, called "laurel" by the people who live there, is that part of northwest North Carolina which borders on Tennessee.

This woman who "lived everyday as if it were her last" was described as having "dozens of ballads at her command" and having the ability to "roll out verse after ... verse with no faltering or seeming effort." Her youngest daughter, while a student at Duke University, said that her mother had "a wonderfully retentive memory," and all these songs she had learned by rote from her mother and from other folk-singers in her community."[1]

This remarkable lady was the bearer of a tradition of songs, ballads, tales, and riddles that came to her from her maternal grandfather, Council Harmon. His descendants have carried on the richest and liveliest heritage of Jack Tales in America. Jane Gentry was the first member of this extended family to be discovered by collectors and folklorists. She was a major contributor to Cecil Sharp and provided the first texts of the Jack Tales for Isabel Gordon Carter. Members of this family with such names as Ward, Harmon, Hicks, and Presnell have made valuable contributions of songs and stories. Ransom Hicks, Mrs. Gentry's father was also a member of this family.

Jane Gentry was born in Watauga County in 1863, the daughter of Ransom and Emily Harmon Hicks. Ransom Hicks was a minister, a farmer and a Federal soldier. About 1875 he moved his family from Watauga County to the Meadow Fork section of Spring Creek in Madison County, some twenty miles from the town of Hot Springs. Jane Hicks married Jasper Newton Gentry in 1879 and they built a home on Meadow Fork in 1880 near Keenersville Christian Church. Ransom Hicks was the church's first preacher and Jane became the singing leader.[2]

Jane and Newt (as he was commonly called) Gentry reared nine children, seven of them born while they lived on Meadow Fork. They farmed the rocky hillside and Newt raised a tobacco crop every year, taking it to market in Marshall in his wagon in the fall.

Although Jane Gentry had little education, she valued it and was a "born teacher." She was described by her daughter, Nola Jane, as being "a very unusual person who could always figure out things." The Gentrys wanted their children to have as much education as they could get. They moved the family to Hot Springs in 1898 so that the children could attend Dorland Institute (to become Dorland-Bell School in 1918), a Presbyterian mission school, for eight months of the year instead of three or four months afforded by public schools. All nine children attended Dorland Bell and eight of them graduated. Mrs. Gentry did laundry, cleaned faculty rooms and paid tuition with apples, vegetables, and handwoven coverlets.[3]

The town of Hot Springs is located in a fertile valley on the French Broad River, six miles east of the Tennessee border. It is surrounded by the high crests of the Pisgah and Unaka Mountains and is bounded by Pisgah National Forest. Because of the warm springs in the town it became famous as a resort area as early as 1800. The Western North Carolina Division of the Richmond and Danville Railroad was completed through the town in 1882 and in time six passenger trains stopped every day. The Mountain Park Hotel with its 175 rooms and ballroom, billiard room, bowling alley, tennis courts and golf course, as well as several boarding houses, accomodated the tourists who came to Hot Springs, "The Healthiest Place in America."[4]

The move to Hot Springs must have been quite an experience for the Gentry family. They had always lived up a "holler" in a rural area, living off the land, resourceful and self-sufficient. Hot Springs was a thriving community at that time. However, there is no evidence that Jane Gentry was uprooted from the mountain culture in which she had grown up. The family was known to be "hard working" and "close knit," and continued to be so.[5]

Irving Bacheller, a famous writer of that day, was a great admirer of Mrs. Gentry. We cannot know how closely he adhered to her words, but he did record his conversations with her and used them in his stories. They certainly give an impression of how life was on Meadow Fork for this young family. He quoted her as saying, "Often in plantin' or hoein' time, Pappy an' me u'd work all night together in the cove. 'Bout the only chanst we had to visit like we used to done. We'd have our suppers at midnight, an' go back an' scratch around on the slick mount'inside 'twil daylight come an' the babies 'gun to holler. Nex' day I'd be kindly tired—I would. I'd lay down on the bed 'twil I'd see some little feller come in with holes in his breeches. Then I'd clomb out, an' pray, an' take up my burden."[6]

Those early years must have prepared her for almost anything. She said, "I just saved every feather an' put 'em away in a poke that hung by the fireplace. Never see no money. Saved everything else er I reckon we'd 'a' starved. All summer I'd kindly scratch up the sunlight an' save hit for the dark days. Hit come handy when the childern got the measles an' I got hit too. Holped me when one got the tyford fever. I 'member I had to give her a teaspoonful o' milk every five minutes. When I'd go to sleep in the night the spoon would drop out o' my hand an' wake me up an' tell me to get up an' tend to my work."[7]

Mellinger Henry could have been describing Jane and Newt Gentry when he wrote, "They still have in them the stuff of their pioneer ancestors and are able to endure hardships without murmur and stubbornly wrest a livelihood out of the mountain soil. Apparently this continuous life of hardship has not made them bitter. Rather they have seemingly grown richer in the eternal verities of human life. In doing so, they have acquired qualities so rarely found in the human race. They have a sane and healthy independence, a practical philosophy learned from Nature and severe environment, a kindly human relationship one to another, and an innate culture that shows itself particularly in their fine courtesy."[8]

Jane Douglas, daughter of Maud Gentry Long, in commenting on a description of the lives of her mother and her grandmother as being "hard," said that neither one of them would have wanted that said about them. She spoke of her mother as always being "on top" and "exuding hope."[9] Mrs. Gentry was invariably described as being "happy" and "cheerful." By most people's standards Jane Gentry's life was not easy, but there is not a trace of self-pity in remembrances of her.

She said: "Sometimes the neighbors would send for me to get the blues tuk off 'em, an' I'd go an' pray with 'em, nurse the sick an' tell 'em stories an' cheer 'em up."[10] This attitude of neighborliness and hard work continued when the family moved to town. Although Hot Springs attracted tourists and temporary residents, the local people agree that there was little cash money and that people in the town raised most of what they ate. They say that neighbors and families looked after each other.[11]

In 1905 Emma Bell Miles wrote, "Nearly all mountaineers are singers. Their untrained voices are of good timbre, the women's being sweet and high and tremulous, and their sense of pitch and tone and rhythm remarkably true."[12] There are few people alive today who heard Jane Gentry sing. Her songs were written down, tunes and lyrics, by Cecil Sharp and his assistant, Maud Karpeles, but there are no recordings of her voice. Mr. Bill Moore, who lives on Meadow Fork, called "Aunt Janie" a "singer among singers." He described her as a wonderful person and "the most beautiful singer you ever heard." He also said that Maud Long was just like her mother and "because her mother liked to sing so well, she went and took music lessons and became a music teacher."[13]

Elizabeth ("Peggy") Dotterer, age 85, was a contemporary of Nola, the youngest Gentry daughter. She has a remarkable memory and is generally accepted as the historian of Hot Springs. She was fascinated by Jane Gentry's singing. She said, "I have never heard as good a ballad singer as she was. She was a generation back more genuine than anyone else I have ever heard. Maud Long was a good singer, but there was something pure about Mrs. Gentry's singing. She was absolutely natural." Mrs. Dotterer described Mrs. Gentry as "the sweetest, most cheerful, pleasant person always . . . There was a special kind of atmosphere in her house. It seemed natural for her to sing and tell stories. I was fascinated by her."[14]

Cecil Sharp talked of how this art form was woven into the everyday life of the people, how some songs were even connected to certain chores.[15] Emma Bell Miles wrote, "Had I but words to say how these tunes are bound with the life of the singer, knit with his earliest sense-impressions, and therefore dearer than any other music could ever be —impossible to forget as the sound of his mother's voice."[16]

In 1947 one of Jane's daughters, Maud Gentry Long, recorded for the Library of Congress ballads, songs and tales she had learned from her mother. The following was her introduction to the Jack Tales and Mrs. Long's granddaughter, Daron Douglas said that her grandmother always gave the same introduction whether she was telling them to one child or to a group.

> "I cannot remember when I heard the Jack, Will, and Tom tales for the first time. For we grew up on them like we did the mountain air and the lovely old ballads that my mother used to sing to us.
>
> "But the occasion for the tales is a very vivid memory: It would be on a long, winter evening when, after supper, all of us were gathered before the big open fire, my mother taking care of the baby or else the baby was in the cradle very near to mother. And she would be sewing or carding.
>
> My father would be mending someone's shoes or maybe a bit of harness. The older girls were helping with the carding or the sewing. And all of us little ones would either have a lapful or a basket full of wool out of which we must pick all the burrs and the Spanish needles and bits of briars and dirt against the next day's carding. For my mother wove all of this wool that had

been shorn from the backs of our own sheep—raised there on the farm that was in the heart of the Great Smoky Mountains in North Carolina—into linsey-woolsey, or hers and our dresses, or into blue jeans for my father's and brother's suits, or into blankets to keep us warm, or into the beautiful patterned coverlets, to say nothing of all the socks and stockings and mitts and hoods that it took for a large family of nine children. And so she needed every bit of the wool that she could get ready.

And to keep our eyes open and our hearts merry, my mother would tell these marvellous tales—the Jack, Will, and Tom tales."[17]

Mrs. Gentry was said to have had "back trouble" and to have been "terribly bent over." In spite of this, "she never complained nor let it interfere with her work. When I think of her," Peggy Dotterer said, "I always think of 'busyness'. Her hands were always busy and she kept everyone's hands busy. She never let anyone sit emptyhanded." The people who lived in Mrs. Gentry's boarding house, some of whom were teachers, always helped out. She wove, spun, tatted, knit, and crocheted, and she was always teaching other people to do things with their hands. Said Mrs. Dotterer, "I could go there and before I knew it I was peeling apples, shelling peas, or stringing beans. And she would sing and tell stories while we worked."[18] Apparently for Jane Gentry songs and stories were not performances. They were a natural part of her everyday life.

Richard Chase speaks of this practical application of the Jack Tales, "That of 'keeping the kids on the job' for such communal tasks as stringing beans for canning or threading them up to make the dried pods called 'leather britches'." Mrs. R. M. Ward tells: "We would all get down around a sheet full of dry beans and start in to shelling 'em. Monroe would tell the kids them tales and they'd work for life."[19]

Elmer Hall, in his proposal which resulted in Sunnybank being placed on the National Register, said that Mrs. Gentry and Mrs. Long "shared mountain food, songs, and tales with hundreds of students, boarders, and travelers who passed through Hot Springs."[20] Everyone who remembered Mrs. Gentry recalled the long table filled with delicious food. James Gentry, a grandson, spoke of how she "baked wonderful bread. I could smell it baking down the street."[21] And after supper there would be songs and storytelling.

In 1916 Cecil Sharp came to Madison County. He was interested in the songs and ballads of British origin. The "Laurel Country" proved to be fertile ground for traditional music. He wrote of his experiences " . . . I discovered that I could get what I wanted from pretty nearly everyone I met, young and old. In fact I found myself for the first time in my life in a community in which singing was as common and almost as universal a practice as speaking.[22] But in any community there are those who know more songs and sing them better. When Cecil Sharp came to Hot Springs he was referred to Jane Gentry, and he made at least eight visits to listen to her.

In 1923 Isabel Gordon Carter collected folk tales from Mrs. Gentry and fifteen of these were printed in *The Journal of American Folklore*. She told the collector she had learned the "Old Jack, Will and Tom" tales from her grandfather who had learned them from his mother. At first she did not take seriously the collector's request for stories. She had sung ballads and songs for Cecil Sharp and other collectors, but no one had asked her for the stories which she told to amuse children. But she kindly agreed, saying: "Old Jack, Will, and Tom tales they are called. They're the oldest stories that ever been in existence, I reckon. Old Grandpop aluz told us—we'd hire him to tell us. Law, he could tell 'em!"[23]

Before her death in 1925 Jane Gentry had a reputation as story teller and singer which extended far beyond Madison County and Hot Springs. A picture of Jane Gentry appeared in *Wide World Magazine* ca. 1923 with the caption: "Mrs. Jane Gentry of Hot Springs, N. C. who is credited by Dr. C. Alphonso Smith, the noted English authority, as knowing more folk songs and old English ballads than any other person in the United States and probably in the world. She can sing 67 ballads which have been handed down to her from generation to generation by word of mouth."[24]

The local children knew her because she went to the school every Friday afternoon and sang and told stories. She was often invited to The Asheville Normal School to entertain with stories and ballads. Mary Kestler Clyde in her book about The Asheville Normal School, *Flashbacks to Dawn*, has written an account of a memorable concert by Jane Gentry in the fall of 1920. She called it "Gentle Jane's Recital."

> "Since she was a natural and humble storyteller, "Lady Jane" captured and held our attention with a fascinating medley of songs, stories, riddles, and tales from her own personal experience. She had reared a large family and had learned a rich lore and a great deal of wisdom. Dozens of ballads seemed to be at her command, all learned orally from her forebears and friends, and all just seemed to be waiting on her tongue and humming in her heart. Even in the long ballads such as "Barbara Allen," she could roll out verse after cumulative verse with no faltering or seeming effort. Then to get her breath, she would toss off a riddle and wait for an answer that seldom found voice from our audience save for an occasional muted giggle."[25]

Her program might have included such ballads and songs as "The Golden Vanity," "The Daemon Lover," "The Cherry Tree Carol," "Born in Bethany," "Edwin in the Lowlands Low," or "The Broken Token." She would almost surely have sung such songs as . . .
. . ."The frog went a-courting he did ride, h'm, h'm. . . ."
. . ."Soldier, soldier, will you marry me? . . ."
. . ."Oh, where have you been, Billy Boy, Billy Boy? . . ."
. . ."We'll climb up Jacob's ladder. . . ."
. . ."Says the robin as he flew: When I was a young man I choosed two . . ."
. . ."Had me a cat and the cat pleased me . . ."

She not only told the traditional tales learned from her family, she related stories from her personal experience. She might give instructions on how to court a man, or give an account of a conversation with a revenuer, or tell about her trip to New York as a guest of the Irving Bacheller family.

Jane Gentry had a thirty year association with Dorland Bell School in Hot Springs which began when her first child, Nora, started to school there. For many of those years she lived next door to the school.

"She had befriended Dorland in a multitude of ways, since the time her first children entered school there, eager to show her gratitude to the Presbyterians. For the Yankee educators she had been a rock to lean upon. If an emergency occurred in the kitchen or the laundry, she was willing to lend a hand. If the Northern missionaries needed the raveling of a Southern mountain mystery, she applied her age-old wisdom. If the teachers wanted a delicious mountain-style meal at reasonable cost, her inn's board was bountiful. When a chapel program or subject course needed a speaker, she was there in her forte, regaling the English ballads and stories of her heritage for which she was sought by collectors. If times were blue and drear, with nothing going right, Jane Gentry was reliable as a lifter-of-spirits. When Dorland had out-of-town guests, Mrs. Gentry was often invited to dinner, bringing "life" to the party with her poise and wit."[26]

Irving Bacheller came to Hot Springs for a vacation. Subsequently, an article titled "The Happiest Person I Ever Knew" appeared in the March, 1925 *American Magazine*. The short story tells of Bacheller's search for a happy person among the talented, rich and famous. Then he met Jane Gentry, whose back was bent because of spinal trouble, whose hands were rough with toil, but "in her eyes and her voice was a singular quality akin to the divine." He saw her often and took her to New York as a guest in his home for a month and "always in her voice and look and manner was the unmistakable note of happiness."[27] His interviews with Jane Gentry provided material for other short stories in books and magazines.

Known to be a wonderful story-teller, Jane Gentry was also the subject for stories, some of which she told and some of which were told about her. The best known story is sometimes called "The Baby in the Briar

Patch." Both Irving Bacheller and Mary Kestler Clyde included it in their books. Their versions are very different, as one would expect them to be in a story which has been learned from oral interpretation.

This is the story as told by Betty Rolfe, daughter of Mae, the Gentry's fifth child. The story was told to Mrs. Rolfe by her aunt, Maud Long. Mrs. Rolfe and her two young sons lived with Aunt Maud in Sunnybank for several years.

> "Grandmother and the two oldest, and I think it was Lalla who was in the cradle had gone out to—she was hoeing corn out in the field. And she had cut a birch bark—where the men had been cutting wood, and you know how they split the bark off the wood so it won't rot. Then they can use it for barns and houses and whatever needed building. Grandmother had gone to the field to hoe corn and she put the baby in the bark; laid it down with its blanket and put it under the shade of a tree. And she went off and started hoeing corn. She told the two girls to look after the baby. And they got to playing and got a little off from the baby. The sun came out and it got hot and grandmother worked right on until it came time to stop for lunch. She went back to get her lunch and feed the children. In the meantime the sun had come in under the tree and closed up the birch bark and the baby got restless and started squirming around in there and when that happened, it started rolling down the mountainside. They couldn't find the baby anywhere, so they didn't know what had happened to the baby. So they ran and got Grandfather and everybody started looking. They had searched all over for quite a long time—four or five kids looking by that time—scattered all over looking. Finally one of them looked down and in a briar patch down—quite a way down the mountain they saw this little log, and sure enough, the baby was inside and almost closed up tight by the time they got to it—but not a scratch on her. And that's the tale Aunt Maud told me."[28]

Another story told by Tinha Anderson, daughter of Lalla, next to the youngest Gentry child is called "The Ghost Story." It concerns a visit of some relatives from California who came in late one night. Aunt Maud prepared supper and then everybody went to bed. One member of the visiting party was a baby who was put to bed in a cradle. In the night the mother woke up and saw someone bend over the cradle, cover the baby, and then go out onto the balcony. Some of the bedrooms at Sunnybank open out on to a long balcony. She thought it was Aunt Maud and so she went back to sleep. In the morning at breakfast she thanked Aunt Maud for covering the baby. Aunt Maud's reply was: "Oh, that wasn't me, honey. That was Mama. She always looks after the babies in that room." This happened several years after Jane Gentry's death.[29]

If Jane Gentry were to "return" she would certainly look after the babies. She told Irving Bacheller that she took her sister's five children when she "broke down" and raised her brother's children when he died of typhoid fever. Bacheller quotes her as saying: "We loved the childern. Good land, mister, when the last baby walked out o' my arms I felt kindly cold an' lonesome. Babies are good company. Ye can visit with 'em. Ye don't know what heaven is, honey, 'twil ye've held it in yer arms, year a'ter year as I done."[30] She was proud that in spite of sickness and injuries, she never lost a baby.

The Ransom Hicks family left Watauga County and moved to Madison County ca.1875 when Jane was about twelve years old and her grandfather in his seventies. She probably saw little of her grandfather, "Old Counce," after that. There were few roads and the trip would have been long and difficult. However, she gave him credit for being her source for the Jack tales, while she named her mother as the source of her ballads and songs.

Mrs. Gentry was the daughter of a preacher, had close ties with a mission school, and lived in an area where there were people who objected to the "old love songs." Samuel Harmon, another of Council Harmon's grandchildren who moved to Tennessee, realized that most of his songs were indeed "devil's ditties," and that they were not tolerated by some of his more strict neighbors.[31] And yet we know of no prejudice against Jane Gentry's songs and tales. Some say that she was so loved and respected that when she broke up an illegal still she was not harmed and there was no retaliation.[32] Perhaps her neighbors knew her too well to see anything "evil" in the songs she sang.

It also is not known if Mrs. Gentry censored her selection of songs to suit her listeners. Daron Douglas, Maud Long's granddaughter, remarked as an introduction to "Young Hunting," that she had learned it from Sharp's book because her grandmother did not sing it. She said her mother had told her that Mrs. Long didn't sing the more explicit ones about lovers.[33] Mrs. Long was an elder in the Presbyterian Church and may have considered those ballads inappropriate for her to sing.

Something is known of "Old Counce" Harmon's problems with the church. Richard Chase quoted some of his relatives, among them, Smith Harmon, the postmaster at Beech Creek: "Old Counce sure did like to have a good time. When he was younger he'd get read out of the church ever' now and then. He'd behave for a while, and not make music, or dance, or sing any love songs. But seemed like he loved the old music so much he'd bust out again and get the church folks down on him once more. When he got to be an old man, though, they didn't pay him much mind."[34]

Jane Gentry's life with her great talent and her rich store of oral literature came to an end the hot summer of 1925, the summer it didn't rain at all. She had raised her children well. Among her descendants there are grandchildren in their seventies who remember vividly the stories told by their parents, both traditional tales and family stories; there are teachers who have told the stories and sung the songs to children in classrooms; there are young people who still sing the ballads. Maud Long's name might be recognized for she was recorded by Artus Moser and Duncan Emrich, and some would know Daron Douglas as a fiddler and ballad singer. But there are many others who still cherish this tradition of marvelous songs and tales.

Notes

1. R. P. Harris, "Miss Gentry Collecting Folk Songs of Mountains Just Like Her Mother." Unnamed newspaper article, ca. 1925.

2. Interview with W. T. ("Bill") Moore, Meadow Fork, Madison County, August 29, 1985.

3. Letter from Nola Jane Gentry Yrjana, September 17, 1987.

4. "Land of the Sky," Pamphlet, late 1800's. Berea College Special Collections.

5. Interview with James and Dorothy Gentry, Hot Springs, N. C., July 23, 1985.

6. Irving Bacheller, "The Happiest Person I Ever Knew," *American Magazine*, March, 1924.

7. Ibid.

8. Mellinger Henry, *Songs Sung in the Southern Appalachians*, London: The Mitre Press, 1933. p.xii.

9. Interview with Jane Long Douglas, Athens, Georgia, October 8, 1985.

10. Irving Bacheller, "The Happiest Person I Ever Knew."

11. Elizabeth B. ("Peggy") Dotterer, "Hot Springs," Lecture, Hot Springs, N. C., September 29, 1987.

12. Emma Bell Miles. *The Spirit of the Mountains*, Knoxville: University of Tennessee Press, 1975. (Reprint of 1905 ed.), p. 147.

13. Interview with W. T. Moore, August 29, 1985.

14. Interview with Elizabeth Dotterer, Hot Springs, N. C. January 25, 1988.

15. Cecil Sharp, *English Folk-Songs from the Southern Appalachians*, London: Oxford University Press, 1973 (Reprint of 1932 ed.) p. xxv.

16. Emma Bell Miles. *The Spirit of the Mountains*, p. 170.

17. Maud Long, *Jack Tales*, Library of Congress Recording L-47.

18. Elizabeth Dotterer, Interview January 25, 1988.

19. Richard Chase, *The Jack Tales*, Houghton Mifflin Co., 1943, p.viii.

20. Elmer Hall, "Sunnybank: The Inn at Hot Springs."

21. Interview with James Gentry, July 23, 1985.

22. Cecil Sharp, *English Folk-Songs from the Southern Appalachians*, p. xxv.

23. Isabel Gordon Carter, "Mountain White Folk-Lore: Tales From The Southern Blue Ridge," *Journal of American Folklore*, March, 1927, pp. 340–370.

24. *Wide World Magazine*, ca. 1923, (Library of Congress Collection)

25. Mary Kestler Clyde, *Flashbacks to Dawn*, Vantage Press, 1983, pp. 59–61.

26. Jaqueline B. Painter. *The Season of Dorland-Bell*, Biltmore Press, 1987, p.164.

27. Irving Bacheller, "The Happiest Person I Ever Knew."

28. Interview with Betty Rolfe, Hot Springs, N.C., October 19, 1987.

29. Telephone interview with Tinha Anderson, Atlanta, Ga., September 10, 1985.

30. Irving Bacheller, "The Happiest Person I Ever Knew."

31. Mellinger Henry, *Songs Sung in the Southern Appalachians*, p.xvi.

32. Letter from Jeannette Armstrong, September 22, 1985.

33. Daron Douglas, Gathering to Honor Jane Gentry, Hot Springs, N.C., October 18, 1987.

34. Richard Chase, *The Jack Tales*, p. ix.

This paper is a part of a larger research project. The biographical data suggests issues which are beyond the scope of this paper.

Legendary Places: The Literature of the Great Smoky Mountains National Park

by
James Byer

When Horace Kephart prepared himself in 1904 for a sojourn in the Great Smoky Mountains, he reports that he could find "in no library a guide to that region," no magazine article describing the land and its people, "not even a novel or a story that showed intimate local knowledge" (Kephart,13). Kephart himself made the first attempt at repairing this deficiency when he published *Our Southern Highlanders* in 1913, and his work was followed shortly by several other accounts of wilderness experiences in the Great Smokies or of the lives of the mountain folk who toiled there. It was the conception and creation of a national park, however, which inspired the production of a more varied and extensive literature, produced not only by natives of the region but by travellers who, like Bartram and Guyot and Michaux of old, found themselves drawn by the wonder of some of the oldest mountains and one of the richest repositories of botanical species on earth. And like Bartram, Guyot, and Michaux, they have left their imprints upon the landscape. In recording sensory impressions, the human and natural history, or the biological complexity of the Great Smokies, they have made themselves a part of our imaginative conception of the land. In so doing they have helped us to see and to value the wilderness while paradoxically making the wilderness more accessible to our imaginations and therefore, in a sense, less wild.

In his book *Man in the Landscape* Paul Shepard shows that the original impulse to establish national parks arose not because nineteenth century Americans wished to preserve wilderness in its original state but because they saw in the hot springs and geological formations of Yellowstone and in the sheer cliffs of Yosemite the closest parallel the new world afforded to the romantic ruins and the formal gardens of the Old World. The term oark, in fact, as applied to Yellowstone, associates that landscape not with a forbidding wilderness but with the inviting, carefully managed grounds of an English or European estate, an association heightened by the fact that the relatively dry climate of the west produces not the dense forest of the Appalachian Mountains but instead many large meadows containing well-spaced individual trees.

The concept of the national park as an area of outstanding scenery, but not as a wilderness per se, was well established in the west before attention was directed in the second and third decades of the present century to several possible areas of preservation in the east, including present-day Acadia in Maine and the Appalachian Mountains of Virginia, Tennessee, and North Carolina. When that attention was turned on the Great Smoky Mountains, it found an area quite different both from the national parks of the west and from the Great Smoky Mountains National Park of today. In the first place, the denseness of the vegetation, particularly in the laurel slicks and rhododendron jungles, made it difficult to see any resemblance between these natural areas and European parks. Indeed, in this density there is something both imaginatively and literally threatening: one of the greatest dangers the hiker or explorer has always faced in the Great Smokies is that he will simply vanish. As Ross Hutchins in his book *Hidden Valley of the Smokies* observes, "It is not at all difficult to be lost in these mountains; there have been many instances of people, including adults, completely disappearing. As recently as 1969, a small boy was lost along the Appalachian Trail near the southern end of the Park and was never found, even though he had been wearing a bright red jacket. This is spite of a massive search carried out over many weeks(4). In the second place, as such writers as Harvey Broome, Paul Fink, and Paul Adams have documented, the Great Smoky Mountains in the first three decades of the twentieth century were both more and less wild than they are today. More wild, in that many of today's popular hiking destinations, such as Mt. LeConte and a number of peaks along the State Line Range, were much less accessible, reached by very primitive trails or by none at all, but less wild, in that farms and settlements covered much of the park that is today wilderness, in that logging operations with extensive networks of rail lines extended up many valleys, and in that even some of the highest and most remote areas such as Spence Field above Cades Cove were used as summer pastures by herdsmen.

    The nature of the Great Smoky Mountains both as a densely forested wilderness and as a comparatively heavily settled and logged area and the changes that have occurred as a result of its designation as a national park have greatly affected the literature which the park has produced. This literature spans the period from the 1920's and 30's to the present and ranges in genre from the scholarly history of Michael Frome to the personal hiking diary of Harvey Broome to the keenly informed naturalist observations of Ross Hutchins to the environmental polemic of Edward Abbey. This literature reveals over the past 50 or 60 years a growing understanding of the importance of wilderness and its preservation at the same time that it serves to humanize and to make less alien the very wilderness it celebrates. It has contributed, in other words, both to the name and to the history of the Great Smoky Mountains.

    In his journal for 1962 Harvey Broome meditates on a friend's opposition to the practice of giving names to mountains or other features of wilderness landscape. Broome concludes: "Such a practice would impose a terrific curb on use. People would not be inclined to go to places that had no names. Maps would be next to useless . . ."(238). Paul Shepard, in explaining how language is necessary to man's control of his environment, observes similarly: "The words mediate between the otherness, the incredible and seemingly chaotic diversity, the existential solitude, and our necessary construct of the world." He adds: "An environment without place names is fearful" (41). If Broome and Shepard are right, then literature and wilderness would seem to be incompatible since to name is a primary literary act and all literature and all recording of history are a form of naming. Yet without the name, the history, and the literature, we would have no conception of wilderness and no way of valuing it.

One means of humanizing the non-human and of creating a history and a value for the wilderness is to associate the mountains with particular individuals and to lend to those individuals an almost mythical stature, to link them with values which the writer associates with the mountains. At times one finds this linkage creating a kind of chain, connecting a man in the present with one in the past who was closer to the "original" wilderness and the latter with one in the more distant past who was yet closer. Michael Frome, for example, in his *Strangers in High Places,* the most scholarly, complete, and conventional of the "histories" of the Smokies, uses this technique throughout. He opens his history by recalling a hike up the Chimney Tops which he took one January day with Harvey Broome and John Morrell, both old men who had hiked the Smokies all their lives, men capable of recalling what it had been like in 1913 or 1918, and both with impeccable conservationist credentials, Harvey a past president of the Wilderness Society, friend of Olaus Murie and William O. Douglas, and John, a land buyer for the Great Smoky Mountains Conservation Association which acquired parcels of land for the park. Although Broome was, as Frome says, in anything but robust health, he was able to leave the younger author gasping for breath, becoming for Frome an emblem of an indomitable strength and courage drawn from intimacy with the natural world. Frome develops even further this association of Broome with the Smokies in his later essay called "When the Mysterious Owl Called in the Great Smokies" published in the collection *Promised Land.* There he recalls Broome's death and a hike in Greenbrier Cove where Broome's ashes were scattered by his wife, making him physically at one with the land with which he had long been spiritually kin. As Frome eulogizes him, "He was out there when the temperature dropped to fifteen below zero, and the trees cracked and popped throughout the night, and the ice froze on his eyebrows and eyelashes, and the water froze in his canteen. And yet without complaint because this was, after all, part of experiencing the natural world" (101).

In *Strangers in High Places* Frome also recounts the stories of other, more distant, men, who are thereby even more easily converted into legend, men like Little Will Thomas, the white chief of the Cherokee, William Bartram, the gentle botanist of unimaginable courage, Arnold Guyot, the Swiss geologist who first charted the mountains. But perhaps the most important of these figures for Frome is Horace Kephart—important because, like Frome, he was the outsider who came to know both the land and its people intimately and because in a time when relatively few people were concerned about conservation, Kephart recognized the danger of uncontrolled logging in the Smokies and urged the establishment of a national park there. It is Kephart who serves as the model for Frome and who defines the role Frome strives to play. In one chapter Frome joins local hunters for a bear hunt and in another he seeks out and wins the trust of a moonshiner, in both cases closely paralleling chapters in Kephart's *Our Southern Highlanders*. Thus Frome's history becomes not only a chronological account of human events but a linked series of human beings all related in similar ways to the land.

Harvey Broome's journal *Out Under the Sky of the Great Smokies* also creates a human history for the mountains by linking together a series of outdoorsmen and conservationists, some native, some not, who are in touch with the true values of wilderness. He describes a hike, for example, with Wiley Oakley, the already legendary "roaming man of the mountains," who died in 1954 and whose jokes and tall tales had been recorded in Laura Thornborough's 1937 volume *The Great Smoky Mountains*. Of similar importance in Broome's journal, although of greater national fame, is Justice William Douglas, with whom Broome often hiked and camped. Douglas, like Broome, suffered a childhood and adolescence plagued by ill health, which he describes in Of Men and Mountains, and like Broome, through his love of the outdoors developed strength and endurance. Similarly in the chapter on the Smokies in Douglas' *My Wilderness: East to Katahdin*, Broome figures as prominently as he does in Frome's *Strangers in High Places* so that for Douglas, as for Frome and Broome, the significance of the land is mediated through the men who are identified with it.

Another way in which the literature of the park serves to humanize the wilderness is through the memory of previous experiences in an individual's life. In a Romantic, almost Wordsworthian way the writer remembers the landscape as it was linked to his own life in the past. The result is a poignancy which deepens the reader's sense of the land as having a history because it is a fixed point in the history of the man. Broome's *Out Under the Sky of the Great Smokies* is particularly rich in such memories, and the further one progresses in the journal the more prominent do the memories become. One can watch in these pages the history of man and the land accrue over the years. Two quotations from the journal for 1959 will illustrate this quality well:

> We climbed on steeply and with some fatigue. But eventually the massed laurel thinned out and broke into clumps. Broad sods of grass appeared and we emerged upon Spence Field, which I had first trod through an impenetrable fog on the Easter weekend 37 years before (214).
>
> By coincidence I met Marcovitch on the street today and he recalled the trip to LeConte with "Prof" Essary in 1922. He remembered that when we worked our way out to what is now known as Myrtle Point, the top of LeConte was so untrailed that we had to nick blazes into the trees to find our way back to Cliff Top.
>
> 'That was the best trip I ever had,' he said. He remarked on the changes that have taken place—the roads, the lodge on LeConte—and finished, 'It'll never be like that again'" (212).

The land is not only connected to our history, it has its own history as well. Partly that history is geological and occurs in geological time. Several books—Frome's and Abbey's for instance—describe this geological history—the formation of the mountains hundreds of millions of years ago and their service as a refuge for botanical species during the last ice age. But the surface of the land has a history too, and it can be observed in much less than millions of years. In September of 1951, for example, a once-in-a-century storm struck Mt. LeConte, dumping four inches of rain in an hour and creating a savage flash flood. On Sept. 16 of that year Broome surveyed the damage: "The destruction in the Alum Cave Prong outdid all the rest. There was no semblance of the usual boulder strewn creek bed. Gravel had been deposited evenly in what was the stream bed. ... The confusion of trunks and limbs was undescribable" (103). And seven years later in 1958 Broome was still recording the devastation wrought by the flood.

The creation of the national park made possible the observation of another kind of process in the Smokies—the process of nature's healing the scars left from the logging and farming of earlier years. For those who can read, the surface of the earth, its texture and form, and the vegetation it supports are a language and embody, just as words do, a history. A virgin forest looks different from a second growth forest, not only in size of trees but in species. A heavily grazed field feels different to the foot from an ungrazed one. Broome and Hutchins are two writers who can read this language. For example,

> The even growth of the tulip trees around the Chimneys campground told the story of former occupation and open fields better than words (Broome, 235).

> Surface conditions in western Smoky have changed greatly since the termination of grazing, now about a quarter of a century ago. During the grazing era the ground was tough, firm turf. On this most recent trip, each time we left the trail I was struck by the sponginess of the earth all the way from Double Springs to Buckeye Gap (Broome, 278).

> On the side of Clingman's we could see the converging bands worn into the surface by the log skidders, now grown up in briars and undergrowth. But the spruce and balsams were absent from those belts of use and grew only in the less disturbed areas between. The broad outlines of man's doings could be read at a glance (Broome, 267).

The appearance of the Great Smokies has changed radically since the establishment of a national park. So too our ability to see, to understand, and to value the land has altered, as has our conception of the purpose of a national park. Books on the national park written early in its history, such as those of Laura Thornborough and Elizabeth Skaggs Bowman are filled with pride in the land that both authors knew well and with a desire to share its natural beauty. Yet there is lacking in these books any sense that the mountains are finite and mortal and can be as irreparably harmed by the administrative exigencies of a national park as by the depredations of a logging industry. Bowman, for instance, in describing the grandeurs of a drive from Newfound Gap to Clingman's Dome, the highest point in the park, along the crest of the main range, writes hopefully of the expectation that that road will be extended along the state line crest some 35 miles further west, to Deal's Gap, thus bisecting the park lengthwise as was done in the Shenandoah. This road plan, once a cherished goal of Tennessee Senator Kenneth McKellar, has not been even mentioned for decades and is now as inconceivable as clear cutting on the sides of Mt. LeConte. Another road plan, to cross the main range from Bryson City, NC, to Townsend, TN, was a very real possibility about 20 years ago, but far from being welcomed it was angrily attacked in the literature of the late sixties and early seventies, and in fact was probably the reason for the existence of some of this literature. Michael Frome, for instance, in his essay in *Promised Land*, speaks of the conception of *Strangers in High Places*, which he says was originally intended as a guidebook, but was redesigned as a much more complete history and appreciation of the wilderness as a way of participating in the transmountain road controversy. The *Promised Land* essay is itself a more overt polemic against the highway as Frome celebrates the leaders of the fight against the road, including one Rufus Morgan, 81 years old and a fifth generation mountain man.

Another polemic, more acerb but ultimately less successful, which appeared at this time, was the text contributed by well known novelist and naturalist Edward Abbey to accompany the photographs of Eliot Porter in the Sierra Club book *Appalachian Wilderness*. Although Abbey lived for a time in Western North Carolina and worked at what he calls the University of Western Carolina, his text shows all the marks of being written on assignment and his familiarity with the park restricted to one impression-gathering trip of a couple of days in the winter of 1970. His impressions are therefore rather thin, being limited to a drive across the transmountain highway (although he deplores automobiles) and two short walks to the most popular tourist destinations—the two mile walk to Alum Cave and the half-mile walk to the Clingman's Dome summit. A three and a half mile walk to Charlie's Bunion proves a little too daunting for him—it's thirty degrees outside and as he says, "No day for a walk to Charlie's Bunion" (40). He fills the space his assignment requires with quotations from the informative signs provided by the Park Service and with his polemic against towns like Gatlinburg and against all roads in national parks. He had made the same points before in *Desert Solitaire*, and in fact the argument deserves to be made. Abbey's tone, however, is so uncontrolled and his persona so out of harmony with his argument that had the road controversy not already been settled by the time his book appeared, his book would probably have done more harm than good. After insisting, for example, that roads have no place in national parks, Abbey happily presses the accelerator: "Without any sense of self-contradiction, I drive my own little car up into the mountains. The road is here, I might as well make use of it, I've been taxed cruelly to help pay for it, I'd be a fool to walk and let the other motorists blow their foul internal-combustion gases in my faces" (37).

A far more persuasive document in the road controversy of the late sixties is the last entry in Broome's journal, dated October 28, 1966, describing a Save-Our-Smokies hike from Clingman's Dome to Elkmont, a total of seventeen miles. 576 had begun the hike; a remarkable 234 had finished it. A few weeks earlier Broome had proven conclusively the existence of red spruce on Miry Ridge, part of the route of the hike and part of the area that would have been seriously disturbed by the new highway. These red spruce grew beyond what had been previously regarded as the westernmost limit of the species in the park, enabling Broome to demonstrate that "the engineers for the proposed new road had picked the precise point where the northern conifers gave way to the southern hardwoods" (Broome, 283). If the road were built, "The rearguard of the last ice age, along one of the great ecotones of the continent, would be wiped out" (284).

As a result of the diligent and determined efforts of many private citizens, writers, and members of the Park Service, that road was never built, nor in the last 20 years has anything comparable even been suggested. Jesse Helms now leads a lastditch struggle to build a road along the north shore of Fontana Lake, but his success seems improbable. One can now wholeheartedly agree with William Douglas when he remarks in *My Wilderness* that in respect for wilderness values and in restricting the encroachments of civilization the Great Smoky Mountains is "close to a model" for national parks (180). And through a study of this national park literature one can recognize and applaud the extent to which our understanding of the purpose of the national park has grown from the concept of a managed "park" with an emphasis, as Broome says, "on scenery and size" to a concept of unmolested wilderness with an appreciation for "the complexity of the land organism" and "the infinitely interlocking animal and plant worlds" (Broome, 169).

In describing how the landscape comes to have such significance for us, Paul Shepard says: "Because the environment echoes dream and visionary forms, is dotted with named, sacred, anthropomorphic and specially remembered places, and comprises a ground of intermediate space arrayed with plant and rock entities to which our apehood responds in entangled and impulsive ways, we are always on the threshhold of legendary places" (46–47). For the best of these writers and for their readers, the Great Smoky Mountains National Park becomes a legendary place, humanized through a history and a set of human associations yet ultimately mysterious and strange, beyond our comprehending or possessing. As Douglas writes, "This is a forest filled with so many wonders, one man could not ever know them all, even if he saw it every season and examined it from the fungi of the forest floor to the tops of the wild black cherries" (161). Ross Hutchins does examine the forest almost this minutely and the marvels he lays bare for us intensify the mystery. He finds things most of us miss: the ant-spider, a spider which is antlike in body form and coloration; the ant-loving cricket, living within an ant's nest and feeding upon secretions from the ants' bodies; the oil nut, a member of the sandalwood family and parasitic upon the roots of rhododendrons. This wonder of a book, focused on a mountain valley above Elkmont shows us how much stranger than we ever thought the world really is.

The literature of the mountains gives names, records history, and strives to know the unknowable. But it must ultimately confront the mystery, which is communicable only through symbol. For several the symbol is an owl. For Douglas: the Smokies "mean the barred owl calling on a moonlight night" (156). For Broome: " . . . I heard the truncated call of an owl. That broken falsetto—whoo-whoo—is the wilderness articulate. Man must not drive the owls to extinction; he needs these windows of sound and sight for a look into a world other than his own" (130). For Frome, who, significantly, writes of an owl that cannot be identified or named:

> During the night we heard a really beautiful owl call. I don't know what kind it was, but it was a different kind of owl than I've ever heard. . . . It could have been a saw-whet or a short-eared or something weird—it was not a great horned or barred owl.
>
> It was something mysterious that seemed to come out of the wilds of Mount LeConte as the voice of the wilderness. . . . It's calling to say it needs a place to be wild in (*Promised Land*, 112).

References Cited

Abbey, Edward. *Appalachian Wilderness: The Great Smoky Mountains*. New York: Ballantine, 1973.

Adams, Paul J. *Mt. LeConte*. Knoxville, 1966.

Bowman, Elizabeth Skaggs. *Land of High Horizons*. Kingsport, TN: Southern Publishers, 1938.

Broome, Harvey. *Out Under the Skies of the Great Smokies: Personal* Journal. Knoxville: The Greenbrier Press, 1975.

Douglas, William O. *My Wilderness: East to Katahdin*. Garden City, NY: Doubleday, 1961.

Fink, Paul M. *Backpacking Was the Only Way: A Chronicle Camping Experiences in the Southern Appalachian Mountains*. Johnson City, TN: Research Advisory Council, East Tennessee State University, 1975.

Frome, Michael. *Promised Land: Adventures and Encounters in Wild* America. New York: Morrow, 1985.

———. *Strangers in High Places: The Story of the Great Smoky* Mountains. Garden City, NY: Doubleday, 1966.

Hutchins, Ross E. *Hidden Valley of the Smokies: Naturalist in the Great* Smoky Mountains. New York: Dodd, Mead, 1971.

Kephart, Horace. *Our Southern Highlanders*. New York: MacMillan, 1913.

Shepard, Paul. *Man in the Landscape: A Historic View of the Esthetics of Nature*. New York: Knopf, 1967.

Thornborough, Laura. *The Great Smoky Mountains*. Rev. Ed. Knoxville: Univ. of Tennessee Press, 1956.

Jesse Stuart's Archetypal Vision of Appalachian Culture: The Thread Still Runs True

by
Edgar H. Thompson

Jesse Stuart was a natural-born storyteller so driven by the urge to create, to share his world, that he had neither the time nor the patience to hone his writing into great art. Still, in his fiction and non-fiction, Stuart created an image, a perception, an archetype that I think captures the essence of the Appalachian region. From my first acquaintance with his work in high school to my subsequent reading of most of his writing, I gained a sense of my cultural heritage that has never left me.

My life, however, has certainly not been a carbon copy of Stuart's, nor have the lives of other readers whom his writing has touched. I have never lived in a small cabin or shack; never ridden a mule anywhere. However, there is something about his experiences, the themes and feelings that arise from them, that do ring true to me and I think to most Appalachian people, whether from small towns or large cities or from the highlands or the lowlands within the region. In this paper, I will explore some of the themes and feelings that arise from Stuart's writing and relate them to both the Appalachian culture and to the larger consciousness of main-stream America.

TO WIN RESPECT BY BEING UNIQUE, BY OVERCOMING GREAT ODDS

In the first two paragraphs of "A Ribbon for Baldy," Stuart's narrator describes feelings that most native Appalachians have felt, usually with great pain, at one time or another.

The day Professor Herbert started talking about a project for each member of our General Science class, I was more excited than I had ever been. *I wanted to have an outstanding project. I wanted it to be greater, to be more unusual than those of my classmates. I wanted to do something worthwhile, and something to make them respect me.*

I'd made the best grade in my class in General Science. I'd made more yardage, more tackles and carried the football across the goal line more times than any player on my team. *But making good grades and playing rugged football hadn't made them forget that I rode a mule to school, that I had worn my mother's shoes the first year and that I slipped away at the noon hour so no one would see me eat fat pork between slices of corn bread.* [179–180]

The italicized lines in the above passage [The added emphasis is mine] reveal a tremendous sense of inferiority in relation to others. They also reveal an equally powerful desire to somehow win respect, and to do so by doing something unique, something to make "them," whomever "them" might be, to recognize the spark, the genius, the human being beneath the dress, the behavior, or the language that didn't fit the norm.

This feeling of inferiority described in Stuart's story reveals a very real and never-ending conflict within many Appalachians. We typically have not felt inferior to anyone. However, people from outside the region have laughed at us and cast us in a negative light, suggesting that something about our background and experiences, our social context or milieu, was *lacking in relation to the rest of the world. We have been angered by this. Sometimes we've kept our mouths shut; other times we've "set people straight." No matter how we have responded to such inaccurate aspersions, many of us have come to feel defensive about our backgrounds, at least when talking to "outsiders." Part of this defensiveness may come from the geographic isolation that exists within the Appalachians. The inability of people within the region to maintain contact with the rest of the world, has created a sense of alienation, of being out of step, though satellite televison has diminished this feeling somewhat.*

Whatever its source, most of us have been made to feel inferior, or at least defensive, about our backgrounds, and many of us still feel it. Thus, when we read Stuart's description of his feelings about the upcoming science project, though many of us may never have worn our mother's shoes to school, we know what he is talking about, since we too have felt this way before. As a result, we eagerly read to see whether or not he is going to succeed at the task he set for himself, which was to plant the longest corn row in the world. It turned out to be approximately 23 miles long, corkscrewing its way up and around Old Baldy. At the end of the story, a picture of Stuart's narrator and a story about his corn row appears in the local paper: "When the article and pictures were published, a few of my classmates got a little jealous of me but not one of them ever laughed at me again" [182]. Though the ending to the story is formulaic, we celebrate and cheer when he receives the recognition he so dearly wanted, because we also want such recognition.

This feeling of wanting to win recognition and respect never left Stuart, just as I suspect it has never left many of us. Such behavior is not uncommon among Appalachian people, nor is it in anyway unique. For example, I've been a magician, finished college in three years, and earned a doctorate, among other things. What's your story? Being laughed at or belittled does something to us that we never forget, though hopefully we learn to deal with it. In the *The Thread That Runs So True*, Stuart's success gives us added confidence to continue our own struggle.

NATURAL KNOWLEDGE VS. BOOK KNOWLEDGE

Stuart's characters are more than just colorful in speech and dress. They are smart. Some possess great school knowledge; others, like Stuart's father, have great knowledge of the natural world. Both kinds of knowledge play important dual roles in Stuart's writing. He believed and respected both kinds equally. In his story "Testimony of Trees," Stuart shares a good example of how natural knowledge can make an important difference in people's lives.

Jake Timmons, a coniving land-grabber, conspires with the county land surveyor to prove that commonly accepted line boundaries specified in the deeds of several parcels of land are inaccurate. With the surveyor's support, he has won 40 court cases and confiscated hundreds of acres of property for himself. When Timmons challenges Mick Stuart, Mick decides he isn't going to give in. He goes to West Virginia to get his uncle who has previously been involved in many line disputes.

Uncle Mel turns out to be quite a character:

> Carrying a double-bitted ax and a turkey of clothes across his shoulder. . . . Uncle Mel was eighty-two years old, but his eyes were keen as sharp-pointed briers and his shoulders were broad and his hands were big and rough. He had been a timber cutter all his days and he was still a-cuttin' timber in West Virginia at the age of eighty-two. [111]

Uncle Mel helps Mick, and a lot of other men to get their land back, because he knows so much about trees. If a tree has been blazed or marked, it maintains a scar on the outside bark as well as on the inside. As a result, when Uncle Mel followed the description in the deed, he looked at the outside of the trees for the outward scar and then chopped into it to find the original blaze. By then counting the number of growth rings from the original scar, he could substantiate that each tree was one of the orginal trees described in the deed. Unless you had worked in timber, you might not know this information. Book knowledge is important, but then so is natural knowledge.

This love of both book knowledge and natural knowledge still exists in many people in this region. My colleague Bob Raines is a good example. A professor of mathematics and education at Emory & Henry, he is a superb teacher, writer, and speaker. He also loves the outdoors, rides horses, knows wildflowers, and is a walking encyclopedia on Appalachian lore. Such a combination of interests is not that uncommon in the region.

LOVE OF THE LAND

Though Stuart himself went beyond what he called the dark hills for a time, he finally had to return. It was among the hills that he felt at home, at peace, in touch with who he was as a person. In his first collection of short stories, *Head o' W-Hollow*, the last line of his prose-poem introduction summarizes his feelings about the Appalachian region, "a place under the sun, walled in by the wind and the hills—nowhere for many—somewhere for some" [5].

Often, people in the region become frustrated at the difficulties of day-to-day living caused by geography. As a result, they loose sight of what they have. In "This Farm for Sale," it takes Melvin Spencer, a real estate agent who has a gift for writing descriptively about the places he plans to sell, to convince Uncle Dick Stone that he has far more "wealth" than he realized he had. Stuart, through the real estate advertisement of Melvin Spencer, describes the Stone farm in such a romantic, alluring way that only a fool wouldn't be attracted to the place.

Consider Spencer's description of the land:

> This peaceful Tiber River, flowing dreamily down the valley, is a boundary to his farm. Here one can see to the bottoms of the deep holes, the water is so clear and blue. One can catch fish from the river for his next meal. Elder bushes, where they gather berries to make the finest jelly in the world, grow along the riverbank as thick as ragweeds. [42]

Consider Spencer's description of the lunch that he had when he visited the farm:

> The proof of what a farm produces is at the farm table. I wish that whoever reads what I have written here could have seen the table prepared by Mrs. Stone and her two daughters. Hot fluffy biscuits with light-brown tops, brown-crusted corn bread, buttermilk, sweet milk (cooled in a freestone well), wild-grape jelly, wild crab-apple jelly, mast-fed lean bacon that melted in my mouth, fresh apple pie, wild-blackberry cobbler, honey-colored sorghum from the limestone bottoms of the Tiber, and wild honey from the beehives. [42]

The above passage almost sounds like Grandpa Jones on Hee Haw describing "what's for dinner." Who, in their right mind, wouldn't want to live in such a place? Uncle Dick quickly changes his mind after reading Spencer's description: "I'm a rich man and didn't know it. I'm not selling this farm" [43].

Perhaps because the outside world seems to offer more in the way of job opportunities and modern conveniences, or perhaps due to the frustration over geographic isolation, at times some of us may have come to believe that living anywhere else would be better than living where we do, in the Appalachians. Stuart points out in this story that when we start to feel this way, we really need to look around us. Maybe we have far more going for us than we think.

Despite complaints about the isolated geography, the difficulty of the terrain has, in fact, not only provided people with sustenance but also provided them with their primary sources of recreation. Almost everything people did in Stuart's part of Appalachia was done in relation to the land and to each other. As Stuart put it in *The Thread That Runs So True*,

> People had learned to play musical instruments to furnish their own music just as they had learned to plant, cultivate, and harvest their crops for their food supply. They depended upon themselves for practically everything. [78]

When Stuart was teaching at Winston high school, the land was almost another member of their family. Their learning, their lives were lived close to and in harmony with the land:

> I went with my pupils, their parents, and neighbors to cornhuskings, apple-peelings, bean-stringings, square dances, and to the belling of the bride when there was a wedding.... There was somewhere to go every night. I couldn't accept all the invitations. [78–79]

Such behavior is still common today. People visit each other frequently within the Appalachian region, depending on themselves, not outside stimuli alone, for entertainment and social contact.

This love of the land is an enduring one that begins in childhood and extends into old age. When Stuart's father was seventy years old and not far from death, he took Jesse with him as they made their way to a small clearing located on the highest point in W-Hollow. An Appalachian's love of the land is probably best described by Stuart's father in "A Clearing in the Sky."

> "Fertile," he laughed as he reached down and picked up a double handful of the leaf-rot loam. "This is the land, son! This is it. I've tried all kinds of land ... !
> "But, Dad——" I said.
> "I know what you think," he interrupted. Your mother thinks the same thing. She wonders why I ever climbed to this

mountain-top to raise potatoes, yams, and tomatoes! But, Jess," he almost whispered, "anything grown in new ground like this has a better flavor. Wait until my tomatoes are ripe! You'll never taste sweeter tomatoes in your life!" [128]

He goes on to tell Jesse that when you get to be his age, seventy years old, "You go back to the places you knew and loved" [129].

No matter where we as Appalachians go, there is always a longing for the land and the people who populate it. The people and places that Stuart describes may not be exactly like people and places we have known, but all natives of the region are familiar with the kinds of things he talks about. What native has not been to a pie social or a cake walk at one time in their lives? Which natives have not eaten the meal of their lives at a farm table? What native has not been at the top of mountain somewhere in the region and been at peace just smelling the fragrances of wood, pine, and wild flowers, celebrating the beauty of a sunset or sunrise, and wondering about what might lie over the next mountain?

When I was in Vietnam, one of the first paintings I did for recreation was a mountian scene. Images of the land and the people and the relationship between the two are powerful ones, and they create very strong feelings within us. There are elements of mystery, suspense, and eternal hope in such feelings, and in almost everything he wrote, Stuart captured these elements. Through his description and attention to detail and nuance of language, his writing stimulates these feelings about the land in us.

THE PEOPLE

Stuart's characters are certainly a colorful lot. For example, notice the way people are dressed for the corn-shucking party in *Hie to the Hunters:*

As the men walked, ran, and jumped over the cornfield, holding to their wives' and their lovers' hands, the handles of their pistols above their holsters on their hips shone like polished silver in the moonlight. The red bandannas around their necks, their red, brown, and gray shirts with stripes and checks, and the gay colors of the women's dresses were autumn colors like the leaves still clinging to the trees. It was a night filled with brightness from the floor of the rugged earth to the tops of the trees. [152–153]

Now most of us have probably not been to a social gathering where the men wore guns in holsters, but we have been to events where everyone was colorfully dressed in clean, colorful, yet common, work clothes.

The language and customs at this party are particularly noteworthy. Notice how Stuart captures the peculiar idiom of speech.

> "Now each man with his wife and each young man git his partner," Peg shouted. "Young couples, ye'll go to the bottom of the slope and shuck the bottom shucks. Yer legs are young and powerful. We older folks have climbed too many mountains."
> "Okay, Peg, we're ready," Slim Winters said as he took Olive Kilgore by the hand. "We're ready and a-rarin' to go!" [151–153]

It's not the dialect but the phrasing and the content of these interactions that is revealing. Many natives of this region, even if their regional dialect has disappeared, will fall back into this kind of speech pattern on informal occassions. For instance, haven't you heard educated people use expressions like "a little skiff of snow," "falling weather," "He really cleaned my plow," or "one brick shy of a load"? Such expressions, which we accept as commonplace, are unique and reveal an Appalachian way of looking at the world.

As hard as life sometimes was in Jesse Stuart's world, many of his characters were humorous. In "Hot-Collared Mule" just simply dealing with the difficulties of working with a mule who had to have its collar hot before it would work were hilarious. It certainly wasn't funny to Mick and Shan, as they were running themselves nearly to death to get Rock the mule warmed up so it would work.

> "Keep that mule a-goin'," Pa hollered as I passed by where he was sitting on a log under the shade fanning himself with sourwood leaves. "Run 'im until he's hot as blue blazes!"
> "He's a-gettin' warmed up," I grunted to Pa as I passed him on the second lap.
> "Fetch 'im around agin and I'll tak 'im," Pa said. "Just be keerful and don't do any hollerin'."
> "All right, Pa," I grunted as I came in on my last lap. "It's your time now."
> "Hit'll be the last time one of us has to run this mule," Pa said as he took the lines.
> Pa couldn't run as well as I could, for he was older and his legs were stiffer and his breath came harder. While I sat fanning, I watched him go out of sight, running stiff-legged like a cold buck rabbit in the winter-time. The twist of burley leaf was jumping up and down in his hip pocket as he made the turn to climb the hill.
> "Hit's a hard way to git a mule to work," Pa grunted as he passed me going into his second lap.

I was fanning fast as I could fan. I had cooled down some, but my clothes were wet as if I had jumped into the river.

When Pa came around on his second lap, I didn't think he'd make it. But he did. His face was red as a sliced beet, and his clothes were as wet as mine were. But a sweaty foam had gathered under Rock's flanks and his shoulders were wet around his collar.

"He's in shape to work now," Pa said as he dropped to the ground. [88–89]

I have excerpted this passage slightly, but still, I can clearly see Mick and Shan running that mule, getting the mule—not themselves mind you—into shape to work. They weren't trying to be funny, but nevertheless, what they were doing was hilarious. Notice Stuart's straight delivery of the facts. He lets the characters' language, their actual behavior, and the situation itself communicate the humor.

THE THREAD STILL RUNS TRUE

I claimed at the beginning of this paper that Jesse Stuart's writing reveals an archetype of Appalchain culture. If this is true, what is this archetype and how is it revealed? Is it suggested through the feelings and emotions that are stimulated in readers by his writing? Are the themes in his writing peculiarly Appalachian? The answer to both questions must in part be no. Even though the experiences he described and wrote about took place in the Appalachian region, the feelings and emotions that arise from his writing can be felt by anyone and ascribed to any culture. His themes are also not uniquely Appalachian in character. People from other cultures also love the land and possess a strong sense of and attachment to place. People in other regions of this country and the world practice customs and dress in ways that we consider quaint. Most human beings who actively participate in life are driven to succeed and to overcome great obstacles. The conflict between book knowledge and natural knowledge certainly transcends this region.

The substance of Stuart's Appalachian archetype relies on more than themes and feelings. As Stuart created his fictional world, or rather described the world in which he lived, i.e., the area in and around W-Hollow in Kentucky, he accomplished something of great importance. Through his careful attention to detail, his lively characterization, his ear for the language and idioms of the region, and his narrative power in both fiction and non-fiction, he created a place, a context, a cultural milieu that provides us with a cross-section of life, as he saw it and lived it, during his lifetime in the Kentucky hills. He captured for all time a way of life that, in its detail, has essentially disappeared. To read his fiction is to enter a world, magical in quality, that doesn't really exist anymore. Our imagination combined with our own experiences—which have taken place in similar, yet different, situations or contexts—meld with Stuart's world or vision. The end result is an Appalachian world picture created during reading that is unique in structure.

Probst claims that:

> literature should enable readers to find the connections between their experience and the literary work. If it does so, it may enable them to use literature, to employ it in making sense of their lives. [34–35]

Jesse Stuart managed to foster such a link between his writing and his readers' imaginations and personal experiences. The synergy created by this link results, I think, in an archetype of both what readers and natives of the region know and feel about Appalachian culture. It is a common thread, first woven by our ancestors before most of us were born, re-spun by Jesse Stuart, and re-created by us during reading. It is a thread that still runs true.

References Cited

Probst, Robert E. "Dialogue with a Text." *English Journal*, 77.1 (1988): 32–38.

Stuart, Jesse. "A Ribbon for Baldy." *A Jesse Stuart Reader*. New York: McGraw-Hill, 1963. 178–182.

———. "Clearing in the Sky." *Land of the Honey-Colored Wind*. Ed. Jerry A. Herndon. Morehead, Kentucky: The Jesse Stuart Foundation, 1981. 124–130.

———. "Head o' W-Hollow." *Head o' W-Hollow*. Lexington, Kentucky: The University of Kentucky Press, 1979. 3–5.

———. *Hie to the Hunters*. New York: McGraw-Hill, 1950.

———. "Hot-Collared Mule." *Land of the Honey-Colored Wind*. Ed. Jerry A. Herndon. Morehead, Kentucky: The Jesse Stuart Foundation, 1981. 88–97.

———. *The Thread That Runs So True*. New York: Charles Scribner's Sons, 1958.

———. "This Farm for Sale." *Land of the Honey-Colored Wind*. Ed. Jerry A. Herndon. Morehead, Kentucky: The Jesse Stuart Foundation, 1981. 36–44.

———. "Testimony of Trees." *Clearing in the Sky*. Lexington, Kentucky: The University of Kentucky Press, 1984. 105–117.

Across the Mountains: Appalachian Literature and the Unsuspecting Student

by
Teresa Wheeling

"My name's Alpha Baldridge," I said as I walked into the classroom. "Ever since I married Brack I've been driven from one coal camp to another. I've lived hard as nails. There's lots of coal camps in eastern Kentucky, and I reckon I've lived in half of them." This was my introduction to James Still's *River of Earth*, and my students didn't know what to do. A few giggled, some fidgeted uncomfortably, others merely sat there, their mouths agape. Soon, though, everyone was caught up in the story, following Alpha through her family's struggle with hunger, the death of her baby, the death of her mother, and the birth of another child.

James Still created Alpha Baldridge and her family in 1940, and forty odd years later, Still's characters are still alive, still growing, and still affecting an ever wider range of readers, among them, my own freshman writing students at Radford University. Appalachian literature has as Wilma Dykeman says, "dealt with experiences as unique as churning butter and as universal as getting born" (18). Though it details the culture of the Appalachian mountains, the region's literature has a universality which enables students to make connections with their own lives, whether they be from the mountains or urban Washington D.C.

My first experience teaching *River of Earth* was not an overwhelming one. The response of my students, most of whom originated from urban Northern Virginia and the coastal areas, was not staggering. Still, the few native Appalachian students I had made vital connections with their own experiences, and several of the others progressed from an immediate dislike of the novel to some kind of appreciation for what Still was attempting.

And so last year I assigned the novel again, this time determined to do anything I could to see to it that the novel had an effect on them. At first their reactions were the same as the previous year's. "It's so boring I fall asleep when I try to read. I can't understand the language." All the same, something was different, and the more I examine that difference, the more I see that it was a difference in me, not my students. The year before I had felt I had to defend the novel and my heritage; I had felt threatened by unflattering comments directed at the novel and the way of life it represented. Even after years of soul searching and trying to understand what it meant to be Appalachian, I was still falling for the stereotypes. I was still defending "us" against "them." No wonder I often felt like I was pulling teeth when we discussed the novel in class. My students weren't stupid; they knew I had created opposing teams.

Then as I was preparing my syllabus last year I found a quote by Jim Wayne Miller. "This is the function of the writer—," he said, "to help us see, and see into, our place, our experience, our lives in the world" (20). At that moment I realized what I was after. I didn't want my students to judge the people in *River of Earth* or their lifestyle. I didn't want them to dwell on the differences. I didn't want them to say, "Those people have nothing to do with my life." I wanted to push them to find similarities, strands that bound them together with the people in the novel, strands that bind all of us together as human beings.

And so, in early March I plunged ahead once again. One of the novel's themes is the conflict between Still's husband and wife, Brack and Alpha Baldridge. The best starting point, I thought, would be to engage the students in that conflict. Through much of the novel Brack gives food and shelter to his uncle and cousins who abuse the family's sacrifice by grumbling about what they have and taking far more than their share. Alpha is appalled by Brack's actions, for they are depriving her three children and infant son of the food they need to survive, and as a last resort she burns the house, the only way she knows to ensure that Brack's kin will leave. To highlight this struggle, I walked into class on the first day of discussion dressed as Alpha. My students were, as I said earlier, unsettled at first, but Alpha quickly captured their attention.

After hearing Alpha's side of the story, it was time for the students themselves to wrestle with the issue which confronted Brack and Alpha. Was Brack right to share the family's food and shelter with others and in doing so endanger the lives of his own children, no matter how noble his intentions? Did Alpha overstep her bounds when she burned down the house? Was it possible to say that either character was right or wrong, or was it simply a case of two people struggling for survival, each handling the situation in the way he thought necessary? Such was the task of the students as they drew from the coffee mug slips of paper which would determine which side of the argument they were to defend. Then, lined up facing each other on opposite sides of the room, the battle began. One group slithered to the back to relieve themselves of the burden of arguing, leaving those who were more intense in front to fight it out. It quickly became apparent that Brack and Alpha would each have one principal proponent, while the others defended their champion's points. At times the argument became vicious, and one student refused to say anything in class for a week because many in the class took issue with her relentless argument for Alpha's point of view. When the argument was over and hurt feelings soothed, one thing was clear—Still's characters had become more than words on paper to these kids. They were real people, people worth arguing about, people worth caring about.

Seeing their reactions in class, I was even more curious to see how my students would respond in writing, both in their response logs and critical essays. Again, I saw that Still had struck a chord. Though the Baldridge family's lifestyle was far different from that of my students, they had found a way to connect with the novel. "All this time I've snided off all this Appalachian 'stuff,'" responded one student in her log. "Well if this is what it's like, bring it on! I expected the book to be some dumb mountainy thing. I'd eat my words in a heartbeat. I love it. I cried with the family when things were hard and when the baby died. Are all of James Still's novels this good? If so—look out library, here I come" (Leftwich).

The authenticity of Still's characters as human beings was backed up by my students' ability to draw parallels between the Baldridge family and their own relatives. Sarah wrote:

> In many ways, the Baldridges with their strength and feeling of family togetherness help me to see my own family through different eyes, through eyes of courage, respect, and oneness. I realized after reading River of Earth, how special and important my family is to me. And I think that each of them, the Baldridges, helps to make up each one of us. I see parts of Alpha, Brack, Grandma, and the others, in my mother, my father, my brothers, and mostly in my grandfather, "pop." I feel more closely bonded with my family and that I have a better understanding of them since I read James Still's *River of Earth*, (Atkinson)

Several students from the Appalachian region were able to draw more detailed parallels, for example, this young man from the coal fields of southwestern Virginia.

> My grandfather stayed in my mind as I read the novel. He was a working coal miner all his life, but the coal mines being as unstable as they were, and still are today, left him unemployed a great deal of the time. As far as I know he never had another job, when the mines closed down he farmed and occasionally logged, making barely enough to keep food on the table. When my grandmother and grandfather were married they lived in a twelve by twelve one room cabin with four other family members. My grandmother has told me about her just sitting and crying all day long because there was no food, and they had no land to farm. (Hayes)

I was especially interested in Timmy's response because he showed an understanding and deep appreciation for the hardship his grandparents endured. I think Timmy realized that his grandparents' perseverance helped make it possible for him to attend college instead of spending long days in, as he once called it, "that endless black hole in the ground."

Linda, a middle-aged student also from Southwest Virginia, found similar comparisons:

> Just as Brack seemed to be a "born coal miner," my Father seemed to be a "born farmer." He never worked in a government-sponsored job; he was always his own boss and strove to make a better life for his children and my Mother. Mother feels sad when she remembers how hard my father worked, how many joys he passed to his family yet died before he could see the fruits of his labor. (Nye)

Ironically, the response that showed most eloquently and passionately the effect of Still's writing came from Murdock, a native of the Eastern Shore.

> Being a person who grew up never hearing the word Appalachian, much less about its people, places, or culture, I placed the book down with a sense of being allowed through the author's eyes and words to actually step into another world alien and unknown, and through the course of the story learned about the mountain people as if I had actually lived there. . . .
>
> In many ways my people were similar to the Mountain Folks in that they were proud, and somewhat secluded people who lived off of the land around them, in that while the boys were trained to help their father's father, and their own so that they could take their place when the time came, the girls were raised to be homemakers, and tempered to support their men when fishing was poor, and crabs hard to find. Until as late as the 1940's to be raised in a fishing family meant that a fisherman you would be, and a pride was held in knowing that your labors (sometimes fatal) went to feed thousands of people, most of whom never knew you existed, or for that matter cared. It was a hard life with days starting before the sun, ending hours after dark. Many times the men would place nets and crab-pots in the murky bay for four days straight, returning only long enough to send off the fish, and get supplies for the next trip. My own grandfather would sit with the children, and he would tell us of things that happened while out on the Bay, while he would carve a duck-decoy from a piece of drift-wood. I have seen his hands scarred from the razor shells of clams, and the spikes of horseshoe crabs. I remember his face wrinkled like a

piece of sail, and the texture of his skin rough from years spent in the salt air of the Bay, that murky-blue mistress that greeted him at birth, fostered him through life, and ultimately advanced him to his death. He was no mighty sailor like those he would tell us about, nor was he a mighty fisherman like those he worked under. My grandfather was just a man, a proud one, but a man all the same who worked hard to survive, and meet much of his labor with pain, and finally death. I was of the later generation, and wasn't brought up in the ways of my grandfather, and I regret not knowing more of that man and of his life. To James Still I owe a debt that I cannot repay because through his story, and living with his people through his book I have been given a greater insight into my own heritage, and a deeper respect for it, and for its people.... (Hodges)

That *River of Earth* could evoke such a response is a credit both to the power of Still's writing and to the universality of Appalachian literature.

Though I was pleased with the writing the novel had prompted, my students' most invigorating response to *River of Earth* came in another form. In addition to teaching the novel in class, I was also in the process of writing my Master's thesis, a dramatic interpretation of Still's story. Because I needed to see and hear the characters in action, I asked for volunteers from my classes to put together a small production of the play. Even I was amazed at what happened. Five of the six people needed volunteered the first time I asked, and only one needed to be enticed with the promise of a grade before consenting to take part. Watching that play come together was a wondrous event, one I'll never forget. There was, of course, the normal horsing around, for example, the soap bubbles which mysteriously appeared in Alpha's churn during one practice, but as the weeks wore on I was impressed with the commitment with which each student attacked his or her role.

The cast list sounds like a cultural and geographic who's who. Christi, a native of Roanoke, Virginia who never knew she was Appalachian before reading *River of Earth*, brought life to Alpha, and though a woman of the eighties, she seemed to draw strength from the hardship Alpha had endured. For a short time Tim, a heavy metal rocker, became Brack, a coal miner doing the best he could to feed his family. Stacia, a native of Maine, worked hard to capture the innocence of the novel's young narrator. Matt, who has spent most of his life moving between Indiana and Richmond, took on the perspective of the narrator in later years, a young man reflecting on his childhood in the mountains of Kentucky. Billy, a punk rocker who sported a mohawk until several weeks before the play's performance, was drawn to Jolly's devil-may-care attitude and lighthearted humor.

The evenings we spent in Young Hall were long. Memorizing several pages of dialogue in an unfamiliar dialect wasn't easy; it was difficult to remember to say "seed" instead of "saw," "heered" instead of "heard." Although the dialogue surely didn't sound like James Still's intention, that wasn't important. It was important that the Baldridge family had come to life, regardless of the dialect in which they were portrayed. Still's characters had spoken to these students not in any dialect, but in a universal language, a language expressing the feelings and emotions we all share as human beings. A month and a half before, most of those students had never heard the word Appalachian, but on that night the words they spoke and the feelings they portrayed transcended any region. On that night my students took their final steps across the mountains.

References Cited

Atkinson, Sarah. "*River of Earth*, A Story of Familyhood." Unpublished essay, 1987.

Dykeman, Wilma. "The Literature of the Southern Appalachian Mountains." Mountain Life and Work 40 (Winter 1964): 7–18.

Hayes, Timmy. Unpublished essay, 1986.

Hodges, Murdock. Unpublished essay, 1987.

Leftwich, Christi. Reading response log, 1987.

Miller, Jim Wayne. "Jim Dandy: James Still at Eighty." *Appalachian Heritage 14.4 (Fall 1986)*: 8–20.

Nye, Linda. "*River of Earth* Analysis." Unpublished essay, 1987.

Agriculture in Preindustrial Appalachia: Subsistence Farming in Beech Creek, 1850-1880

by
Paul J. Weingartner, Dwight B. Billings, and Kathleen M. Blee

Beech Creek, a neighborhood first defined and studied by James Brown (1950/1988) in 1942, is situated in the hills of eastern Kentucky in the heartland of Central Appalachia. In his ethnographic account of Beech Creek, Brown described isolated portions of East Kentucky outside the coal mining districts as being still engaged in the subsistence oriented farming which had been characteristic of Appalachia nearly a century before. He comments that, "Then, as now, the Mountains had an economy of subsistence farming" (1950, p. 36). Brown also described Beech Creek as a relatively isolated area, noting that entry into the neighborhood was only possible by maneuvering over harsh terrain and up a dried creek bed either on foot or by pack animal. Linking the reality of geographical isolation to the state of the local economy, Brown claimed that, "the effect of geographic isolation was increased by the region's economic self-sufficiency which made contact with other areas relatively unnecessary and infrequent" (1950, p. 37).

Although Brown's work on Beech Creek focused on kinship structures and social stratification, the first chapters of his ethnography provide a historical account of eastern Kentucky and Beech Creek in the mid to late nineteenth century. Brown's account incorporated what Beech Creek inhabitants themselves were saying about their ancestors and vividly described what the life of the region's earlier inhabitants had been like. The information contained in these chapters and the rich genealogical information which Brown obtained from the inhabitants of Beech Creek provide the starting point for our work.

The value of ethnographic information must not be understated. In other interest areas of social history, abundant primarily historical sources such as church and court records, personal diaries, and business logs facilitate historical reconstruction. Social historians have been able to rely upon such sources in writing detailed accounts of New England farm families and their agricultural relations of production, for instance, which suggest new directions for Appalachian scholars (Billings, Blee, and Swanson, 1986). Many social historians of the Appalachian region, however, find their work made more difficult by the shortage of such sources, in a region with predominantly oral traditions. In the absence of such sources, ethnographies of rural community life in preindustrial Appalachia often provide valuable historical insights (Billings and Blee, 1987). But many of the accounts that provide us with the views of the Appalachian farmer, such as the literature of local color writers from the late nineteenth century, have almost exclusively been written by persons who were not from the region and have been subject to exaggeration and distortion. Shapiro (1978) suggests that many writers erred in stressing the "otherness" of Appalachia as a region set off from modern life. Some such accounts, as in Pearsall (1959), document the production methods of Appalachian farmers with the effect of imposing an inferior status on them while excluding the socio-economic realities that they faced. These accounts often speak of subsistence production but offer little or no evidence as to its actual extent or its mix with commercial farming.

Our particular approach in writing a social history of agriculture in Beech Creek is one which intersects primary data on agricultural production and demographic change with Brown's research on the Appalachian rural community and other recent literature on the Appalachian region. We attempt to avoid the negative stereotypes and condescending notions of the literature of the pejorative tradition by relying on Brown's ethnography—one which is the result of Appalachians talking about their ancestors—as a secondary source of information about Beech Creek during the preindustrial era. To supplement Brown's text, we utilize primary historical data compiled from US censuses and Kentucky tax rolls.

The question we have chosen to ask in this paper—whether or not Beech Creek farmers were producing at a subsistence level—is one that is often asked by social historians of Appalachian communities. Until recently, however, the answers researchers have given have been based mostly on the speculative writings of a variety of authors. No one has shown definitively that Appalachian farmers were primarily subsistence *oriented* producers or that market relations were based on a kinship network because of the *conscious* choices of producers and consumers as others such as Hahn (1985) contend. In fact, some recent accounts, such as Dunn's (1988) study of Cades Cove, Tennessee, posit commercialized farming as the predominant form of nineteenth century agriculture in the mountains. By integrating data from historical records with what Appalachians say about their past and their ancestors, we hope to be able to provide a more informed account of preindustrial agriculture and its characteristic social relations of production practices in Beech Creek.

This paper is a preliminary description of our current research. First, we describe the methods we have used to create data sets from the manuscript records of the US Census. Secondly, we illustrate a particular method we used for calculating the level of agricultural production in Beech Creek in 1880. This method estimates whether individual farm units were producing at merely a subsistence level or on a level at which production exceeded the consumption needs of farm families. Lastly, we integrate the information generated from these methods with what Brown has said about preindustrial agriculture in Beech Creek.

In his ethnographic study "Social Organization of an Isolated Kentucky Mountain Neighborhood" (1950), the isolated rural neighborhood of Beech Creek and the surrounding neighborhoods of Flat Rock and Laurel were defined by Brown not only in terms of geographical proximity but by the specific nature of relational ties which "connected" the farm families in a social grouping: "By 'neighborhood' (Brown) meant a 'real social group . . . a group of individuals . . . bound by some ties or bonds . . . which unite them into one social group in life and not only on paper'" (Brown, 1950, p. 142).

In reconstructing the Beech Creek community for the years 1850–1880, we employ a historical method that includes farms in the Beech Creek area based on the sequence and proximity of farms enumerated on the agriculture census schedules for the respective years. The method does not capture first hand observations of real life social ties but it does assume that proximity on census pages reflects geographical and, consequently, social proximity. The genealogies traced by Brown in 1942 were the starting point for this data collection. Names of the ancestors of Beech Creek inhabitants were found listed on the population schedules for the census years of 1850, 1860, 1870, and 1880. Those persons (and their neighbors) who were listed as heads of households and who were designated as "farmers" were then located on agricultural census schedules for the corresponding years. When exact matches resulted, the names of farmers and information about their farms were included in the data sets for each year.

Additional names and farms were also included in these data sets according to the following method advanced by Daniel (1978). The enumeration pages of agriculture schedules for each census year are read starting with the names of families who were directly matched from the population census. Assuming that the census takers walked up and down creek beds, from farm to farm, while soliciting census information, names which were listed on the census pages between the names which were directly matched are also included. Although this method includes more families than actually existed in what was later defined as Beech Creek by Brown, a rigid definition of Beech Creek is not important because we are primarily tracing family groups rather than merely a geographic area.

The agriculture data sets created by this method for 1850, 1860, 1870, and 1880 contain information on land, cash value, and production yields for 56 farms, 59 farms, 133 farms, and 86 farms, respectively. We have used these data sets to generate information concerning average cash value of farmland and farm production, average size of farms, average numbers of livestock, and average yields of crop production over time in Beech

Creek. (Table 1 contains a partial account of this information for the census year 1880.)

TABLE 1
LAND, CASH VALUE, and PRODUCTION YIELDS
BEECH CREEK, KENTUCKY, 1880

VARIABLE	MEAN	NO. OF FARMS REPORTING
Unimproved Acres	160.1	65
Improved Acres:		82
filled acres	21.3	
acres of pasture	14.0	51
Cash Value of Farm	$460.77	83
Value of Machinery and implements	$ 22.35	79
Value of Livestock	$140.95	82
Value of All Farm production	$150.50	80
Value of Forest products	$ 67.28	76
Horses	1.4	47
Milk Cows	1.9	72
Swine	11.6	50
Sheep	14.4	46
Indian Corn (bushels)	251.3	74
Wheat (bushels)	39.2	37
Oats (bushels)	36.9	25
Dried Beans (bushels)	2.6	38

Total Number of Farms: N = 86

Preliminary research tells us how much each farm unit produced, what the value of that production was, what the value of the farm itself was, and how each of these variables changed over time. This information alone, however, does not provide information relative to the topic of subsistence. Hence we searched for a method whereby we could determine whether Appalachian farmers were producing at a subsistence level or at a level which resulted in surplus. Tentatively, we are suggesting the use of a method adopted from two historical economists, Roger Ransom and Richard Sutch (1977) that relies on data available in the Agriculture Census of 1880 to determine whether or not the particular farmers in that year were producing a surplus. This method utilizes data on crop yield, crop acreage, number of livestock, number of farm laborers and family members and informed estimates on seeding requirements, the corn-equivalence of crops based on nutritional information, and reproduction requirements for livestock, farm laborers, and family labor. It requires that the total production of all basic food crops be converted into corn-equivalent units and that the requirements for reproducing the farm unit be deducted from this amount. The result indicates either a level of production below subsistence or one at above subsistence, e.g., a "surplus."

Similar methods have been used by other researchers with substantially different emphases. As suggested by Ransom and Sutch, many studies have de-emphasized the extent of food production while exaggerating the farm unit's consumption (see, Gallman, 1970). In their research, Ransom and Sutch suggest estimates that are more "conservative" in order to exaggerate production and de-emphasize the amount consumed by the farm unit.

We are using the revised estimates of Ransom and Sutch in this project to provide empirical evidence of whether or not each productive unit in Beech Creek was producing at or above a subsistence level. Subsistence, in this analysis, is thus defined as the level at which the production unit, the farm, can reproduce itself. Calculations which yield a zero or non-negative sum indicate production at or above subsistence level for particular farm units. We consider a farm unit to be capable of sustaining itself if the production of the unit exceeds the estimated required consumption. In using the conservative estimates of Ransom and Sutch, we have thus biased analysis in the direction of exaggerating production and de-emphasizing consumption. Therefore, the likelihood of a zero sum or non-negative sum resulting from the calculations is increased.

The calculation of surplus in corn-equivalent bushels is as follows: The estimated seeding requirement percentages provided by Ransom and Sutch are multiplied by the number of acres cultivated of a particular crop, and this product is subtracted from the total outputs of eleven essential grains and food crops produced. This net output is then converted to corn-equivalent units by multiplying it by estimated corn-equivalent conversion ratios also provided by Ransom and Sutch. This product is then aggregated and equals the total net crop production (TNGP) in corn-equivalent units The product of the feed allowance in corn-equivalent bushels for five basic farm animals (horses, oxen, mules, milch cows, and sheep) and the actual number of each on the farm, the total livestock consumption (TLC), is then subtracted from this total. Likewise, the product of the necessary requirements for reproducing the farm laborers and family members and the actual number of each on the farm, the total unit consumption (TCU), is subtracted from this difference. The resultant difference, the surplus food residual (SFR), is the surplus in corn-equivalent units produced by each farm in 1880.

Having described these methods, we now turn to an integration of Brown's work with the information provided by the data from 1880. Brown described Beech Creek as having been isolated from national and international economic markets by self-sufficiency. Though Brown characterizes late nineteenth century agriculture in Beech Creek as small scale production oriented toward sustaining the farm unit, he also indicates that small surpluses were produced.

In determining levels of production, we attempted to differentiate between crops that were used to sustain the farm unit and those which may have been produced for market. In looking at the historical record of Beech Creek farming, therefore, we concentrate on crops that were produced to sustain the farm. (These averages and totals are listed in Table 1.)

In 1880, production was focused on diversified staple crops. Indian corn was produced by seventy-six of the eighty-six farm units and average production was of 247 bushels produced on an average of thirteen acres. Corn was used as a staple crop for feeding the farm family and other persons on the farm and also to feed livestock, although open grazing was probably more important for the latter. Wheat production was less common among Beech Creek farmers—only thirty-seven out of eighty-six produced the crop. Of these thirty-six producers, an average of 39 bushels was produced on an average of seven acres. Another feed grain, oats, was produced by twenty-six farmers. These farmers produced an average of 37 bushels of oats on an average of six acres. Other crops that were specifically grown to feed the family were beans and potatoes: thirty-eight farmers produced an average of three bushels of dried beans, and irish and sweet potatoes were produced by ten and eleven farmers, respectively, at an average of 13 bushels and 26 bushels.

Tobacco was also produced on a small minority of farms: four farms produced the crop, three of which produced less than forty pounds and one which produced 300 pounds. Wool was produced on 46 of the 86 farms at an average of 19 pounds per farm. There was no cotton produced in Beech Creek. Further research is required to determine the significance of these crops to the local economy.

Almost all the farms had some sort of livestock. Most common were milk cows and swine—milk cows were present on 73 farms with an average of two per farm and swine were present of 51 farms with an average of twelve per farm. Forty-six farms raised sheep with an average of 14 sheep per farm. Barnyard poultry are also found: 81 farms raised poultry—averaging 23 birds per farm—and produced an average of 47 dozens of eggs.

Work animals were also kept. The most common were horses, mules, and working oxen: forty-seven farms had at least one horse per farm;

twenty-one farms had at least one mule; and eighteen farms had an average of 2 working oxen. The average value of livestock on 84 farms was $142.38

All but two farmers indicate that they utilized at least one acre of their farm in 1880 for crops. The average tilled portion of 84 farms was 21 acres. Fifty-two farms indicate an average of 14 acres of cleared pasture and 66 farms had an average of 160 acres of woodland. The value of the land on 85 farms averaged $473.81, however, the lowest land value was $4 indicated by one farmer and the highest value was $2000 indicated by three farmers. Only thirteen of the 85 farms were valued at more than $1000 while 64 of the farms were valued at or less than $500. Despite an egalitarian ideology, Beech Creek farms were stratified by differences in landownership and the wealth in 1880 just as they were when Brown first observed them in the 1940s. The average value of all farm production on 82 farms was $148.11 with no farm exceeding $500 in total farm production value.

This information indicates production level amounts and values of Beech Creek farms in 1880 but it does not provide sufficient information to determine the social significance of such amounts and values. Intuitively, it is obvious that there is a difference between producing 10 bushels of corn and producing 200 bushels, but how can this difference be made significant in determining what effect producing either 10 bushels or 200 bushels of corn had on respective production units. How are the effects of differential production to be ascertained? At this point we turn to the method of calculating surplus food residuals.

The case of Charles Barker illustrates the utility of our methodology. In 1880, Barker, at thirty-four years old, was the owner of 103 acres, of which 19 were cultivated, 9 were in pasture, and 75 were woodland. The value of his land, buildings, and fences was $500. With his wife Nancy, who was twenty-one years old, and four children, he produced indian corn, wheat, beans, and rye. The Barkers had two horses, one milk cow, and several sheep. The value of these animals was $200. Including the production of fifty dozens of eggs and fifty pounds of butter, the total value of all farm production for the year, consumed, sold, or on hand, was $100.

To calculate the production of surplus, the known variables are: 200 bushels of corn produced on 12 acres; 12 bushels of rye produced on 4 acres; 25 bushels of wheat also produced on 4 acres; 2 bushels of dried beans; 2 horses, 1 milk cow and 7 sheep; and the six family members. The corn-equivalent ratios for wheat, rye, and dried beans are 1.104, 1.05, and .946 respectively. The seed allowance for indian corn is .125 bushels per acre; for wheat, 1.5 bushels per acre; and for dried beans, .08 per bushel yield. The feed allowances for the animals are 35 bushels per horse, 5 per milk cow, and .25 per sheep. Lastly, there is a 15 bushel per family member allowance for the reproduction of labor. With this information, then, the calculation of the production of surplus in corn equivalent units for 1880 on Charles Barker's farm can be represented:

$$\text{Total Net Grain Production} =$$
$$(200-.125(12)) + 1.104(25-1.5(4)) + 1.05(12-1.5(4)) + .946(2-.08))$$

$$= 227.5 \text{ bushels}$$

$$\text{Total Consumption of Livestock} =$$
$$35(2) + 5(1) + .25(7)$$

$$= 76.75 \text{ bushels}$$

$$\text{Total Consumption Of Unit}$$
$$15(6)$$

$$= 90 \text{ bushels}$$

$$\text{Surplus Food Residual}$$
$$227.5 - 76.75 - 90$$

$$60.75 \text{ bushels}$$

With these calculations we have established that the production on Charles Barker's farm exceeded the amount needed to sustain the farm unit by almost 61 corn-equivalent bushels. According to our definition of subsistence production, then we would conclude that this particular farm was producing at a greater than subsistence level of production.

An example of a farm not producing at a subsistence level is that of Joseph Andrews. Andrews, who in 1880 was 46 years old, lived with his wife, Nancy, 45, their eight sons, one daughter, one daughter-in-law, and a niece and nephew, on 742 acres of land. 650 of these acres were woods, 32 were pasture, and sixty were used for crops. The total value of the land and buildings was $1750. Andrews produced just two crops: corn and wheat. In 1880, he produced 500 bushels of corn and 65 bushels of wheat. Andrews had 3 horses, 1 mule, and two oxen on the farm, as well as 2 milk cows, 40 sheep, and 15 pigs. His livestock was worth $400. Including 200 pounds of butter and 100 dozens of eggs, total farm production was valued at $300. When the surplus food residual is calculated for Andrews, we find that his farm was producing at below the subsistence level by 34 bushels.

We have calculated the surplus food residual for 84 farms in 1880 to determine the average total net grain production, the total consumption of each farm, and how many farms were producing at or above a subsistence level of production and how many were producing below subsistence. The average surplus food residual for 84 farms is 82 corn-equivalent bushels. 29 farms were producing below subsistence level and 55 were producing above subsistence level. The average total consumption of livestock is 65 corn-equivalent bushels. The Andrews case illustrates that even though the historical record may show high value, an abundance of land and livestock, and what appears to be high production, when the consumption level of the farm unit is considered, actual production was often less than at a subsistence level. The importance of this method, then, lies in its consideration of not only the objective production amounts obtained from the census records but also of the necessary consumption of the farm unit. When consumption is used as the second variable in the equation that indicates subsistence level of production, the information concerning production becomes more relevant to the topic of subsistence.

Social historians of the Appalachian region have begun to understand the significance of the manuscript census records in light of the available ethnographies of the region's rural communities in the preindustrial era. The agriculture census schedules from 1850 to 1880 provide a wealth of information about agricultural production on individual farms in many of the region's areas, including Central Appalachia. When this information is utilized in conjunction with the economic methods of Ransom and Sutch, levels of production can be assessed which indicate whether or not farms are producing at or above the level at which the farm unit can sustain itself, the subsistence level. The use of all three of these types of information—ethnographies, census records, and data generated from the methods of Ransom and Sutch—is extremely important in presenting a more informed description of agriculture in preindustrial Appalachia.

How did so many farm families that remained in Beech Creek survive below the level of subsistence in the late nineteenth century? Pruitt, in a study of 18th century Massachusetts which found 38% of all farms falling below the standard for self-sufficiency, suggests that 18th century New England farms were integrated into networks of production, cooperation and exchange that made "subsistence possible on farms that were not sufficient" (1984:349).

A similar inter-household economic subsistence network clearly operated in 19th and early 20th century Beech Creek. Some farm households supplemented below-reproduction level farm production with the proceeds of hunting, fishing and trapping, sources of food supply not measured in the Ransom and Sutch equation, yet we speculate that the major factor in their survival was the kin network.

Although census manuscripts do not record kinship relations beyond that of households, we believe that we will be able to show that the strength of family groups that Brown documented in 1942 was rooted in a pattern of interdependent subsistence from the previous century. Family and kin relationships made possible the reproduction of marginal and below-subsistence farms through inter-household strategies of survival. Case by case examination of the census materials reveals numerous examples of young household heads producing at the edge of subsistence (or below) but living up or down creekbeds near households headed by fathers and brothers, both producing a surplus. Extra-household strategies of cooperation, which the original Beech Creek researchers found to be so important for understanding the migration experience and urban adjustment of rural Appalachians as they relocated in Midwestern cities after the Second World War (Schwarzweller, Brown, and Mangalam, 1971), seem already to have emerged as an essential feature of nineteenth century Appalachian family life.

Bibliography

The authors would like to recognize James S. Brown for his initial work on Beech Creek. The authors also thank Gaye Holman, Jack Thigpen, and Jane Bagby for their help in collecting the data and Cecil Tickamyer for his assistance with computer programming. Data collection was supported with a grant from the Economic Research Service of the USDA. Requests for reprints of this article should be addressed to: Paul J. Weingartner, Department of Sociology, University of Kentucky, Lexington, Kentucky, 40506.

Billings, Dwight B., and Kathleen M. Blee, "Household Structure in a Preindustrial Appalachian Community: Beech Creek, Kentucky, 1850–1942." Forthcoming.

Billings, Dwight B., Kathleen M. Blee, and Louis Swanson, "Culture, Family, and Community in Preindustrial Appalachia." *Appalachian Journal*, 13:2 (Winter 1986).

Brown, James S., *Beech Creek: The Social Organization of an Isolated Kentucky Mountain Neighborhood*. (Berea, Kentucky: Berea College Press, 1988).

_____. "Social Organization of an Isolated Kentucky Mountain Neighborhood." Phd Dissertation. (Cambridge, Massachusetts: Harvard University, 1950).

Dunn, Durwood, *Cades Cove: The Life and Death of a Southern Appalachian Community, 1818–1937*. (Knoxville, Tennessee: University of Tennessee Press, 1988).

Gallman, Robert E., "Self-sufficiency in the Cotton Economy of the Antebellum South." *Agricultural History* 44 (January 1970).

Hahn, Steven, *The Roots of Southern Populism: Yeoman Farmers and the Transformation of the Georgia Upcountry, 1850–1890*. (New York, New York: Oxford University Press, 1959).

Pearsall, Marion, *Little Smokey Ridge: The Natural History of a Southern Appalachian Neighborhood*. (Birmingham, Alabama: University of Alabama Press, 1959).

Pruitt, Bettye Hobbs, "Self-sufficiency and the Agricultural Economy of Eighteenth Century Massachusetts." *William and Mary Quarterly*, 41:3 (July 1984).

Ransom, Roger and Richard Sutch, *One Kind of Freedom: The Economic Consequences of Emancipation*. (New York, New York: Cambridge University Press, 1977).

Schwarzweller, Harry K., James S. Brown, and J.J. Mangalam, *Mountain Families in Transition: A Case Study of Appalachian Migration*. (University Park, Pennsylvania: Pennsylvania University Press, 1971).

Shapiro, Henry, *Appalachia On Our Mind*. (Chapel Hill, North Carolina: University of North Carolina Press, 1978).

Smith, Daniel Scott, "A Community-Based Sample of the Older Population From the 1880 and the 1900 United States Manuscript Census." *Historical Methods*, 11:2 (Spring 1978).

Government Documents:

United States Census Office. *Tenth Census of the United States, 1880*. Vol. 1 (Population) Washington Government Printing Office, 1884.

───. *Tenth Census of the United States, 1880*, Vol. 3 (Agriculture) Washington Government Printing Office, 1884.

Biculturalism: A Comparison of Central Appalachians and the Inupiat of Alaska

by
Nelda K. Daley

Abstract

Biculturalism is a term used widely to discuss the conflict between Appalachian and dominant culture and is found often in the writings of Appalachian scholars. This term is not used widely by other subgroups in the United States such as Native Americans, Blacks, and Hispanics. The term is used extensively by the Alaskan Eskimo. In interviews with native people of the Inupiat, a subgroup of the Inuit, at Point Barrow Alaska during the winter of 1987 the term was frequently used to describe their efforts to accommodate themselves to the impact of the petroleum industry on their native culture which is based on hunting and gathering.

Several parallels between the development of coal in Appalachia and oil in Alaska lead to comparisons of how biculturalism played an adaptive role. Both regions were isolated with little or no infrastructure. Both regions maintained a subsistence barter economy with marginal participation in a monetary economy before development of an extractive single industry economy. Both regions had gone through periods of boom and bust and there has been little attempt at encouraging a diversified economy or an indigenous professional/middle class. In both cultures education tended to be brought to the region by "missionaries" who denigrated the indigenous culture and encouraged outmigration of the "better" students.

Although there are similarities in economic development and both groups now identify themselves as bicultural, biculturalism has developed somewhat differently in the two regions. These similarities and differences will be explored in the paper.

Introduction

In interviews in Central Appalachia, especially southwestern Virginia, and Barrow, Alaska, the term biculturalism was used or eluded to by informants who felt that 1) they wished to preserve values of their subculture that differed from dominant culture and 2) they needed to accommodate dominant culture in order to survive and prosper.

These two groups, mountaineers and the Inupiat, at first glance appear to be very different. Central Appalachia is a fertile ecological niche while Barrow on the Arctic north slope is frozen tundra that is virtually a dessert. Mountaineers are western Europeans, except for the black population, and therefore physically indistinguishable from other Americans. The Inupiat are Inuit and considered part of the mongoloid grouping with features that clearly distinguish them from whites. Central Appalachians are not an indigenous people but in migrants who drove out Native Americans. The Inupiat are Native Americans who have been dislocated by whites.

Closer analysis show some significant similarities. Both areas were developed by outlanders and in both cases the primary development occurred around a single non-renewable resource, coal in Central Appalachia and petroleum on the North Slope. There are also parallels in how these resources were developed. Both regions were isolated before development, Central Appalachia by the mountains and Barrow by the cold, with little or no infrastructure. Both regions had developed a subsistence barter economy with marginal participation in the monetary economy. Through development both regions had gone through boom and bust cycles and there had been little attempt by developers at encouraging a diversified economy or an indigenous professional or middle class. Both cultures had developed a set of values which are strikingly similar, emphasizing self-reliance, operation and sharing (Lewis, Kobak. and Johnson,1978; Chance, 1966). These values are at loggerheads with the values of competition, individualism, and self-achievement brought into the regions by developers. In both mountain and Inupiat cultures education tended to be brought to the area by "missionaries" who denigrated the indigenous culture, substituted dominant white values and encouraged outmigration of the "better" students.

The response of both Central Appalachians and the Inupiat to development and to the assault on their culture has been to develop ways of "acting" dominant while thinking and feeling in ways that preserve their culture. Unlike Blacks and Native Americans who also behave in bicultural ways. Central Appalachians and Inupiats identify themselves as bicultural. This biculturalism has developed somewhat differently in the two regions and the similarities and differences will be explored below.

Biculturalism Defined

Lewis, Kobak, and Johnson (1978) use the term biculturalism to illustrate the tension during the process of development between mountain values of equality, noncompetitiveness and family-neighborhood solidarity and dominant culture values of competitiveness, individualism, and selfachievement. Relying heavily on Memmi's *The Colonizer and The Colonized* (1965) they point to the family and the church as two refuges where mountain culture is maintained.

The tension occurs according to their view as missionaries follow developers into an underdeveloped region. As Mrs. Campbell pointed out: "suddenly the retarded frontier was rediscovered by two classes: those who saw the natural resources and sought them regardless of the interests of the natural owners: and those who with missionary zeal rushed in to educate and reform" (1925;8). As Lewis, et al. and Memmi indicate these educators and reformers tended to see indigenous culture as backward, arrested, primitive, and they tended to denigrate the culture, pushing to replace it with the culture of the colonizer. This denigration included all phases of the indigenous culture from arts and crafts to language to norms and values. Education tends to stress not only formal learning but also stresses resocialization and enculturation into the "right" culture. the culture of the missionary educator.

As Lewis, Kobak, and Johnson point out the tension between the family and the school create a dualism, indigenous culture at home and dominant culture in public. This biculturalism is a source of great unresolved stress because it causes the native to act in ways that denigrated his own "true" self.

> The family encourages biculturalism. The schools create a duality—a world different from the family environment. Branscome speaks of the "annihilation of the hillbilly" by the institution. Many mountain youth remember the shaming process when they had to deny their "mother tongue'" reject their music and religion.
> ... Mountain children are taught early to act properly in public and hillbilly at home. Mountain people learn to deal with medical, welfare, educational, government institutions and speak their language and use their techniques. They learn to use institutions, outsiders, etc. selectively. But the strain is great. The mountain person is taught how to use the hillbilly stereotype for his own protection and to confound, aggravate, harass, and thwart the colonizer. (They leave the program planner wondering why that didn't work.) One example is the stereotype of the laziness, dependency, and irresponsibility which the Appalachian has learned to manipulate effectively in order to sabotage the colonizer's attempts to organize the mountaineer into pseudo participatory democracy rituals which further splinter Appalachian solidarity. (Lewis, Kobak, and Johnson. 1978:134–135)

Biculturalism as defined here is a learned adaptive behavior in which the person maintains their native culture, away from the eye of the outlander but tends to enact cultural stereotypes of himself when dealing with members of the dominant culture. The conclusion drawn by Lewis, et al. with regard to biculturalism is ambivalent. They quote Memmi's point that in order to preserve indigenous culture the native must cut himself off, live in cultural isolation which leads to a situation in which the culture "hardens, petrifies, and degrades its own life in order to save it"(1978;136). On the other hand Smathers is quoted as pointing to enacting stereotypes as "resistance strategies" which could further the saving of Appalachia (1978,136). In the extended quote above biculturalism sounds much like the shucking and giving of whitie or Uncle Tomming done by Blacks to conceal one's real abilities.

Since this article the view of biculturalism and the ambivalence generated by it has been modified by at least one of the authors. Sue Ella Kobak has indicated that she now sees biculturalism in more positive terms, namely a combination of the cooperative sharing values of the mountains with the technical skills and competencies offered by the dominant culture (Conversations, 1987–1988). For example mountain young people who seek higher education frequently go into the helping professions. This allows them the professional status and selfachievement approved by dominant culture while maintaining a commitment to others, a mountain value. Further, these professions tend to allow them to return to their communities, i.e. back to their kin and to the land. as both one of their own but also someone who can help. These young people can become professionals while "not getting above their raising." On the other hand, biculturalism can create some negative combinations. When the personableness of mountain culture gets combined with a desire for acquisition of material goods and an elite status, traits of the dominant culture, a very manipulative personality can emerge. Whether positive or negative, this revised view of biculturalism does not see the indigenous person as "shucking and jiving" to conceal their "true personality" but rather combining aspects of both cultures to create a "new" character.

It is this latter use of biculturalism that was found among the Inupiat. Biculturalism was seen as a very positive and desirable ability, one to be encourahed. It was seen as adaptive rather than as a resistance strategy and a strategy that allowed for the preservation of Inupiat culture while being able to use what was usable from white culture and technology.

Chance (1966) in discussing how greater contact between whites and Inupiat will impact on Inupiat leadership stresses biculturalism (without using the term).

> ... the leadership role becomes complex. In addition to being technically proficient at the appropriate tasks, initiating and directing action, and showing consideration for followers, the Eskimo leader must have an overt awareness of the conflict-

ing patterns and values of white and Eskimo culture and be able to deal effectively with them.

This requires not only sufficient command of English, but an adequate understanding of those aspects of white society that have a bearing on community life in the north. . . . [but]

. . . he must be careful not to identify himself too closely with his white counterpart for fear that community members will believe he no longer is representing their needs and interests. The leader who ceases to share the norms, objectives, and aspirations of the group ceases to be a leader. Nor may he be authoritarian or aggressive in his actions for this goes directly against Eskimo values. (Chance, 1966:63–64).

These differing views of biculturalism reflect slightly different events in economic development in the two regions as well as differences in the ecology of the regions. Below we will explore some striking cultural parallels and then turn to important differences to see how biculturalism has evolved in the two regions.

Parallels

Appalachian and Inupiat cultures contain values that are very similar. These values revolve around self-reliance and individualism, sharing, cooperation and the family as the basis of society and community. Lewis describes Appalachian culture as follows:

The main aspects of the culture that were fought for and were the hardest to change were mainly patterns of relationships which can be described as basically *non-competitiveness*. Family members and neighbors depend on each other, but it is a dependence which also encourages independence of "let the other fellow alone." People help each other in time of need; they share the load; but this help is not imposed nor organized and leaves room foe independence and individuality.

. . . To keep a sense of equality and noncompetitiveness, a "local success" or ambitious hillbilly almost has to leave his family and neighborhood and live with the colonizers. In his small neighborhood he will be sabotaged and people won't help him. He will be put down as not neighborly and "out for himself."

. . . Equality is still important. Mountain people resist experts, titles, and people who put on airs or get above their raising. (Lewis, Kobnak and Johnson, 1978: 133–134)

Jones confirms these values by pointing out that Appalachian society stresses self-reliance, neighborliness, familialism, and personalism. He points out that we "do not want to be beholding to other people" (Jones, 197:102), but at the same time it was a compliment to be "clever," i.e. "to be hospital, quick to invite you in and generous with food" (102). Further, "we will go to any lengths to keep from offending others" (102) and have a sense of "responsibility to one another that extends to cousins, nephews, nieces, uncles and aunts and to in-laws" (102). Finally, "we know that he [man] fails, often, and we are not disillusioned when he does ... These beliefs keep us at peace with ourselves. We don't pretend we are something we are not" (103). Jones also points out that Appalachians have a keen sense of place and a strong identity with the land. In speaking of his sense of locale he says "and this place is tied in my mind along with my family and with the people I knew in the growing process" (103). As Eller points out the "essence of community life" was familialism (Eller, 1982:33).

This society then was one that stressed a sense of equality, that no one was better than anyone else and that he who was most capable at a given task made the decisions as to what action to take. A sense of social class and lines of authority are foreign to this society.

Chance (1966) identified very similar values among the Inupiat. He points out that there as a "strong current of individualism" in the culture which "stressed respect for the thoughts and feelings" of others (73). This individualism was combined with "self-reliance, self-confidence and generosity" (74). Child rearing practices stressed the need for co-operation and that wishes were more likely to be fulfilled if the child was not "lazy" (75).

> Children soon learned that family members were highly dependent upon each other for many of their comforts and conveniences in daily life ... Achieving manhood, the adult continued to maintain a strong sense of identification with members of his own kin group and as such, was more likely to subordinate his own personal interests to the welfare of the group ... it is easy to understand why the "poorest" Eskimo was a person without kin, the individual who had no one to turn to in time of need. (Chance, 1966:75)

Like the Appalachian the Inupiat stressed equality and leadership was based more on ability than authority. The leader of a whaling expedition had:

> no clearly defined authority over others, for his role as leader was determined by his own personal qualities and skills. Except within the family orders and commands were not ex-

pected from others, and the authoritarian bull met with great resentment (Chance, 1966:74).

The Inupiat also have a strong sense of place and resist mobility, a quality frequently seen as problematic by whites (Chance, 1966; Stabler, 1985; Whittington, 1985).

Similar disruptions occurred to both the Appalachian and the Inupiat with the development of the non-renewable resource, coal and petroleum. Both moved from a barter economy to a wage economy. Males moved into the wage economy as unskilled labor. During boom times, 1880–1926 in Appalachia and 1970–1986 in Barrow, work was plentiful and wages adequate to good. The development of a diversified economy did not occur however and was not encouraged. No indigenous educated middle class was encouraged and the main employer of educated indigenous people was the public service sector of government (Eller, 1982; Whisnant, 1980; Page, 1986; Stabler, 1985; Whittington, 1985).

These economic changes had very similar impact on the culture which is best summarized by Whittington in writing about the Eskimo. He points out that removal from the land and native subsistence patterns in effect mean cultural displacement as well. Native economy is based on a culture which places high value on the oollectivity, stress communal sharing, has no clear sense of private property, and has a reverence for the land.

> The wage economy implies individualism, competition and inegalitarianism, while the native culture espouses collectivism, consensus, and egalitarianism. Similarly, where the native social structures see authority in terms of a functional division of labor based on ability, the wage economy implies that power and status are determined by income. (Whittington, 1985:68)

Eller (1982) points to a very parallel problem in Appalachia and the development of coal. As the mountaineer moves from agriculture to company towns he also looses his sense of identity with the land. As taxes and land prices soared, opportunities for mountaineers to acquire homes near coal mines diminished. "This lack of home ownership sorely disturbed many mountain residents ... whose family and culture tied him to the region" (Eller, 1982:196). Dependent on company town facilities and paid in scrip that could only be spent in these towns the mountaineer became a tenant in what once was his. Further, the towns created living conditions foreign to mountain culture. Disposal of refuse was a problem, child and spouse abuse increased as did divorce. Illnesses uncommon in the mountains as well as malnutrition also increased. A generation of children were raised removed from the land yet unable to leave (Eller, 1982:232–234).

Differences

Despite these parallels there are some significant differences between mountaineers and the Inupiat. The primary difference was in the definition given them by outlanders. Inupiat men who define themselves primarily as hunters and outdoorsmen found that unskilled day labor could be combined with traditional subsistence activities of hunting and whaling Secondly, the extreme conditions of the Arctic made whites dependent on the survival skills of the Inupiat. Inupiat men are seen as hard working and industrious by whites and the men have made efforts to adapt to white ways such as accommodating themselves to white work schedules (Chance, 1966:92).

Eller on the other hand points to the mountaineers resistance to the ways of outlanders.

> The tendency of mountain laborers to take off during certain times of the year to participate in farm activities and traditional customs was especially irritating to the mine operators . . .
> Absenteeism, however, was only one way that the mountaineers rejected the industrial norms of the mine managers. By ignoring work schedules, mining routines, and other innovations which worked at cross-purposes with their traditional way of life, they sought to maintain their individualism and freedom from authority. (Eller, 1982:167)

Coal barons felt that mountain men might make good hunters and guides but were useless as a reliable labor force. Immigrant labor was preferred and blacks and mountaineers were seen as shiftless and unreliable.

Inupiat men had made some essential and inevitable compromises in order to adapt to the white system. As Chance points out the Inupiat are quite pragmatic and accept or reject an idea or technology based on their view of its usefulness. Mountain men were more resistant to these compromises.

The Present Situation

Currently among the Inupiat there has been a decline in the high wage but unskilled jobs in construction traditionally held by Inupiat men. As capital improvement projects decline and a cutback to maintenance jobs occurs, there are fewer jobs available and at lower wages. Those jobs that are available tend to be in the service sector of the government. These jobs are indoor jobs, require advanced levels of education, and are work that women have traditionally held in white culture (Worl and Smythe, 1986). These jobs are seen by the men as incompatible with their hunting schedule (Kruse, 1986) and incompatible with their definition of themselves as hunters (Interviews, 1987). Women are now the main wage earners with 60 percent employed fulltime, year round in white collar jobs (Worl and Smythe, 1986). Women have moved into these positions because their work in offices is compatible with traditional subsistence activities such as skin sewing and such activities have been abandoned to some extent by the women (Worl and Smythe, 1986; Kruse, 1986). These traditional activities conferred less status on the women than did hunting on the men and was less central to their identity. More women have become well educated and have been encouraged by whites to take these service occupations that are traditionally female.

The Inupiat women of Barrow see themselves as bicultural, use the term, and believe that biculturalism is the hope for the future. They admit that the men are less enamoured of biculturalism and link the men's lack of enthusiasm to their identity as hunters. Professional Inupiat women plan to encourage Inupiat children to go to university and return to Barrow systematically replacing whites in the schools, in the scientific installations and in the professions. (Interviews, 1987). To that end the North Slope Borough was incorporated and Inupiat language and culture are encouraged in the schools. However, very serious efforts are being made to get Barrow children into the University of Alaska and keep them there. Currently, nearly 50 percent of all Barrow High School Graduates enter university.

This biculturalism and the role of women in its latest development has created some problems. Men are still the primary political leaders but still define themselves as hunters. They resist this new biculturalism and see many of the activities of the women as unimportant and/or undercutting their authority. There have been problems of family breakdown, alcohol and drug abuse, and spouse abuse. The women through the mother's club established the Arctic Women in Crisis which is staffed half and half by white and Inupiat women. The white staff fully intends to turn the project over to the Inupiat women (Interviews, 1987). However, these facilities and the staff positions as well as positions in the government service sector are dependent on huge government expenditures. As petroleum profits decline and reserves are used up, as capital improvement declines, less revenue will be generated. If the men, the government leaders, decrease funding in these areas because they see them as "white" activities that are irrelevant to Inupiat culture, the role of the women will deteriorate and biculturalism will deteriorate. In interviews in a small southwestern Virginia community (Interviews, 1986) it was clear that men in the community had not only experienced a long period of unemployment but were also demoralized. The community had a high illiteracy rate and there was low motivation for men to seek employment. Many of these men defined themselves primarily as outdoors men and hunters and saw little value in acquiring skills or education for jobs that did not exist (Shifflett, 1977; Carawen and Carawen, 1982). The women in the community had worked in the local sewing factory and when that burnt down worked with the local development commission to develop both jobs and education. The development commission itself, an incorporated non-profit corporation, had been developed by the local women's club to deal with local community needs. Although the goal of the commission was not to help women, in fact it was women who took advantage of and benefited most from the commissions projects. It was primarily women who enrolled in the GED and AA programs, obtained degrees, and worked with the commission to develop jobs. Women then were the most likely to be bicultural, to acquire the skills and knowledge that make them competitive in the labor force. Men, on the other hand, were more likely to act out the stereotypical roles of a "hillbilly or redneck." Men were referred to as "real go getters" which meant they were willing to give up time from their outdoor activities to "go get her [the wife] from work." They tended to be less interested in the educational programs and were less involved in the development commission. Local male political leaders had in fact actively worked against the commission (Interviews, 1986).

This community also had experienced some serious dislocations. Family breakdown was common as well as alcoholism and spouse abuse. Further, the development commission had not been able to generate jobs for the women commensurate with their education nor had economic diversity occurred. The main goal of the commission to establish a community owned sewing factory would generate over 100 jobs but these jobs did not require higher levels of education.

Unlike the Inupiat these mountain women have not found a ready market for their education and skills. If these women are to find employment commensurate with their education, if they are to continue to develop, they will have to outmigrate. In effect, they will cease to be bicultural, giving up their commitment to family and the land.

Summary and Conclusion

There are some clear parallels between mountain society and Inupiat society with regard to values, patterns of development and the impact of development on those values. Both societies have utilized biculturalism to deal with those changes. In both societies it was the men who were initially bicultural. However, Inupiat men were not negatively stereotyped by white culture while mountain men were.

Inupiat men could more easily combine their traditional activities with wage labor than could mountain men. For Inupiats biculturalism was functional while it was not for mountain men. However, for both societies as job opportunities declined and/or shifted, men's motivation to be bicultural also shifted. Inupiat men have decreased their investment in white culture while mountain men have acted out dominant culture's stereotypes.

Women in both societies are currently more likely to benefit from biculturalism. However, for both groups the conditions that support this biculturalism is fragile. Among the Inupiat it depends upon continued government funded white collar and professional jobs. Among mountain women it depends on the development of jobs commensurate advanced education.

The future does not look good. Feelings in Alaska are that as oil revenues decline, the Inupiat villages will disappear. Mostly likely these women will migrate then to urban areas in southern Alaska where it will be impossible to maintain traditional Inupiat culture of co-operation, sharing, selfreliance and family solidarity linked to the land as noted by Whittington. The same is true for mountain women unless job opportunities expand which does not seem likely (Caudill, 1986). These women will migrate to urban areas outside the region and their mountain ways, so similar to the Inupiat, will also disappear.

Biculturalism may be a transition adaptive strategy. As development based on non-renewable resources and a single industry economy fluctuates, so does the need for biculturalism. In the final analysis it appears that the indigenous culture is absorbed by dominant culture.

Bibliography

Carawen, Guy and Candie Carawen. 1982. *Voices from the Mountains.* University of Illinois Press.

Caudill, Harry. 1986. Comments. conference entitled *Appalachia: The Land and The Economy* The University of Kentucky, Lexington.

Chance, Norman A. 1966. *The Eskimo of North Alaska.* Holt, Rinehart and Winston.

Eller, Ron. 1982. *Miners, Millhands, and Mountaineers.* The University of Tennessee Press.

Jones, Loyal. 197 . "Appalachian Values." In Ergoode and Kurhe, Kendall/Hunt.

Kruse, John A. 1986. "Subsistence and the North Slope Inupiat: The Effects of Energy Development," in Steve J. Langdon (ed.) *Contemporary Alaskan Native Economies.* University Press of America.

Lewis, Helen M., Sue Easterling Kobak, and Linda Johnson. 1972. "Family, Religion, and Colonialism in Central Appalachia or Bury my Rifle at Big Stone Gap," in *Colonialism in*

Modern America: The Appalachian Case, Lewis, Johnson, and Askins (eds.), Appalachian Consortium Press.

Memmi, Albert. 1965. *Colonizer and Colonized*. Grossman.

Page, Robert. 1986. *Northern Development*. McClelland and Stewart.

Shifflett, Peggy. 1977. *Women in Appalachia*. Unpublished Masters Thesis.

Stabler, Jack C. 1985. "Development Planning North of 60: Requirements and Prospects," in Michael S. Whittington *The North*. University of Toronto Press.

Whittington, Michael. 1985. "Political and Constitutional Development in the N.W.T. and Yukon: The Issues and Interests," in Michael Whittington (ed.) *The North*. University of Toronto Press.

Whisnant, David E. 1980. *Modernizing the Mountaineer*. Appalachian Consortium Press.

Worl, Rosita and Charles W. Smythe. 1986. *Barrow: A Decade of Modernization*. U.S. Department of the Interior, Technical Report 125.

Appalachian Culture As Reaction To Uneven Development A World Systems Approach to Regionalism

by
Roberta McKenzie

Introduction

The region called Appalachia in the United States has been defined over the last half century as a culture apart from mainstream America (Billings, Blee, Swanson, 1986). Such perceptions of Appalachia as different from the rest of society has fostered not only volumes of research on the nature and causes of this difference, but a reactionary literature to the negative implications of many analyses.

Since the advent of a coal-boom inspired infrastructure in World War II, the historically isolated mountain region has been percieved, in the extreme, as harboring descendants of criminals who were responsible for their own "backwardness" and poverty (Raitz and Ulack, 1984:336). A softer, and in some ways more exploitive, image of Applachians is that they were simply behind and needed to "catch up" to the modern world. Two important themes, one pervasive during the 1970s, and a second one which has been developing recently, are intellectual responses to the explanations of Appalachians as possessing a culture that is out-of-step with the rest of society: 1) The application of the internal colonialism model to the situation of Appalachians, and 2) the question of an emerging Appalachian ethnic identity. In general, the internal colonial model has been applied to explain the conditions of Appalachian development as due to uneven capitalist relations between the region and the rest of the country (Walls). The question of "Appalachianness" is explored here as a reaction to these uneven relations and to the definition given to Appalachians by outsiders.

The World System and Social Order

World Systems theories are anchored in the premise that the components of the world, i.e., nation-states, governments, groups and individuals, are integrated politically and economically within a system. Whether this notion arises from a perspective which equates internal dynamics with the capitalist mode of production (such as Wallerstein, Feinberg, Frank) or from a view that there are diversified systems in ideological as well as economic conflict (Krasner, etc.), the basic contention is that the peoples of the world interact on an institutional level and that these relationships are often uneven. Imperialism and colonialism are concepts which delineate the exploitative nature of these relationships. Smith (1981:5) defines imperialism " ... as the effective domination by a relatively strong state over a weaker people whom it does not control as it does its home population, or as the effort to secure such domination." Colonialism is the forced entry into and domination of a region by outsiders and is characterized by cultural and social restructuring and by "racism" (Lewis, 1978:16). In most analyses of such relationships investigators deal with the colonization of a nation or region by a foreign culture (Hechter, 1975:30). The *internal* colonial model is used to analyze a "peripheral" or underdeveloped area *within* the national boundaries of a "core or highly-industrialized area (Hechter, 1976; Lewis, 1978; Walls, 1976). This model was particularly important in Appalachian studies during the 1970's.

In an external colonial situation, less advantaged groups may adopt an ideology in opposition to racist perceptions of their dominators in order to claim economic and political rights. Nationalism since the nineteenth century was forced reaction to the spread of capitalist relations (Nairn, 1977:27). The movement for Scottish separatism within the British Isles, Nairn (1977:126–128) argues, was a "neo-nationalistic" response to "relative deprivation." "Neo-nationalism arises at a different much later point in the same general process [of capital expansion] ... at a far more advanced stage of general development" (Nairn, 1977:128). Likewise, Beers (1979:202) examines ethnic activism in France in the dual framework of *internal colonialism* and relative deprivation. "While internal colonialism explains the preservation of ethnic regions, rapid economic development and its attendant rising expectations explains the extra-electoral ethnic protests of the present time" (Beers, 1979:217). Hechter (1975) takes a similar view, using the internal colonial model to define nationalism as *ethnic* reactions to domination from the core. The question to be asked is whether or not there can be detected such a tendency among the people of the Appalachian region and what it indicates about institutional relationships. Specifically, is identification with a group a cultural manifestation of the political and economic conditions of a capitalist world economy?

Internal Colonialism

As stated before, colonialism and imperialism are related and sometimes interactive processes. Melizia (1973:130) claims imperialism is not just a capitalist phenomona: "Broadly speaking, imperialism refers to a complex set of unequal relationships—economic, political and cultural, where the strong take advantage of the weak." He (Melizia, 1973:132–134) delineates three types of economic imperialism: 1) Unequal real wage distribution between metropolitan and non-metropolitan regions; 2) Unequal amounts of profits on same production processes across regions; and 3) unequal market relations.

British expansion in the nineteenth century was still characterized primarily by imperialism that was both a consequence and a motive of British economic policy (Smith, 1981:35). The political dimension of imperialism developed due to competition among Western powers that forced projections into other regions (Smith, 1981). Thus imperialism predicated on capitalism may be seen as an antecedent or previous state of colonialism. "Imperialism was particularly apt to become colonialism in those areas where the native political organization was unable for local reasons to exercise its authority effectively" (Smith, 1981:85).

While overt imperialist expansion and colonialism are no longer part of European and American international policy, the legacies of the processes are still very much a part of the economic world order and colonial relations persist (Smith, 1981). One of the manifestations of these relations is the racial basis of differentiation among groups. This carries over from the colonial justification for dominating and administering to an "inferior" populace. Thus colonialist relations are not only characterized economically and politically, but ideologically. "Colonialism, racialism and racialist ideology are the products and component parts of the capitalist system" (Klaus, 1980:454).

"One of the defining characteristics of the colonial situation is that it must involve the interaction of at least two cultures—that of the conquering metropolitan elite and of the indigenes" (Hechter, 1975:73). Indigenous culture is denigrated and results in the native's will being undermined to resist the colonial regime (Hechter, 1975:73). Ultimately this translates into the "culture of poverty" perspective that the indigenous culture is responsible for its own backwardness. Regarding Appalachia: "Generally, such explanations tend to identify subcultural traits (or behavior) and compare these against some 'norm' usually the larger American culture" (Raitz and Ulack, 1982:341). Thus, the denigration and appropriation of culture is indicative of such an exploitative situation as the appropriation of resources.

Lewis (1978:16) borrows Blauner's rather straightforward distinction between classical colonialism and internal colonialism. In the former, the colonizers move in; in the latter, the colonized are brought into the situation as well. Otherwise, relationships between the dominant group and the subordinate group differ little between the two situations. Internal colonialism occurs in the uneven development of state territory settled by different groups (Hechter, 1975:9). "As a consequence of this initial fortuitous advantage, there is crystalization of the unequal distribution of resources and power between the two groups" (Hechter, 1975:9). This results in a diversified industrial core and a complimentary dependent periphery (Hechter, 1975:9).

Emergent Ethnicity

Hechter (1975:28) applies the internal colonialism model to the relationship between the Celtic regions of the British Isles to England as a way to explain the "survival of traditionalism within a sea of modernity." "From the seventeenth century on, English military and political control in the peripheral regions was buttressed by a racist ideology which held that Norman Anglo-Saxon culture was inherently superior to Celtic culture" (Hechter, 1975:342). When one group is denied access to high prestige roles which the superordinate group reserves for its members this "contributes to the development of distinctive ethnic identification in the two groups" (Hechter, 1975:9). Further, . . . "to the extent that social stratification in the periphery is based on observable cultural differences, there exists the probability that the disadvantaged groups will, in time, reactively assert its own culture as equal or superior to that of the relatively advantaged core" (Hechter, 1975:10). The specific form of a culture is incidental to the function culture performs in maintaining social order (Hechter, 1975:35). In this way, an ethnic group is defined by cultural traits (Hechter, 1975:35). This definition is inadequate to explain social change and the maintenance of cultural differences between groups in close, continued contact (Hechter, 1975:35). For Hechter (1975:37), cultural distinctions can be deliberate and purposeful: "It is clear that culture maintenance in the periphery can be regarded as a weapon in that it provides the possibility of socialization, as well as political mobilization, contrary to state ends." Ethnic solidarity is an instance of political mobilization that can result when individuals see inequality as a pattern of collective oppression (Hechter, 1975:41–42).

Another way to view ethnicity which may be concommitant to Hechter's (1975) perspective is to see it as a psychological "anchor" for personal identity in a changing world (Obermiller, 1977), an in-gathering of human resources for group economic and political participation (Isaacs, 1975: Glazer, 1983; Eisinger, 1978), or as developing from both processes. Ethnicity becomes more of a rational "option" (Eisinger, 1978). "Rather than viewing it as a primitive holdover, the optionalists conceive of ethnicity primarily as a strategic possibility peculiarly suited to the requirements of political and social mobilization in the modern large-scale state" (Eisinger, 1978:90). However, this may be taken further: " . . . as more groups choose the option of exploiting ethnicity for political mobilization—as American blacks have done most recently—other groups feel compelled to use ethnicity as a defensive response" (Eisinger, 1978:93). It is necessary for survival.

To put this into a simpler framework, the emergence or salience of ethnicity may be seen as based on interactions between distinct groups within facilitating circumstances: " . . . ethnic distinctions do not depend on an absence of social interaction and action, but are quite to the contrary often the very foundations on which embracing social systems are built" (Barth, 1969:10). In this way, ethnicity is more of an instance of active participation distinctly different from anthropological definitions which are based primarily on cultural and geographic distinctions. However, this fact—anthropological definition, that is—may be a part of the process. In other words, pushing a group into a particular definition may spark a reactionary self-definition.

Appalachian Underdevelopment

The cultural definitions of Appalachia are generally limited to the coal-rich Central Plateau in parts of West Virginia, Kentucky, Tennessee, and North Carolina even though the mountains range from upper New York to central Alabama. "Appalachia was not recognized as a distinct sociocultural region until the latter part of the nineteenth century" (Raitz and Ulack, 1984:18). It was delineated first by the "local color movement," then cultural regionalizations and governmental regionalizations (Raitz and Ulack, 1984:26). Even sociologists and anthropologists perpetuated an image of a traditional, isolated society that ran counter to mainstream America.

Pearsall (1959:127) described the folk culture of Appalachia based on fieldwork done in 1949–50:

> "Through continued isolation, the world of the Southern frontier became a folk world of small isolated, homogenous societies with a simpler and almost self-sufficient economy. In such societies there can be little occupational specialization or differentiation of roles beyond those of male and female, adult and child."

However, even then, Pearsall (1959:137) noted the tendencies for missionaries and social workers from the outside "to lump the entire mountain population together, seeing 'quaint' folk traits but also seeing 'appalling' characteristics of a rural lower class." What seemed to be happening was both a process of definition of Appalachians and explanation of their society that was centered in the region and concentrated on Appalachian resistance to outside influence.

In the 1970's, along came an upsurge in studies on the Third World that charged that the age of colonialism is still affecting the political processes and social organizations of Third World countries. This view was "borrowed" to some extent and applied to the Appalachian region as "victim" of uneven capitalist relations to counter the culture of poverty definitions. Whereas the prevailing view in the mid-century was of a traditionalist subcultural "remnant," political and economic interpretations of Appalachia began to replace these views in the 1970's (Billings, Blee and Swanson, 1986:154).

"The internal colonialism model has emerged from a background of the history and theories of colonialism and imperialism, and is most directly related to the theories of neocolonialism and dependency that have been developed in the post-World War II period" (Walls, 1978:234). The model is attractive because of its powerful analysis of the destruction of indigenous culture by the dominators (Walls, 1976:238). Caudill (1965), Walls (1976:237) claims, while not naming it outright, was using it when he outlined the relationship between the coal boom and the discovery of Appalachia: "When the construction gangs laid down their tools ... the vast, backward Cumberland Plateau was tied inseparably to the colossal industrial complex centering in Pittsburgh, and a dynamic new phase in the region's history had begun" (Caudill 1965:93).

In a similar fashion, but with a different tone, Eller's (1982:xviii) later analysis of Appalachian history discussed the penetration of the industrial North and the disparaging attitudes toward Appalachians as a tendency in core/peripheral relationships:

> "Blaming the victim, of course, is not a uniquely American phenomenon. Rather, it is a misreading that takes international form. French intellectuals talk about the Alps and Spanish intellectuals talk about the Pyrenees in much the same simple if condenscending way as urban Americans talk about Appalachia. Ironically, it was during the same years that the static image was emerging as the dominant literary view that a revolution was shaking the very foundations of the mountain social order."

The nature of the "invasion" of the Appalachian region was a negative one, bringing " ... bitter civil war followed by vicious exploitation of timber and mineral resources" (Pearsall: 1959:61). Pearsall (1959:58) noted the encounter with the outside left Appalachians not only negatively defined but in a negative economic position.

Along with the coming of railroads, towns and expanding industrialization, " ... there emerged in Appalachia a constructed political system based upon an economic heirarchy" (Eller, 1982:xxi). Those in economic and political power exploited the region's natural wealth (Eller, 1982:xxi). Behind this transition in political culture lay the integration of the region into the national economy and the subordination of local interests to those of outside corporations (Eller, 1982:xxi).

To get down to a specific instance of outside exploitation and the application of the internal colonial model, Gaventa (1980) analyzed a small coal town in Central Appalachia. He (Gaventa, 1980:52–53) described the appropriation of resources as " ... the industrial colonization of ... valleys of the Cumberland Gap region ..." which was undertaken by the American Association, Ltd.—an English company incorporated in 1887.

Further, Gaventa (1980) contended the valley's apparent disinterest in contesting their unequal treatment was due to past experience, a phenomena not unique to America. "As much of the under-developed area is owned and dominated by a British-based corporation, an understanding of the situation involves examining the contemporary role of the multinational in the affairs of a local community, as well as the means through which protest may emerge against landholders who are corporate and absentee" (Gaventa, 1980:viii-ix.)

The mechanisms by which the multinational, American Association, Ltd., maintained its hold on the community was three-dimensional (Gaventa, 1980:13). The first dimension of power is a straightforward conflict with emphasis on who prevails in decision-making: the second dimension is a "mobilization of bias," the institutionalization of systematic rules in favor of certain groups (Gaventa, 1980:13–14). The third, or "hidden" dimension of power is descriptive of colonial relationships:

> "Their [mechanisms of power] identification, one suspects, involves specifying the means through which power influences, shapes, or determines conceptions of the necessities, possibilities and strategies of challenge in situations of latent conflict. This may include the study of social myths, language and symbols, and how they are shaped or manipulated in power processes" (Gaventa, 1980:15).

This is tied, then to the the ideological aspect and leads to the appropriation of culture, a process which ranges from new place names in an area that reflect outside influence to the control of socializing agencies such as churches and schools (Gaventa, 1980:62).

The evidence of a colonial relationship between Appalachia and the rest of the United States "cannot be disputed" according to Lewis (1978:24). Uninvited coal interests controlled the region from outside and impacted the cultural patterns (Lewis:24). Especially supportive is ."..the fact that racism exists to perpetuate this pattern ..." (Lewis, 1978:24). Additionally, Lewis (1978:17) claims the domination of the region is based on technological superiority and the "broad-form" deed. These deeds were instituted during the early industrialization of Appalachia and ceded to coal operators all minerals and rights to remove them any way necessary (Lewis, 1978:17018). Much of the evidence of colonialism is centered around the broad-form deed (Raitz and Ulack, 1984:344-345), the legality of which is still being contested.

Melizia (1973:130) claims a scientific application of the imperialism concept in examining statistics in a non-metropolitan region of Central Appalachia. Despite a lack of statistical support for unequal wage, values of capital and trade between core and perhipheral areas, he (Melizia, 1973:132-136) switches to a logical argument: "The region appears to continually suffer from a net drain of economic surplus to other areas without making gains in relative income or productivity growth."

However, Walls (1976:232), while contending that Central Appalachia "is a peripheral region within an advanced capitalist society," claims internal colonialism must be carefully defined to be more than a "catchword" (Walls, 1976:235) and that Lewis' application is "strained" (Walls, 1976:237).

The establishment and maintenance of dominance over others is a pervasive process in America extending to all ethnic and working-class cultures in advanced capitalist societies (Walls, 1986:239). Walls (1976:234-235) says, internal colonialism is popularly useful to counter exploitative situations or to justify what he calls "regional or ethnic chauvinism." "The model suggests the need for an anticolonial movement and a radical structuring of society, with a redistribution of resources to the poor and the powerless." (Raitz and Ulack, 1984:343). Thus, the internal colonial model not only raises the question of ethnic reactions but might be viewed as founded on an agitation for an Appalachian "identity movement."

Billings, Blee and Swanson (1986:155) argue that ethnographic accounts of Appalachia that concentrated on traditionalism looked at communities outside the industrialized regions of coal extraction. "What Pearsall [1959], Stephenson [1968] and to a lesser extent, Brown [1950], frequently saw as *antiquated* behavior were traces of a social logic and a set of values distinct from those of more advanced capitalist societies but nonetheless shaped by economic rationality" (Billings, Blee and Swanson, 1986:156). Whereas Billings, Blee and Swanson (1986:157) see the colonial model as somewhat reactionary to these accounts, what would be more appropriate, they (Billings, Blee and Swanson, 1986:168) conclude, is a "'second oppositional challenge'" to Appalachian exceptionalism: "that is an historically-based understanding of unique cultural trends and power relationships.

Appalachian ethnicity?

If the internal colonialism model is a valid perspective on Appalachian underdevelopment and accepted as the basis for ethnic momentum, then two more questions must be asked: First, what are the specific economic and political links to colonialism? Some of this has been explored in defining relationships between the dominant and subordinate groups.

A second question, to be explored briefly, is who among the Appalachian populace will define themselves as uniquely Appalachian?

In many of the studies of colonialism, boundaries set up by conquerors that gave no attention to existing social allegiances and the unequal treatment of and partitioning of resources to the existing groups were faciliting circumstances for ethnic allegiances. A similar process occurs in internal colonialism, however, it may work to dispel ethnic tendencies among certain segments of the indigenous population. Groups in the urban areas within a peripheral region, those who are quicker to adopt "modernization," are viewed differently from the most rural populace. Hechter (1975:122) explores this in Great Britain: " . . . the docility of late eighteenth-century Wales and Scotland was achieved by the co-optation of regional elites, rather than the direct intervention of the state." Likewise, Gaventa (1980), found middle-class elites less resistant to changes in the social order.

An essay by Lewis (1967:7) that predates the development of her internal colonial model charged: "The coming of coal-mining did not open up the mountains. It facilitated three subcultures." One of these subcultures, located in the mountain settlements, was traditionally-minded and presented a solid front to outsiders. This was necessary, she maintains, for security and adjustment in the face of change. She predicted then an eventual breakdown in segregation with full integration of the mountaineer into main stream capitalist culture. "Instead of reticent and retiring, he will become blase, gregarious and sophisticated" (Lewis, 1967:16).

For Obermiller (1977:148,345) . . ."the key issue in urban Appalachian studies is ethnicity . . . Many Appalachians in the cities and mountains need the opportunities afforded by ethnic recognition."

What Billings and Walls (1980:137–138) conclude is that ethnic politicalization and reactions to prejudice are salient to urban Appalachian migrants. "Hillbilly stereotypes cause some migrants to disavow their Appalachian origins, but they also function to pull the group together" (Billings and Walls, 1980:127). There exists in Cincinnati, Ohio, an Urban Appalachian Council and an Appalachian Identity Center (Billings and Walls, 1980:127). Returning migrant professionals may also be more ethnically "aware" such as scholars and professors involved in Appalachian Studies in many universities and colleges in the region. On the other hand, Billings and Walls (1980:178) say "Appalachia" is not as an important symbol of identity as are other affiliations. Further, these authors call for a reassessment of Appalachia that synthesizes the traditional subculture view and outside domination (Raitz and Ulack, 1984:346). This could take the form of assessing the difference between "hanging on" to culture and being culturally defined.

Finally, one last point is raised that ties culture to capitalism in a most direct manner. When Stephenson (1984) returned in the 1980's to Shiloh (1968) where he had studied the extension of modernity in mountain culture, he found what he called "culture-brokering." The elites of Shiloh were "commodifying" the place (Stephenson, 1984) by selling it as a traditional community offering escape from the alienated metropolis (Stephenson, 1984).

References Cited

Barth, Fredrik
    1969 *Ethnic Groups and Boundaries*. Little Brown and Company: Boston.

Beers, William R.
    1979 "Internal colonialism and rising expectations: Ethnic activism in contemporary France." *Ethnic autonomy—Comparative Dynamics: The Americas, Europe, and the Developing World*. Raymond L. Hall (ed.). Pergamon Press: New York. pp. 201–233.

Billings, Dwight, Kathleen Blee and Louis Swanson
    1986 "Culture, family, and community in pre-industrial Appalachia." *Appalachian Journal*, Winter.

Billings, Dwight, and David Walls
    1980 "Appalachians." *Harvard Encyclopedia of American Ethnic Groups*. Stephan Thernstrom (ed.). Harvard University Press: Cambridge, pp. 125–128.

Brown, James Stephen
    1950 "The social organization of an isolated Kentucky mountain neighborhood." Dissertation. Harvard University. Department of Social Relations.

Caudill, Harry M.
    1963 *Night Comes to the Cumberlands*. (Little, Brown and Company: Boston and Toronto.

Eisinger, Peter K.
    1978 "Ethnicity as a strategic option: An emerging view." *Public Administration Review*, 38:89–93.

Eller, Ronald D.
    1982 *Miners, Millhands and Mountaineers: Industrialization of the Appalachian South, 1880–1930*.

Gaventa, John
    1980 *Power and Powerlessness: Quiescence and Rebellion in an Appalachian Valley*. University of Illinois: Urbana.

Glazer, Nathan
   1983 *Ethnic Dilemmas: 1964–1982*. Harvard University Press: Cambridge.

Hall, Raymond L.
   1979 "Introduction." in *Ethnic Autonomy—Comparative Dynamics: The Americas, Europe and the Developing World*. Raymond L. Hall (ed.). Pergamon Press: New York, pp. xvii-xxxii.

Hechter, Michael
   1975 *Internal Colonialism. The Celtic Fringe in British National Development, 1536–1966*. Berkeley: University of California Press.

Isaacs, Harold
   1975 *The Idols of the Tribe: Group Identity*. Harper and Row: New York.

Klaus, Ernst
   1980 "Racialism, racist ideology and colonialism, past and present. Sociological Theories: Race and Colonialism. UNESCO. pp. 453–475.

Lewis, Helen Matthews, Linda Johnson and David Askins (eds.)
   1978 *Colonialism in Modern America*. The Appalachian Consortium Press: Boone, North Carolina.

Malizia, Emil
   1973 "Economic imperialism: An interpretation of Appalachian underdevelopment." *Appalachian Journal*, 1:2(spring)

Nairn, Tom
   1977 *The Breakup of Britain: Crisis and Neonationalism*. Humanities Press: London.

Pearsall, Marion
   1959 *Little Smoky Ridge. The Natural History of a Southern Appalachian Neighborhood*. University of Alabama Press.

Obermiller, Phillip
   1977 "Appalachians as an urban, ethnic group: Romanticism, renaissance or revolution?" *Appalachian Journal*, 5(1):150–160.

Raitz, Karl B., and Richard Ulack
   1984 *Appalachia: A Regional Geography: Land, People and Development*. Westview Press: Boulder.

Smith, Tony
   1981 *The Pattern of Imperialism: The United States, Great Britain, and the Late-industrializing World Since 1815*. Cambridge University Press: Cambridge.

Stephenson, John B.
   1984 "Escape to the periphery: Commodifying place in rural Appalachia." *Appalachian Jounral*, 11(Spring):187–200.

   1968 *Shiloh: A Mountain Community*. University of Kentucky Press: Lexington.

Thompson, Richard H., and Mary Lou Wylie
    1984 "The professional-managerial class in Eastern Kentucky: A preliminary interpretation." *Appalachian Journal*, 11(1–2):105–121.

Walls, David S.
    1978 "Internal colony or internal periphery: A critique of current models and an alternative formulation." *Colonialism in Modern America*. Lewis, Helen Matthews, Linda Johnson and David Askins (eds.). The Appalachian Consortium Press: Boone, North Carolina.

    1976 "Central Appalachia: A peripheral region within an advanced capitalist society." Journal of Sociology and Social Welfare. 4(2):232–246).

The Influence of the Smoot Tannery on the Economic Development of Wilkes County, N. C. 1897–1940

by
Barry Elledge

Ronald Eller's book, *Miners, Millhands, and Mountaineers*, is considered by many to be a definitive work detailing the industrialization of the Appalachian South. Although mainly focusing on the development of the timber and coal industries, Eller makes brief mention that the abundant tanbark gave rise to a thriving tanning and leather industry in western North Carolina, with nearly 1200 people working in that industry at the height of the industry's activities in 1916. Major tanneries, he notes, had been erected at Morganton, Brevard, Lenior, Asheville, Marion, Hazelwood, Waynesville, Andrews, and Murphy.[1]

Eller omits the biggest and perhaps the most important tannery of them all: the C. C. Smoot and Sons Tannery at North Wilkesboro. This tannery operated from 1897 until crippled by a flood in 1940, and was frequently cited as the largest of its kind in the South. The Smoot Tannery is considered by local authorities in Wilkes county to be of singular importance in the industrialization of that County.[2] As this paper will show, the Smoot tannery made a huge initial contribution to the economic growth in northwestern North Carolina.

In 1914 the local newspaper described the tannery as embracing 25 buildings in all, with the largest 42 x 465 feet.[3] The tannery maintained its own steam plant, electric power plant, and water works. The tanning industry was slow to mechanize, but evidently the Smoot tannery was state of the art. It was not until about 1880 that tanners began to use machinery, and even then it was primarily confined to steam power for bark crushing and grinding and the generation of electricity.

THE PROCESS OF TANNING

A brief description of the tanning process provides a better understanding of the total economic impact of the tannery. The Smoot tannery used the conventional tanning procedures of that time. Tanning a hide required four basic operations: 1) the preliminary washing and soaking to clean the hides; 2) a long soaking in lime water to loosen the hair, followed by scraping the skin to remove the hair and loose flesh; 3) tanning by soaking the hides in a solution of a tan liquor consisting of water and tannin; and 4) the drying, finishing, and oiling of the hides to a durable and attractive leather. The entire process of tanning normally took several months.[4]

Unslaked lime was the conventional agent used to open the pores of the hide so the hair could be easily removed. The lime was shipped in by railroad car. The lime vats for soaking hides were made of wood or masonry and about five feet square. After removal from the lime vats, the hides were taken to the beam room, where the worker placed a hide upon a broad wooden beam and scraped both surfaces free of hair and surplus flesh, with the hide being washed several times as necessary. The hides were then taken to "the yard" for immersion into the vats containing the tanning solution. When completely penetrated by the tannin, which could take several weeks, the hides were removed to the "loft," where they were dried, brushed, smoothed by mechanical rollers, oiled, cut into sections and made ready for shipment.

During the lifetime of the Smoot tannery, the end product was sole leather intended for the manufacture of shoes. The Smoot tannery tanned only cattle hides, and contrary to some local beliefs, local hides from the area were an unimportant trade for either the tannery or local farmers. The hides, a byproduct from the meat industry, arrived by the boxcar load, previously salted and rolled up at the packers to retard spoilage. The normal source was midwest meat packers, but hides from South America were also commonly used. Typically tanners sought hides where they could find them and where prices were lowest.

Unloading the hides was done by hand labor and was a dirty and odious work, as was the immersion and removal of the hides from the lime vats. This work was typically done by the black employees of the tannery, with whites shunning this work, hoping for an assignment further up the tanning process. Many of the jobs involved the handling of bark and wood, since the tannery purchased and stored huge quantities of chestnut wood and chestnut oak bark.

The chestnut wood and bark were ground and crushed by a large steam-powered grinder called "the hog." It made a fearsome racket during operation that reportedly could be heard all over town. The tannic acid was then leached from the crushed material in the extract plant, a freestanding building. Later, as the local tanbark supply dwindled, some wood and bark rich in tannin were imported, such as kuebracho from Argentina, cutch from the Philippines and Borneo, myrabalams from Ceylon, and wattle bark from South Africa.[5]

THE FLOODS

The tannery demand for tanbark and chestnut wood resulted in local residents cutting and selling large quantities of these materials. In addition, the railroad provided access to markets for the region's vast timber resources. The denuding of much of the timbered landscape, plus the logging trails, accelerated the runoff following rains and contributed to two major floods.

The first major flood came in June 1916. The tannery lay in the floodplain very near the Yadkin river and was heavily damaged by the flood waters. The second major flood came in August 1940. The flood waters crested six feet higher than in 1916. Damage from flood waters was again extensive; however, damage to the tannery was also heavy from a fire caused by the chemical combustive reaction of the flood water penetrating a rail car of unslaked lime. The tannery elected not to repair the damage to the facility and sold the property to local interests for alternative uses.

Apart from the fire and flood damage, the future of the tannery was in doubt before the 1940 flood. The supplies of chestnut wood and tanbark were nearly exhausted by this time. The chestnut blight had spread throughout the Appalachian forest in the twenties and thirties, killing nearly all the chestnut trees. The dead trees could still be sold for tan wood, but were mostly gone by 1940. The extract plant managed to continue operations until 1945, then it too closed for good.

THE ECONOMIC IMPACT

The tannery presence had the obvious direct effect of providing many jobs through direct employment and a considerable injection of cash income through the payroll; there was also much indirect employment spread over a wide area for those who cut and sold tanbark. A total assessment of the tannery influence must also include its contribution to the local tax base, to local population growth, to purchases from the local economy, to pollution and environmental problems, and to the business and social climate in the community. And, like any enterprise, there was a beneficial multiplier effect from the money injected by the tannery into the community as portions of that money were spent and respent again in the normal spending patterns of a money-based exchange economy.

Since the tannery changed ownership in 1925 and later closed for good in 1940, most company records have long been lost or are in private hands and unavailable for study. It is therefore impossible to provide precise data on the financial impact of the tannery. The following account, however, was given in the local newspaper shortly before the 1940 flood abruptly halted operations.[6]

"Employees numbered 155 men, the payroll was $150,000 per year, over $12,000 was paid yearly for city, county, and state taxes. These and other local expenses total over $325,000 which is largely spent in the local community. The capacity of the tannery was listed as 600 finished hides per day, or 24,500 pounds per day. Normally one rail car of leather was shipped each day. The extract plant had a capacity of producing 45,000 pounds of 25 percent tannin extract daily. The extract not used locally is shipped in tank cars to other tanneries. Five tank cars were available for this purpose. The tannery purchased three million cubic feet of chestnut wood, 4,500 tons of chestnut oak bark, and 500 tons of hemlock bark yearly. The chestnut wood purchases were valued at $90,000, the tanbark at $55,000."

It is commonly accepted by local residents that the tannery was the economic backbone of Wilkes county during its operation. The facts support this notion only during the initial years of the tannery, but not during its latter years; other industries developed rapidly after 1900 and, collectively at least, exerted a stronger economic presence than the tannery. Furniture manufacturing became strong, e.g. the Forest Furniture in 1901, the Oak Furniture and Turner-White Casket in 1903, Home Chair in 1919, and the American Furniture in 1927, and rapidly added to the industrialization and payrolls of the area. The Wilkes Hosiery Mill, established in 1918, became a major employer and the first industry to offer employment for women. The Carolina Mirror Company, established in 1936, offered the highest industrial wages in the area at the time and became a major competitor for the local labor force. Concomitantly, the service industry, including banking and finance, insurance, transportation, and communications developed during this interval. By the time the tannery closed in 1940, the economy had grown and diversified to such an extent that the closing did not have a devastating impact on the economy. And as the economy continued to grow, especially after World War II, the loss of the tannery jobs was quickly recovered through the expansion of other enterprises.

Clearly the tannery made a rather dramatic initial impact, but one that waned over time, certainly in the relative sense if not absolutely. The exact impact is examined in some more detail, although the paucity of records hampers the effort.

Direct Employment. Direct employment by the tannery is easiest to account for; but even this is a matter of dispute. Judge Hayes, as cited in the *Land of Wilkes*, claims employment was " ... up to 200 men," a figure not corroborated elsewhere. The last newspaper account of the tannery cited employment of 155; earlier accounts vary from 125 to 150. This range is corroborated by those who worked at the tannery or are knowledgeable of it.

Direct employment evidently was relatively steady over the life of the tannery, even suffering little from the depression of the thirties. Census data for 1900 gives 377 as the "average number of wage earners" in Wilkes County; the tannery probably accounted for one third of these jobs. In 1940, the census gives 12,081 as "employment" in Wilkes; tannery employment of 155 would account for less than two percent of this. Interestingly enough, there is no record of labor strife during the lifetime of the tannery; historically the local labor force has shown an indifference if not hostility toward organized labor and few outsiders that might have been sympathetic to labor unions were brought in for employment.

Indirect Employment. There are no extant data on indirect employment, and such information was probably never collected; yet indirect employment of those cutting and selling chestnut wood and tanbark probably equalled or exceeded direct employment. Tanning required huge quantities of chestnut wood and tanbark for the tannic acid, and the tannery depended on local and regional people to cut and supply these materials. For every man employed at the tannery, probably three or more were at work harvesting tanbark from time to time as a supplemental activity. It is through the indirect employment that the tannery may have made its greatest impact on the region, where the boundaries of the affected region extended beyond the county boundaries, for there were at least two bark buying stations removed from the tannery—one along the railroad line in Thurman and another in Mt. Airy, a distance by rail of approximately 40 and 60 miles, respectively. Cash was paid on delivery. A good guess is that hundreds of men at one time or another were involved in cutting and hauling tanbark. An early publication of the Yellow Jacket Press in 1906 reported that sometimes as many as 300 wagons a day would be lined up at the tannery to sell tanbark.[7] This picturesque view of the tannery's early impact is still fondly recalled by some of the county,s elder residents.

The importance of the tanbark market is also illustrated by the newspaper account in 1940, cited earlier. The purchases of chestnut wood and tanbark totaled $145,000, virtually the same as the payroll ($150,000). In previous years, when the supplies of wood and bark were more plentiful, and more men were working the land and forests as a livelihood, the tanbark market was probably even more important. It is worth noting that chestnut wood could be harvested and sold anytime. It was crushed by the tannery and used in its entirety. Harvesting chestnut oak bark was a seasonal activity; the bark could be easily cut and peeled from the tree only in the springtime when the sap was rising. The timing was ideal for many farmers, being a slack time prior to crop planting; moreover a coincidental benefit also occurred, as the bark harvest resulted in more cleared land that could be pressed into cultivation.

Income. No company payroll data for the tannery still exists. One former employee interviewed recalled being hired in 1907 at ten cents per hour, with a standard workday of ten hours. It is not unreasonable to assume that ten cents per hour was the initial wage when the tannery opened in 1897. There is much anecdotal evidence regarding the "dollar per day" as a standard during this time. Another former employee interviewed recalled being hired in 1926 at thirty cents per hour. The last newspaper account of payroll as cited above suggests a wage range probably between 40 to 50 cents per hour. These wage rates appear to be typical for the times and location, and the tannery appears to have adjusted its wage rate upward as necessary to remain competitive as diversification in the economy asserted more competition for the labor force.

Although the wage rates were low by national norms and slightly below state averages, they were accepted without serious complaint by men who were initially grateful for any kind of steady cash job. Employees were mostly hired from the local labor force; the opportunity cost for most of these men was the income or product they could produce from working their small subsistence farms. Large families were still common, and some industrial workers were able to continue life on the small farms much as before while generating a dependable cash income by holding a job at "public works."

The tannery paid its employees every two weeks. If initial employment of 125 is assumed with a 50 hour week and ten cents per hour, the payroll would be $1450 every two weeks and about $38,000 for the year. This amount was probably matched, and exceeded by, the purchases of chestnut wood and tanbark. Undoubtedly in the early days this represented the largest single infusion of steady cash into the community. As this income was spent and respent in the multiplier chain, it encouraged the fledgling markets previously hampered by a lack of currency for spending and built these and new markets into a modern exchange economy.

Data from the Census of Manufacturers in 1900 lists the total payroll in Wilkes County as $80,384; the tannery would have accounted for approximately half of this. In 1940, the census data show a total payroll of $1,431,241; the tannery payroll of $150,000 represents less than eleven percent of the total.

Population. The tannery had a slight, but in no way major, impact on population growth. Most of the employees were hired from the local labor force; a few, including some blacks, came from surrounding areas. There are some reports, not completely corroborated, of a nearby house operated by the tannery for its transient laborers. There is no evidence at all of a major immigration of non-locals to provide tannery labor. In 1890, the population of Wilkes County was 22,675; with no major employers this provided a large labor pool for the tannery to draw from. By 1940, the population had grown to 43,003, a 90 percent increase from 1890.

There is little to suggest that the tannery contributed to population growth; the population of the state increased by 120 percent over the same time period, and besides, except for the initial spurt provided by the tannery, most of the industrial growth in Wilkes was provided by other industry. A slight impact on population was provided by the tannery management. While the production workers were mostly local, management was not. The Smoots, as owners and managers, relocated their families from Alexandria, Virginia. About six other men in top supervisory positions also relocated from the Smoot tannery in Alexandria or from other tanneries in West Virginia. These families became permanent residents and contributed socially, politically and economically to the new town.

The Local Tax Base. As the first major industry in the county, the tannery provided a major contribution to the local property tax base for the town and county. There were no local income taxes, and the state income and sales taxes were not initially imposed. Property tax rates were low, especially at first, as there were few government services. The tannery initially provided its own water, sewage system, electricity and security. As the city and county grew, government services expanded, but the tax rate remained low because the tax base was rapidly expanding. There is every indication that the tannery was a good citizen and paid its taxes, and made an important early contribution to the development of education and other government services.

Local Purchases. The importance of the tanbark purchases has been shown earlier. Otherwise, most of the materials used by the tannery were imported from outside the immediate area: hides as byproduct of the meat industry; coal for the steam plant, lime for the soaking vats, and small amounts of imported wood and tanbark from South America and Asia.

In the course of ordinary business operations, the tannery made local purchase of office supplies, building materials, tools, and repair services. These purchases were never a major part of total expenses, and made only a slight contribution to the local economy.

Pollution and Environmental Problems. Some pollution was an unavoidable byproduct of the tanning process. There was the noise from the bark grinder, smoke from the steam plant, polluted water from the soaking and tanning vats, disposal of the hair and surplus tissue from the hides, and the smell of the entire operation. And, in the larger sense, part of the deforestation that contributed to the flooding was due to the harvest of tanbark.

Strangely enough, the contribution to flood conditions may have been the most serious of these. Local residents were unconcerned about the other problems, or bore them gladly as a necessary cost of industrialization and transition to a modern economy. The noise of the bark grinder is remembered, but not as an intolerable nuisance. Nor is the odor recounted with disdain. The smoke was dispersed from the 150 foot high smokestack. The polluted water from the vats was discharged directly into the river or allowed to seep over ground to the river; either way there are no recorded complaints and the river probably suffered much less from the tannery than from the discharge of raw sewage from towns along its banks before sewage treatment plants were built. As for the hair and residual tissue from the hides, there was briefly a time when the hair was cleaned and dried and sold as stuffing for automobile seats. At all other times, this material was dumped in a field behind the tannery and allowed to compost. It was made available to farmers who were willing to haul it away; as farmers learned its value as a useful soil amendment to be spread over their fields it was viewed as an asset rather than a pollutant.

The Business, Social, and Cultural Climate. As the first major industry utilizing an organized and disciplined labor force that took advantage of specialization and division of labor, a modern corporate structure and management team, the reliance on markets and the use of credit and financial services, the tannery played a major role in creating and fostering an entrepreneurial and commercial climate that served other enterprises that followed. This kind of climate was cited by Rostow[8] as crucial in producing a self-generative process of continual economic growth. That the tannery had a significant part in this process is beyond dispute.

Beyond the cultivation of a favorable business climate, the tannery's presence was also felt. The Smoot family and the families of the rest of the management team became an important part of the social, political, religious, and cultural fabric of the town. The perspective provided by these families and others who took an active interest in seeing the town grow played an important role in shaping the new town. In contrast to much of coal-mine Appalachia, the outside capital was provided by entrepreneurs who adopted the area as their home.

Conclusions

The economic development of Wilkes County matches the stages of growth described by Rostow, with the opening of the tannery initiating the take-off period of sustained growth. There is no mistaking its large size and early economic impact, but with the tannery now closed since 1940, there may be a somewhat romanticized local view of the importance of the tannery. Judge Hayes, in his history of the county, observes that, "It is utterly impossible to estimate the enormous influence and financial assistance that one concern has meant to Wilkes County."[9] Even allowing for some possible exaggeration, this does not deny the importance of the tannery in the initial stages of economic growth in Wilkes County. Like much early economic development, the tannery exploited a natural resource, wood and tanbark, but helped create a modern economy based on specialization, division of labor, and exchange. The impetus of the tannery helped give rise to other industry, but also created competition and higher wages for the labor force. The popular view in the county of the tannery as the backbone of the economy is accurate initially but does not give adequate allowance for the emergence of other industry that soon surpassed the tannery's influence.

NOTES

1. Ronald D. Eller, *Miners, Millhands, and Mountaineers*. The University of Tennessee Press. 1982, p. 122.

2. Johnson J. Hayes, *The Land of Wilkes*. Wilkes County Historical Society, Wilkesboro. 1962, pp. 185–186.

3. C. P. Waters, *Resources and Progress of Wilkes County*. 1914: as quoted in J. Jay Anderson, Wilkes County Sketches, monograph printed by Wilkes Community College, Wilkesboro, 1976, p. 58.

4. Peter C. Welch, *Tanning in the United States to 1850*. The Smithsonian Institute. Washington, 1964, pp. 15–35.

5. Personal knowledge of Mary Smithey, as quoted in Absher (ed.), *The Heritage of Wilkes*. Wilkes County Genealogical Society, 1982, p. 36.

6. *The Journal Patriot*, Special anniversary issue of June 27, 1940.

7. Don Laws, *Views of North Wilkesboro*. 1906, as quoted in J. Jay Anderson, Wilkes County Sketches. op. cit., p. 59.

8. W. W. Rostow, *The Stages of Economic Growth*. Cambridge University Press. 1968, pp. 4–10.

9. Johnson J. Hayes. Op. cit., p. 186.

Other resource material:
   I have greatly benefitted from interviews with the following people:

   J. Jay Anderson
   Annie F. Winkler
   Joe Colson, tannery employee, 1907 to 1940 George Brown, tannery and extract plant employee, 1926 to 1945
   Edward Smoot Finley
   Mary Sink Smithey

Mountain Foragers in Southeast Asia and Appalachia: Cross-cultural Perspectives on the "Mountain Man" Stereotype

by
Benita Howell

When and how did Appalachia become identified as a distinctive region, a "strange land inhabited by peculiar people"? In his massive doctoral dissertation, Cratis Williams (1961) catalogued the ingredients of the mountaineer stereotype as they emerged from nineteenth century travel accounts and local color fiction. He found that a consistent image of cultural primitivism, based on "branchwater" Appalachians, persisted well into the twentieth century. Williams argued that this stereotype reflected a real deterioration in living conditions which created a distinct lower class of Appalachians in the decades following the Civil War.

Henry Shapiro (1978) later took up the question of why Appalachia preoccupied affluent urbanites in the latter part of the nineteenth century, and why "branchwater" Appalachians in particular fascinated these consumers of local color literature. Shapiro suggested that Appalachia's emergence as a distinctive region followed upon a growing recognition that "the strange land and peculiar people" were out of place in the new industrial culture of modern America. Lifeways which had appealed to a romantic nostalgia for the frontier past became a challenge to modernization and progress-problems to be solved and deficits to be remedied through home missions work, secular education, community development, or cultural revival.

Both of these accounts explain the emergence of the Appalachian stereotype in the late nineteenth century by appealing to particular events in American history—the Civil War and its aftermath of devastation in Appalachia, industrial growth and urbanization in the North, and Reconstruction in the South characterized by continuing sectional and sectarian rivalries within religious and philanthropic organizations. But explanations phrased in specific historical terms don't account for the Appalachian stereotype's perplexing resistance to the facts.

Why, for example, was the "branchwater mountaineer" made stereotypic representative of the region as a whole, although he was not numerically in the majority, was not particularly visible in the towns and resorts frequented by outsiders, and was not culturally, socially, or economically dominant within the region? Why, towards the end of the nineteenth century, did many scholars and popular writers assert that Appalachians represented a separate genetic stock from other Americans, whether pure Anglo-Saxon, Highland Scots, Scots-Irish, or English poor white, even though there was ample evidence that the region had received settlers from diverse stocks and sent its share of settlers west to become middle Americans? And why have affluent, educated Appalachians themselves become the primary purveyors of the stereotype, whether in casual comments about "holler folk" or in fiction?

As an anthropologist, I would like to propose that we look beneath the particular events of late nineteenth century American history in our attempts to account for the Appalachian "mountain man" stereotype. If we view the Appalachian case in a broader framework of cross-cultural comparison, it appears to be one instance of a more general and fairly widespread phenomenon in which distinctive economic adaptations provide the basis for stereotyping and ethnic labeling. In fact, the Appalachian "mountain man" stereotype has a close parallel in pervasive distinctions between primitive highlanders and civilized lowlanders which have long organized ethnic relations in Southeast Asia.

This cognitive and symbolic contrast quite possibly has been central to ethnic group relations in Southeast Asia ever since the first millennium A.D., when Hindu commercial states began incorporating mountain foragers and shifting cultivators into trade networks. The object was to obtain forest products for international maritime commerce which linked Southeast Asia with the Mediterranean, the Middle East, and China (see Coedes [1968], Hall [1966], Meilink-Roelofsz [1962], and Simkin [1968]). Karl Hutterer (1974), interpreting archaeological sites dating from roughly 1000–1600 A.D., found evidence of trade between the coast and interior groups in the Philippines. Chinese records indicate that a large percentage of Philippine trade goods consisted of forest products such as bees wax, abaca, sandalwood, rattan, civet, and animal hides. Presumably coastal traders did not have access to inland territories and lacked the environmental knowledge to procure these items themselves, so they traded with foragers and swidden farmers of the interior but did not culturally incorporate these peoples into the emerging coastal states. Spanish records indicate that such trading networks definitely were in operation when the Spanish arrived in the Philippines. Hetterer argues that evolution of lowland societies into commercial states entailed deliberate maintenance of foraging and swidden adaptations among peoples geographically situated to supply the prized forest products. Lowlanders depended upon and subsidized the foraging lifestyle but at the same time labeled it primitive and inferior.

Ethnologists observing interethnic relations in the European colonial period and in contemporary nation states of South and Southeast Asia have documented continuing symbiotic and often exploitative relations between foragers, peasants, and traders. Thus it appears that long-standing stereotypic contrasts between "civilized" lowlanders and "backward, primitive" highland foragers have become ingrained in South and Southeast Asian folk notions of culture and ethnic identity (e.g., see Lehman 1967). Culture traits which signal "backwardness" bear an uncanny similarity between Asia and Appalachia.

In the Philippines, for example, Negrito peoples known collectively as the Agta carried on a nomadic, foraging lifestyle in which they traded with middlemen or agents from the coast. John Garvan (1963), an Irish-American amateur ethnologist who studied the Agta in the 1910s, noted that Filipinos circulated many erroneous rumors about them. The stereotypic Agta had a monstrous, ape-like appearance (p. 11), was dirty and diseased (p. 12), subject to drunkeness (p. 54), immodest, promiscuous and incestuous (p. 81), and prone to violence and theft (pp. 157–161). Most puzzling to Filipinos was the Agta preference for an independent, nomadic lifestyle. Agta resisted Filipino efforts to engage them in long-term wage work or share-cropping relationships, but they did on occasion appear in farming villages to exchange work for rice, garden produce, or metal implements as well as supplying forest products—lumber, bark cloth, "rattan, honey, bees wax and whatever else might be desired" (p. 79). Garvan described how the Filipino partners in trading relationships took advantage of Agta ignorance of the market value of their products, exercised debt peonage, or sometimes posed as government officials and extorted trade goods from Agta (pp. 159–163). In response, Garvan wrote, the Agta "has no need and no desire for any relations with the government. He fears taxes. He fears schools. He fears the police and he fears all kinds of things ..." (p. 158).

Jean Peterson (1978) has described more recent relationships between Agta foragers and pioneering peasant farmers, whose encroachment into Agta territory has brought many more outsiders into personal contact with Agta and reduced the primary forest available for Agta foraging. These newcomers have continued to establish patron-client trade relationships which use an idiom of friendship but at least potentially leave the Agta open to debt peonage and other forms of exploitation. While Peterson observed a surface cordiality in relations between rural villagers and "their" Agta, the same old stereotypes persisted (pp. 64–66). Villagers were disturbed by Agta sexuality, their crude humor, and their children's undisciplined behavior. Stories of Agta violence and savagery continued to arouse fear, particularly among townspeople who had little personal contact with Agta. Negrito origins of the Agta have given Filipinos familiar with American racial prejudice an additional basis for stereotyping. Peterson was told, "These Agta are just like your niggers. They're lazy, thieving, and dirty. It's right in their blood and you can't teach them anything" (p. 79).

Physical difference reinforces but does not account for Agta stereotyping, however. The same stereotypic characterizations have been applied to other highland peoples of South and Southeast Asia who are racially indistinguishable from their lowland neighbors. Lowland Malays, for example, have stereotyped tribal groups of the interior of Borneo and the Celibes as backward, dirty, stupid, and savage (Lasker 1944: 37–40). Yet there is a strong possibility that the lowland Malays have their origins in the very tribes which they denigrate. Using ethnographic and ethnohistoric sources, King (1985) has reconstructed a multi-level system of ethnic stratification based on trade between interior and coastal Borneo. Punan foragers (similar in lifestyle to the Agta but not Negrito) and Iban Dayak shifting cultivators supplied trade goods to the Maloh. The Maloh were wet-rice cultivators who also served as middlemen in trade with lowland Malays. Maloh were distinguished from Dayak people not by language or race, but by their economy and more hierarchical political organization. The Malay controlled catchment areas upstream, while coastal trade was in turn controlled by Chinese and Buginese from the Celibes. King found that the "Malay" commercial center had in fact been formed as recently as 1815 by Dayak (or Maloh) who converted to Islam (pp. 59–62), and he suggested that Punan nomads who settled and planted rice became Dayak (p. 206).

King's findings fit a pattern often reported for Southeast Asia in which contemporary boundaries and distinctions between lowlanders and more primitive highlanders have been demarcated and maintained through the use of discrete ethnic labels. Economic specializations form a framework for different lifestyles which, along with particular cultural behaviors such as religious affiliation, serve as ethnic markers. The use of ethnic labels implies a separate historic origin for each group so labeled, but physical similarities, linguistic affiliations, and historical data such as those reported by King tend to invalidate such claims. Moerman (1965), Lehman (1967), Dentan (1975), and Rousseau (1975) all have shown that tribal identifications are notoriously confusing in Southeast Asia precisely because "tribes" are not genetic and cultural units at all, but reflect an ongoing process of ethnic labeling and manipulation of ethnicity. Cunningham (1987) has recently shown how similar processes of constructing ethnicity have occurred repeatedly in the history of the British Isles.

If the mountain foragers of Southeast Asia do not really constitute separate ethnic groups, what is the basis for their being treated as if they were separate? Both Hutterer and King imply that forager to swidden cultivator, to wet rice cultivator, to commercial trader represents an evolutionary sequence of development. If this were the case, then contemporary foragers would represent survivals of a truly primitive hunting-and-gathering adaptation, the "contemporary ancestors" of other Southeast Asians. More recent work by Carl Hoffman (1984), however, suggests that it is equally plausible that these groups, like Appalachian pioneers, went into a mountain forest environment, adapted to its requirements, and in the process shed some cultural baggage and took on the appearance of being more primitive than they actually were.

Hoffman studied a number of different Punan groups in Borneo and concluded that the Punan (the name can be translated as collectors or forest dwellers) do not constitute a homogeneous cultural or linguistic unit. Rather each Punan group is paired with neighboring swidden farmers who share linguistic and other cultural similarities such as burial customs with their Punan trading partners. Punan appear to constitute a distinct ethnic group only because of behaviors directly associated with their forest collecting. Conventional wisdom had it that foragers, isolated and enclosed within complex societies, could continue their primitive hunting and gathering lifestyle only by resorting to trade with cultivators who supplied them with garden produce, metal tools, and other trade goods, but Hoffman's findings turn this reasoning upside down. Hoffman proposes that, rather than being descendants of aboriginal foragers, the Punan are Dayak who have moved into the primary forest to specialize in collecting raw materials to supply the long distance trading networks. The Punan hunt and gather in order to subsist during their commercial collecting activities in the primary forest, rather than using trade to cushion an inefficient, maladaptive, outdated lifestyle.

In South Asia as well as Southeast Asia, forest foragers have been stereotyped and labeled as distinct "tribes," sometimes incorporated into the bottom levels of the Hindu caste system, sometimes left entirely outside of it. After examining ethnographic data on the Kadar, Birhor, Chenchu, Vedda, and Nayadi, Richard Fox concluded that social scientists as well as agricultural neighbors erred in viewing these groups as "cultural left-overs or fossils from pre-literate times" (1969:140). Fox argued that their spatial and sociological isolation from Hindu culture, like their primitiveness, had been exaggerated. He wrote: "Far from depending wholly on the forest for their own direct subsistence, the Indian hunters-and-gatherers are highly specialized exploiters of a marginal terrain from which they supply the larger society with desirable, but otherwise unobtainable, forest items such as honey, wax, rope and twine, baskets, and monkey and deer meat" (p. 141). Fox also explained the often noted social fragmentation of these groups—the mobility of individuals and loose structuring of communities—as an adaptive response to the demands of competitive foraging in which each household tried to maximize its gain (p. 142). Thus, according to Fox, fluid social organization, a trait often denigrated and interpreted as savage by foragers' lowland neighbors, is actually one more indication that these groups are "professional" rather than true primitives.

Brian Morris (1977, 1982) has provided new ethnographic data on another hill tribe of India, the Hill Pandaram, utilizing ecological and economic rather than evolutionary perspectives to account for their foraging adaptation. Within this framework, Morris focuses on Hill Pandaram contacts with the outside world rather than assuming them to be isolated. The Forest Department of India has largely taken the place of independent traders in the old commercial system, but Hill Pandaram are still collecting for trade, and not for trade with local villagers alone, but to supply urban markets (1982:3). As in Southeast Asia, the distinction between country people of the plains and forest people of the mountains has cognitive and symbolic importance. Morris reports that outsiders from the plains feel awe and apprehension in the mountains, that they fear the mountains as an alien environment. These feelings lead to stereotyping of mountain people (1982:44). Before Morris met the Hill Pandaram, he learned from villagers that they were "lacking affectionate ties, sexually promiscuous to such an extent that incestuous relations between close kin were frequent, and lazy and stupid, unable even to discern what their own interests were. Villagers would even say they had no religion or culture" (1982:2). Morris later observed: "they are treated as social inferiors by almost everyone with whom they have dealings.... They are commonly said to live like animals and to lack any notions of decent behavior." (1982:42) "Welfare and other government officials seem to view the nomad life of collectors as somehow 'primitive' and are largely dedicated to making them a sedentary community. Local people in general despise their nomadic, apparently carefree and promiscuous life and their comparatively recent adoption of textile clothing." (1982:45) While Morris observed Hill Pandaram behaving with the subservience villagers expected of them when they visited villages to trade, they were more independent in the forest and able to preserve a large measure of their independence by limiting their contact with outsiders. Because the Hill Pandaram were living in a government Forest Reserve, their hunting and clearing of swidden patches technically were "illegal" activities; this fact colored their dealings with forest wardens and commercial and meant that their attitudes toward the authorities were similar to those of the Agta.

Without belaboring the point further, it should be obvious that stereotyping and labeling of mountain foragers as distinct "primitive" ethnic groups is a fairly consistent phenomenon throughout South and Southeast Asia. As Bruno Lasker observed:

> Not many years ago (the Moi of Indochina) were reported as wearing few clothes, as not being overclean, as building their houses on stilts or in trees, and as being altogether "savage."

The Annamites who now make up the dominant native population of most of Indo-China say of the Moi much the same things that Filipinos say about Ifugaos ... coast Malays about the Dyaks [sic] of central Borneo, Burmans about Kachins—the same things that Greeks said about the barbarian tribes of Macedonia, Romans about Britons.... Always these more primitive peoples are hunters who if they go in for agriculture at all do only a little of it, afraid to take root in an area from which at any time they may be ousted by superior force. Always the "superior" people call them savages and deny that they have any culture or religion (Lasker 1944: 22–23).

Lasker's pointed comparisons with Europe can profitably be extended to Appalachia. Consider the core themes of the Appalachian stereotype catalogued by Williams. While the mountaineer described by travelers before the Civil War resembled the heroic American frontiersman in his self-reliance, love of liberty, and rugged individualism, Williams observed that post-Civil War fiction increasingly emphasized negative traits—lawlessness, violence, ignorance and disdain for education, suspiciousness of outsiders and outside interference, sordid living conditions, sexual aberrations (pp. 77–123). Williams concluded that the "backwoods frontiersman" theme in Appalachian stereotyping was progressively supplanted by two more negative characterizations, the cultural primitive and the buffoon, each a savage in his own way and lacking the nobility of the pioneer frontiersman (pp. 1600–1603).

As appears to be the case for at least some South and Southeast Asian foragers, Appalachian mountain men left more settled, "civilized" communities to enter the mountains, not to farm, but to hunt, trap and forage. Williams makes it clear that early travelers consistently commented on encountering hunters who devoted little effort to farming, readily moved away from populous areas, bartered goods and exchanged labor but resisted regular wage work (see Williams' comments on Toulmin and Michaux [pp. 188–189], Paulding and Featherstonhaugh [pp. 201–203], and Lanman [pp. 226–229]). Lanman observed a vigorous, profitable trade in ginseng in 1848 (Williams 1961:229). Both Muir (Williams 1961:264) and Lane Allen (Williams 1961:292–297) identified hunting as an inducement to settlement of the mountains, though by the time of their travels they encountered fewer active commercial hunters than old men who had been hunters in their youth. Muir and Lane Allen also commented on the commercial importance of ginseng and other medicinal roots, even after the Civil War. Two more travelers, Buckingham and Olmstead, (Williams, pp. 216, 237) indicated that livestock raising was by far the most significant agricultural activity in the mountains during the 1840s and 1850s. This activity was compatible with other uses of the forest environment since it was based on the animals ranging freely and consuming acorn and chestnut mast.

It is generally accepted that the eighteenth-century "long hunters" who were the vanguard of white settlement in rugged sections of Appalachia dealt commercially in hides and pelts; they did not spend winters roughing it in station camps to put meat on their families' tables. Family traditions of early settlers verify travelers' observations that hunting continued to be important, so much so that hunters actually moved away from settlements in good farming areas in their pursuit of game. For example, descendants of Jonathan Blevins sometimes express their chagrin that old Jonathan sold valley land in Wayne County, Kentucky around 1820 in order to move into the rugged gorge of the Big South Fork in Scott County, Tennessee, but they explain that Jonathan felt compelled to seek out more remote hunting grounds when increasing settlement made game scarce in Wayne County (personal communication, Oscar Blevins). Having moved away from settlements, to hunt and trap rather than to farm, these men and their families could supplement their income by taking advantage of other commercial activities afforded by their backwoods environment, such as collecting medicinal roots, tanbark, nuts, beeswax and honey, and raising hogs on forest mast.

In the early nineteenth century, backwoods hunters and foragers were viewed positively as pioneers opening up the old Southwest and claiming it for settlement. The rugged lifestyle of the pioneer was adventurous and ennobling, a powerful symbol of the American experience. But as Shapiro suggests, once Appalachian mountaineers were no longer on the physical frontier, their persisting frontier lifestyle required explanation. Just as Hindus, Filipinos, or Malays viewed their foraging specialists as primitives who had failed to make an evolutionary transition into civilization, other Americans viewed Appalachians as "contemporary ancestors" who had failed to modernize, failed to make a transition from subsistence into commercial farming because they had chosen poorly or been pushed into land ill-suited to farming.

Even while Asian forest foragers continued to plan an important role in supplying essential raw materials to the lowlands, "civilized" Asians misinterpreted the true nature of their economic role in the larger society and the origins of their "primitive" lifestyle. Differences between foragers and farmers were exaggerated and fixed in stereotypic contrasts and characterizations. Thus it should be no surprise that similar stereotypic contrasts and characterizations emerged to explain Appalachian foragers at a time when their economic contributions to the larger society were in fact dwindling in importance. Demand for buckskin decreased, fashions in furs changed; transcontinental railroads made it feasible for huge livestock and meat packing operations in the west to supply eastern markets; improved technologies and larger scale factory production resulted in substitution of synthetic chemicals for tanbark and new drugs for the old pharmacopoeia. Simultaneously, industrial America made incursions into the mountains. It took only a quarter century for industrial-scale timbering virtually to eliminate the primary forest. Mining also was destructive of the habitat necessary for commercial hunting and forest collecting. All that remained for commercial foragers was subsistence-level enterprise, and there was less and less land available and suitable for that purpose.

To local color writers who began to develop the "cultural primitive" stereotype of Appalachia in the 1870s and 1880s, their subjects seemed to be clinging to savage lifeways borrowed from the Indians (see Cunningham 1987 for extended discussion of this point). They seemed unable or unwilling to modernize and too ready to isolate themselves in the mountains. In fact these Appalachians had experienced and were still in the throes of an economic upheaval that rendered their old hunting and foraging specialization useless in the regional and national economy and deprived them of their livelihood. We know that many valley farmers and townspeople recovered from the aftermath of the Civil War and took advantage of new economic opportunities created by industry. It seems plausible that hunters and foragers who did not perceive their situation and adjust quickly became the chronically poor, apathetic "branchwater" Appalachians who were stereotyped in increasingly negative terms toward the turn of the century. Given their economic plight, it is hardly surprising that these Appalachians experienced worsening material conditions and cultural disintegration; but these conditions unfortunately provided added impetus for stereotyping which blamed the victims of modernization for not modernizing and exaggerated the boundaries separating them from other Americans. Thus writers of local color fiction took up the task of describing and rationalizing cultural differences and reaffirming the appropriateness of boundaries between lowlanders and Appalachians (beautiful but uncultured daughters as well as mountain men). Attempts were made to establish historical ethnic origins for these cultural differences in order to further set the group apart as "other" Americans. Appalachians who identified with the wider society, much like Dayak people who became Malay, joined outsiders in their fascination with the primitives who lived upstream.

In an article entitled, "If There Were No Malays, Who Would the Semai Be?" R.K. Dentan, an anthropologist who studied the Semai of Malaysia, described with perplexity how his quest for them always led him further into the hinterland. People in the village of Jinteh "chuckled at the word Semai, saying 'That's what outsiders call us here, but the real Semai live in the mountains.'" Had Dentan been Appalachian, he'd have understood immediately that Semai is the Malay equivalent of hillbilly.

Bibliography

Coedes, G.
The Indianized States of Southeast Asia. Honolulu: East-West Center Press.

Cunningham, Rodger
1987 *Apples on the Flood: The Southern Mountain Experience.* Knoxville: University of Tennessee Press.

Dentan, R.K.
1975 "If There Were No Malays, Who Would the Semai Be?" in *Pluralism in Malaya: Myth or Reality*, ed. Judith Nagata, pp. 50–64. Laiden: Brill.

Foster, Brian L.
1974 "Ethnicity and Commerce" *American Ethnologist* 1:437–48.

Fox, Richard G.
1969 "Professional Primitives: Hunters and Gatherers of Nuclear South Asia" *Man in India* 49(2): 139–160.

Garvan, John M.
1963 *The Negritos of the Philippines*, ed. Hermann Hochegger. Vienna: University of Vienna Institute of Ethnology.

Hall, D.G.E.
1966 *A History of Southeast Asia.* New York: St. Martin's Press.

Hoffman, Carl L.
1984 "Punan Foragers in the Trading Networks of Southeast Asia" *Past and Present in Hunter Gatherer Studies*, ed. Carmel Schrire. New York: Academic Press.

Hutterer, Karl L.
1974 "The Evolution of Philippine Lowland Societies" *Mankind* 9(4):287–299.

Lasker, Bruno
1944 *Peoples of Southeast Asia.* New York: Knopf.

King, V.T.
1985 *The Maloh of West Kalimantan: An Ethnographic Study of Social Inequality and Social Change Among an Indonesian Borneo People.* Dordrecht, Holland: Foris Publications.

Lehman, F.K.
1967 "Ethnic Categories in Burma and the Theory of Social Systems" *Southeast Asian Tribes, Minorities and Nations*, ed. Peter Kunstadter, pp. 93–124. Princeton University Press.

Meilink-Roelofsz, M.A.P.
1962 *Asian Trade and European Influence in the Indonesian Archipelago.* The Hague: M. Nijhoff.

Moerman, Michael
    1965 "Who Are The Lue: Ethnic Identification in a Complex Civilization" *American Anthropologist* 67: 1215–1230.

Morris, Brian
    1977 "Tappers, Trappers, and the Hill Pandaram" *Anthropos* 72:225–41.

    1982 *Forest Traders: A Socio-Economic Study of the Hill Pandaram* (London School of Economics Monographs on Social Anthropology 55). London: Athlone.

Peterson, Jean Treloggen
    1978 *The Ecology of Social Boundaries: Agta Foragers of the Philippines* (Illinois Studies in Anthropology 11). Urbana: University of Illinois Press.

Rousseau, J.
    1975 "Ethnic Identity and Social Relations in Central Borneo" *Pluralism in Malaya: Myth or Reality*, ed. Judith Nagata, pp. 32–49. Leiden: Brill.

Shapiro, Henry D.
    1978 *Appalachia on Our Mind: The Southern Mountains and Mountaineers in the American Consciousness, 1870–1920*. Chapel Hill: University of North Carolina Press.

Simkin, C.G.F.
    1968 *The Traditional Trade of Asia*. London: Oxford University Press.

Williams, Cratis D.
    1961 *The Southern Mountaineer in Fact and Fiction*, Ph.D. Dissertation, New York University. (University Microfilms facsimile, 1973)

Appalachianism and Orientalism: Reflections on Reading Edward Said

by
Rodger Cunningham

Here is a pair of quotations from a sociological work published in the 1960s,

> [They] so far have demonstrated an incapacity for disciplined and abiding unity. They experience collective outbursts of enthusiasm but do not pursue patiently collective endeavors, which are usually embraced half-heartedly. They show lack of coordination and harmony in organization and function, nor have they revealed an ability for cooperation. Any collective action for common benefit or mutual profit is alien to them. (Said 309–10)

> Thus, [he] lives in a hard and frustrating environment. He has little chance to develop his potentialities and define his position in society, holds little belief in progress and change, and finds salvation only in the hereafter. (Said 310)

These are not from Jack Weller or any of his fellow soldiers in the war on mountain backwardness. They come from the pen of the Israeli author Sania Hamady and appear in a book titled *Temperament and Character of the Arabs*. I am quoting them, with the occasional noun left out, from Edward Said's *Orientalism*, published in 1978. I had not read *Orientalism* when I wrote *Apples on the Flood*, but I greatly wish I had, for what I have just quoted is only one example of the striking parallels between, on the one hand, Western views of the Muslim East as analyzed by Said, and on the other the terms in which Appalachia has been viewed by scholarship and journalism since its first "discovery."

Other clear parallels lie close to hand. Just as *Orientalism* is, in Said's words, "a strange, secret sharer of Western anti-Semitism" (27), so stereotypes of Appalachians have strong affinities with stereotypes of blacks and Indians—and in each case, the resultant prejudice is the only halfway respectable outlet for such stereotyping in "enlightened" American society today. The student of Appalachia is also struck by such things as Chateaubriand's judgment that Orientals represented "civilized man fallen again into a savage state" (Said 171); or the American textbook which stated of the Middle East, "Few people of the area even know that there is a better way to live" (287); and in general the fact that, as Said puts it, "for no other ethnic or religious group"—I'm sure we can think of an exception—"is it true that virtually anything can be written or said about it, without challenge or demurral" (287). Again, when Said speaks of Islamic orientalism's "retrogressive position when compared to the other human sciences" (261), we need only think of how articles on Appalachia from the turn of the century were used as the basis for serious studies in the 60s, while books and articles from the 60s retain a popular and even an academic currency today which would be thought scandalous in the study of any other group. Or again, when Said speaks of the importance of travel accounts in establishing the image of the Orient (99), and the disappointment of later writers that the reality was different (100),and when he examines the use of such accounts to construct a picture of a "'cultural synthesis' . . . that could be studied apart from . . . economics, sociology, and politics" (105), the student of Appalachia is on familiar ground. And finally, when Said invokes the assumption "that no Oriental can know himself the way an Orientalist can" (239), we might well think of Rupert Vance's praise of how Jack Weller "came to know these people better than they know themselves" (Vance v).

And in both cases, the Oriental and the Appalachian, the underlying phenomenon is the same: a discourse of power, a way of seeing and talking about things which is conditioned by domination and which tends both to perpetuate itself and to perpetuate that domination. It is a way of organizing perceptions into a closed self-referential system which takes on a life of its own, shaping assumptions and perceptions even among those who are unaware of any motivation to oppress. My editors made me severely prune the use of the word "discourse" in *Apples on the Flood*, but obviously this is one of the main themes of the book. As Said says, "It would be wrong to conclude that the Orient"—or Appalachia—"was essentially an idea, or a creation with no corresponding reality" (5)—*pace* certain crude and ill-digested forms of cognitive dissonance theory. It is simply that one may legitimately take as an object of study not that reality but what is said about it, since the latter constitutes a "regular constellation of ideas" (5) which goes on "despite or beyond any correspondence, or lack thereof, with a 'real'"(5) region of the earth. It is a matter of how "texts can *create* not only knowledge but also the very reality they appear to describe" (94)—can "produce evidence that proves their validity" (239) in what has been called a "near bewitching self-verification" (M. McDonald in Chapman 206).

These qualities of discourse reflect a particular relationship between the author and the subject of the discourse. Since discursive relations are power-relations, in each case the powerful one of the pair is the writer, the other the written-about (cf. Said 308). The one is active, the other passive.

Hence the one is allowed to change without altering its basic nature, while the other is seen as static, as never really moving beyond some "classic" period (cf. Said 79 etc.). And in each case, therefore, the victim is then blamed for the static nature which is an artifact of discourse in the first place; the victim is seen as an example of "arrested development" (Said 145) in a scheme based on the dichotomy "advanced/backward" (207). Hence in each case, finally, the marginalized member of the opposition is neutralized symbolically as well as physically—deprived of self-explanatory power as well as physical power.

In this essay, then, I wish to explore the nature of this relationship in detail with respect to the parallel cases of Orientalism on the one hand and to our own concerns as Appalachian scholars on the other. I shall do so by examining two authors discussed by Said as part of the "Orientalist" phenomenon—authors who also had a large effect on perceptions of Appalachians' "Celtic" or Atlantic ancestors, cousins, and analogues. The latter form another group whose relations with "the West" have been problematic ever since "the West's" birth. The authors I wish to discuss are Bede in the eighth century and Ernest Renan in the nineteenth.

Bede, called "the Venerable," was born in the English kingdom of Northumbria in 673 and died there in 735. He wrote both on a "Celtic" Christianity which in his time was resisting assimilation to the Western Church in Britain and also on an Islam which was rolling that church back on the continent. Said mentions Bede only twice, and in *Apples on the Flood* I also have little to say about him; but as a common father of both sets of "Western" attitudes, he is worth a closer look here.

Bede stood at the beginning of Western civilization. He championed it at a time when it was still in the process of being synthesized out of the remains of Western Roman civilization and the culture of those Germans, including the English, who were Rome's former enemies, new overlords, imitators, and would-be preservers. Bede was born only three-quarters of a century after Christianity had come to the English from Rome. Just eleven years before his birth, the Synod of Whitby had mandated the union of the older churches of the British Isles with the Roman Church, but many areas were still in resistance in Bede's time and for long afterward. Bede, then, was separated by only a few generations from Germanic paganism and by only a few miles from "Celtic" schism. Furthermore, in his lifetime Islam conquered North Africa and Spain, and was barely turned back in the middle of France two years before his death. On his deathbed he prayed the Psalms in Latin, but among his last words were five lines of Anglo-Saxon alliterative verse about the unknowability of the soul's fate after death.

Thus in Bede's time, Muslims and "Celts" were both near, powerful, and threatening; and in consequence, he inscribes them both in a rhetoric of the adult, the male, and the negative. The Arabs to him were "sons of

Ishmael, whose hand is against every man" (Bede 347). Ishmael was, of course, the rejected son of Abraham, as Isaac was the accepted son and the ancestor of the Jews, hence of the "true Israel" of the Church. The Arabs indeed claim descent from Ishmael, while reversing the legend. Thus the quarrel between Christianity and Islam is imaged forth by Bede as a strife between siblings of different and disputed status but of equal manhood. As for the British Christians, their greatest sin in Bede's eyes is not any of their deviations on the date of Easter, the form of the tonsure, and so forth, but rather their refusal to send missionaries to the English—that is, to take on the duty of instructing their younger brothers in the wishes of the Father. It was for this reason, says Bede, that God allowed, indeed appointed, the heathen English to slaughter the Christian Britons (Bede 103–04). Since they have abdicated their fraternal duty and their paternal authority, their very existence is denied them, and their enemies, even when pagan, can be described in terms of Israel (Bede 92).

In all this it is significant that both Muslims and "Celts" are defined as schismatics—not as independent realities but as versions of the perceiver's reality (cf. Said 71–72). Thus, on the one hand, they are denied a reality of their own: their perceived reality is constituted by the more "basic" reality of the author of the discourse, namely Western Roman Christianity, which is thus discursively privileged above its neighbors. And, on the other hand, these marginalized neighbors appear all the more threatening, since they represent alternative modes of being which must thus be defended against with redoubled force. As R.D. Laing says, "The more one attempts to preserve one's autonomy and identity by nullifying the specific human individuality of the other, the more it is felt to be necessary to continue to do so, because with each denial of the other person's ontological status, one's own ontological security is decreased, the threat to the self from the other is potentiated and hence has to be even more desperately negated" (Laing 52).

Romano-Germanic Western civilization never really recovered from the trauma of Islam (cf. Said 59–60)—nor, as I have held elsewhere, from the threat of alternatives presented by Celtic/Atlantic civilization and its descendants—not even when "our" civilization rose enormously in power and complexity and came to dominate first the Atlantic world and then the Near East. The nineteenth century was of course the high noon of Western dominance, and it was also the high noon of the articulation of still-prevailing attitudes toward both "Celts" and Muslims. During this period another man who also wrote about both was Ernest Renan; and as with Bede, his writings on both groups possess striking parallels with each other, as well as instructive comparisons and contrasts with the attitudes of a millennium earlier.

Renan, best known for his iconoclastic *Life of Jesus*, was a "Celt" himself, a Breton. He wrote in a day when both "Celts" and Muslims were perceived as remote, weak, and non-threatening (or no longer physically threatening). Thus, in contrast with Bede, he describes both groups of Others in terms which are feminizing, infantilizing and quasi-positive; that is, in both cases he deals in terms conditioned not by overt boundary-defense, but by the kind of projection and appropriation which typifies those in a position of unquestioned superiority and which masks aggression in the terms of acceptance.

Renan perceives both Muslims and Celts, then, in terms of childhood. He sees the Celts in terms of his own personal childhood in Brittany, and of his mother in particular (cf. Chapman 82–83). He also sees Islam in terms of an "unaging 'gracious childhood'" (Said 306), and he sees Semitic languages as "a phenomenon of arrested development in comparison with the mature languages and cultures of the Indo-European group" (Said 145). Thus Renan constructed his feminized, infantilized "Celt" and "Oriental" from the part of the universe which was left out of his own adult male nineteenth-century rationality. In what Said calls "Renan's . . . peculiarly ravaged, ragingly masculine world of historical learning" (147), he felt a nostalgia for his mother's home (Renan in Chapman 83) and for whatever he could associate with it. But this was that sort of nostalgia which is not only compatible with, but contingent upon, the disappearance of its object, "Alas! It is also condemned to disappear, this emerald of the western seas!" (Renan in Chapman 85: my translation).

Thus we see two ways in which, in two historical moments of the West, two of its neighbor cultures have been dealt with on the level of the sign. In both cases, the threat presented by the alternatives is symbolic before it is physical, and in both cases the threat is neutralized semiotically before it is physically. In Renan, as in Bede, "Celtdom" and Islam represent alternative possibilities of being. In the intervening eleven centuries, however, the relations of power had fundamentally changed, as had the degree of self-definition of the West. These Others were not strong but weak, and therefore they were regarded not as adults but as children. Thus they were semiotically represented not as schismatic but as archaic: not as illegitimate offshoots but as arrested earlier forms—not as rejected brothers but as contemporary ancestors. And they were dismissed from consideration not by calling for crusades (these having long since succeeded) but by a quietly regretful acknowledgment that the archaic must yield to the progressive as childhood to adulthood. Thus the power-relation which assures the victory of Western might is paralleled by a discourse-relation privileging a Western rationality which *constitutes*, in the Derridean sense, its opposite numbers in Near East and Far West. This discourse, in Said's words, "failed to identify with human experience, failed also to see it as human experience" (328).

Yet it must not be forgotten that around, beyond and above the necessities of discourse, there are the possibilities of dialogue. Beyond the dichotomous vision of negations, there is the synthesizing and esemplastic vision which unites contraries. The two types of vision may even occur in the same individual, as in another example I would like to examine.

Another writer who dealt in images of both the "Celt" and the Oriental was W.B. Yeats, whom Said quotes three times, but in two sharply different contexts. Yeats bought into "Orientalism" and used it in his poetry and his occult writings much as he constructed elitist mystifications out of his own nation's history. The Appalachian poet P.J. Laska gives us a telling image of Yeats

> in the streets at night,
> when he walked in dreams
> from the mansioned gardens of the rich
> to the statehouse chambers,
> stumbling over bundles of rags
> which he took for wondrous spirits
> when he heard them groan. (Laska 163)

This strikingly dense image captures the essential problem with Yeats' attitudes toward the Other. This master of masks indeed mistook the garment for the body; and, having done so, he must needs perceive the real cry of the self as a sending from some fantasticized other world. The same image was used in a more unpacked form by Frantz Fanon: "The culture that the intellectual leans toward is often no more than a stock of particularisms. He wishes to attach himself to the people; but instead he only catches hold of their outer garments. And these outer garments are merely the reflection of a hidden life, teeming and perpetually in motion" (Fanon 223–24).

There was a valid core in Yeats' identification with Ireland: and yet the very energy of the identification was turned away by a mystifying discourse in order to strengthen defenses against the truly threatening aspects of the reality he touched. Thus, for example, though he knew the name of an ancestor who had fought at the battle of the Boyne, he always asserted that the latter had fought for King James and the native Irish, while in fact he had been on the other side, as one would expect from Yeats' Protestant background. This falsification of self-identity can stand for a whole array of failures of clear vision—a whole structure of mystifications beclouding the facts of oppression in this case and in many others.

Thus far for Yeats' romantic use of the imagery of his oppressed neighbors. But Said also quotes Yeats in quite another context. To wit, he Cites Yeats' line "the foul rag-and-bone shop of the heart" in appealing for a recognition of "the human ground ... in which texts, visions, methods, and discourses begin, grow, thrive, and degenerate" (110). The line is from "The Circus Animals' Desertion," a poem from the end of Yeats' life in which he repents of a career in which "Players and painted stage took all my love, / And not those things that they were emblems of" (Yeats 185). Thus Yeats himself, speaking in dialogue with his own self and in the name of his own genuineness, points the way to a particularism, an attention to the individual and concrete. Thus the heteroglossia of his poetic practice transcends the hieratic, monological discourse of his visionary theories.

We have seen then that Said's work on the image of the Near East bears important and fertile correspondences with the work which many of us have been trying to accomplish in the study of Appalachia and of the images by which this region has been interpreted. And there are parallels, too—or we may hope there are—in the careers of Said's ideas and of our own. Writing a decade ago, Said complained that Orientalist discourse went essentially unchallenged in the journalistic and even the academic worlds. If this is no longer quite so true as it was then, the difference is largely due to Said's own efforts. He lamented that the official discourse of Orientalism was rarely broken into by native voices answering Orientalist scholarship with scholarship from the inside. One could have said much the same thing about Appalachia at that time. But the same year that saw the publication of *Orientalism* marked the appearance of Helen Lewis' anthology *Colonialism in Modern America: The Appalachian Case*, which (though it has hardly attained the same degree of attention in the "outside world") has meant a great deal to the self-definition of Appalachia on the part of native scholars and students and to the delineation, from the inside, of the problems facing the region—thus breaking the near-monopoly of external and/or elitist views on the "problem of Appalachia." In both the Near Eastern and the Appalachian fields, these pioneering works have stimulated a great deal more such native analysis: and as a result, it is no longer quite so true in either case that virtually anything can be said without challenge.

Said's writing is sometimes said to be tendentious, axegrinding, and overdrawn. But often the real object of his critics' indignation, I feel, is that he is angry at all: and considering what he has had to put up with intellectually, professionally, and personally, that anger is hardly surprising. Again, the position his critics call "overdrawn" is one hardly drawn at all before his time, and certainly not with such learning and cogency. Personally, I like the quality of his anger, which is a function of his engagement, an engagement which energizes his work as I hope my own engagement does mine. In both cases, if what we say is personally colored, then I think it is so in an entirely positive sense—not as a projection of private resentments, but as a rational search for historic roots which can then be worked forward from again in a quest for solutions. On the flyleaf of my own copy of *Apples on the Flood* I have written a quotation which Said reproduces from Antonio Gramsci, "The starting-point of critical elaboration is the consciousness of what one really is, and is 'knowing thyself' as a product of the historical process to date, which has deposited in you an infinity of traces, without leaving an inventory. Therefore it is imperative at the outset to compile such an inventory" (25). This expresses precisely what I was trying to do in writing *Apples on the Flood;* and I hope that what both Said and I are grinding is not an axe but a lens—a lens for the examination and, as Raymond Williams says, "the 'unlearning' of 'the inherent dominative mode'" (Said 28).

References Cited

Bede. *A History of the English Church and People.* Trans. Leo Sherley-Price. 1955. Harmondsworth, Eng.: Penguin, 1968.

Chapman, Malcolm. *The Gaelic Vision in Scottish Culture.* London: Croom Helm: Montreal: McGill-Queen's UP, 1978.

Fanon, Frantz. *The Wretched of the Earth.* 1961. Trans. Constance Farrington. New York, Grove, 1968.

Laing, R.D. *The Divided Self: An Existential Study in Sanity and Madness.* 1960. Harmondsworth, Eng.: Penguin, 1965.

Laska, P.J. "Contrary to Appearances, Belief in the Master Race Is Not a Condition of Greatness in Poetry." *New Ground.* Ed. Don Askins and David Morris. Jenkins, Ky.: White Oak, W.Va.: Southern Appalachian Writers' Co-operative: Whitesburg, Ky.: Mountain Review, 1977. 162–63.

Lewis, Helen Matthews, Linda Johnson, and Don Askins, eds. *Colonialism in Modern America: The Appalachian Case.* Boone, N.C.: Appalachian Consortium Press, 1978.

Said, Edward. *Orientalism.* New York: Random House, 1978.

Vance, Rupert. Introductory note to Jack Weller. *Yesterday's People, Life in Contemporary Appalachia.* Lexington, University of Kentucky Press, 1965. v-ix.

Wallace-Hadrill, J.M. *Bede's Europe.* Jarrow, Eng.: G. Beckwith, 1962.

Yeats, William Butler. Selected Poems of William Butler Yeats. Ed. M.L. Rosenthal. New York, Macmillan, 1962.

Llewellyn and Giardina, Two Novels About Coal Mining

by
Laurie Lindberg

Nothing in the definition of regional literature as "an accurate representation of the habits, speech, manners, history, folklore, or beliefs" (Holman:373) of a particular geographical area suggests that a regional work is somehow second class, less valuable than a work with a more general or an indefinite setting. Yet we've all heard the term used as a pejorative, that writer is only a *regional* writer; that novel only a *regional* work.

The local color movement may be what initially gave regional literature a bad name. The works of popular local color writers such as Mary Murfree were characterized by sentimentality, by an emphasis on the grotesque or eccentric in character, and by a focus on obvious peculiarities with little insight into what went on below the surface of a people or place. Such local writing seemed to be the work of an outsider who invited other outsiders to observe and be amused by the peculiarities of the inhabitants of a specific locale.

Local color and regionalism are both forms of literary realism, but there is an important distinction between them. Whereas local color emphasizes the particularities, the idiosyncrasies of a group, regional writing points out "in the local and the particular . . . those aspects of the human character and the human dilemma common to all people in all ages and places" (Holman:373). Good regional literature has an application far beyond the region it claims to describe.

Two works that represent regional writing at its best are *Storming Heaven*, by Denise Giardina, and *How Green Was My Valley*, by Richard Llewellyn. The two books differ in a number of ways. *Storming Heaven* was published only last year; *How Green Was My Valley* appeared in 1940, almost fifty years ago. *Storming Heaven* is narrated by four speakers in alternating chapters, so the reader views the events of the story from a variety of perspectives; *How Green Was My Valley* is unified by having a single narrator and thus a more focused point of view. Giardina's coal fields are in Appalachia, mostly Eastern Kentucky and West Virginia; Llewellyn's valley is in South Wales.

Yet even the most casual reading of the two works reveals striking parallels. One explanation for the similarities is that both books accomplish what fine regional literature always does, they present what is universal in the human character and the human condition by means of particular characters in particular places. In that sense these books compare to all literary works that comment on what it means to be human in a specific time and place. There is another explanation, however, both books capture a way of life and delineate characters that have been significantly shaped by a mountainous land and by those who seek to profit from the coal that lies beneath it. Although thousands of miles and an ocean separate the Welsh valley in Llewellyn's book and the Appalachian coal fields in Giardina's, the regions as described in the two novels have much in common.

Land ownership is a basic issue in both places and in both books. Land means security, prosperity, power for those who own it. In the case of the Morgan family in the unnamed Welsh community of *How Green Was My Valley*, ownership of a house and land means stability. Gwilym and Beth Morgan are able to establish their house as a home for six sons and three daughters over a period of thirty years because the property it stands on is theirs. In the end, however, even land ownership means nothing when the land surrounding the Morgans' is sold to the coal company, which promptly begins dumping slag on the hillside above the house. Huw, the youngest of the Morgan sons and narrator of the novel, describes the destruction of his home and land by the slag,

> The slag heap is moving again.
> I can hear it whispering to itself, and as it whispers, the walls of this brave little house are girding themselves to withstand the assault.... But the slag heap moves, pressing on, down and down, over and all around this house which was my father's and my mother's and now is mine. Soon, perhaps in an hour, the house will be buried, and the slag heap will stretch from the top of the mountain right down to the river in the Valley. (101)

Huw Morgan is forced from his home because the coal company owns the land above his on the mountain.

In *Storming Heaven* land ownership is a life-and-death matter whenever a coal company wants a tract of land which the owner is unwilling to sell. When persuasion and intimidation fail, the companies are not averse to using stronger measures; for example, after the grandfather of one of the novel's narrators, C.J. Marcum, refuses to sell his property, he is murdered and his widow and grandson forced off the land. C.J. remembers, "Mamaw and me heard a shot. We ran and found him toppled over into one of the hives ... shot once through the head. Sheriff come around in three days and nailed the notice to vacate on our cabin door" (16). Families that have farmed their land for generations find themselves homeless, without ground to raise the produce and livestock that have sustained them, dependent on relatives for shelter. Loss of land means loss of security, even in the face of death. As Carrie Bishop, another of the book's narrators, remarks, "I feared we would lose the Homeplace some day. I tried not to think about it. ... But if there was no place of my own to be, no ground where my bones could be laid beside my kins', would I not be the most miserable creature in God's world?" (141) Both in Appalachia and in South Wales, land is a commodity precious for many reasons, but especially for its power to mark the difference between a sense of belonging and a sense of homelessness.

We see in both novels that when the coal companies take over the land, mining becomes the primary, sometimes the solitary, source of income in an area, and the hazards of mining become a fact of life for those who must go down into the mines as well as those who wait and worry above. The Welsh woman Beth Morgan is bravely matter-of-fact when she sends her husband and sons off to the colliery each day, but she never loses sight of the dangers they face. When her son Ivor is killed in a roof fall only days after the birth of his son and her husband reminds her that "The Lord giveth and the Lord taketh away," Beth refuses comfort and kindles her anger over his loss. When her husband dies under the coal some years later, it signals the end of more than her marriage; it signals the end of her faith, "'God could have had him in a hundred ways,' she said, and tears burning white in her eyes, 'but He had to have him like that. A beetle under the foot. ... If I set foot in Chapel again, it will be in my box, and knowing nothing of it'" (492–93). The necessity of death she can accept, but the thought of death in the mines is almost too ugly for her to endure.

In the West Virginia mines of *Storming Heaven*, the naturally hazardous job of underground mining is presented as even more hazardous because of the carelessness and criminal neglect of the owners. Vernie Lloyd protests when her husband wants to take their sons into the mine with him, but to no avail. Like Beth Morgan, Vernie is a wife and mother terrified for her men; unlike Beth, she reacts to the constant fear by detaching herself from her family. She becomes cold and distant, withdrawing from those she loves in order to protect herself from hurt. After the man with whom Rondal works is crushed to death in a roof fall; she tells her son, "I done lost you. Coal mine will get you sure. You're bound to git kilt. I seen it coming" (39–40). The anger that Beth Morgan turns against God Vernie Lloyd turns against her men—but in neither case can the mother protect herself or those she loves. Beth loses her oldest son and her husband in cave-ins, while Vernie's husband and youngest son are killed in an underground explosion. For the women in coal country, whether Wales or West Virginia, mining means horrible fear and grief.

The men are afraid, too, but their fear seems to be blunted by early, regular exposure to the hazards of their occupation. Leaving school at the age of ten to join his daddy in the mines, Rondal Lloyd tries to quell his initial fear of the darkness and confinement by reminding himself of the other children who must work in the mines to help support their families. But he remains afraid when he is underground, "I tried not to think of the mountain pushing down on us. ... The air was still and our breathing could not move it. The mountain pressed down, uneasy at the violation of its entrails" (35). Rondal leaves the mine, swearing not to return, but his desire to improve conditions for his father and brothers by starting a union brings him back. Eventually his fear eases to become what he describes as a "disregard for danger and even a mocking sort of courage. (He) would look up after the powder had blown and dare the son of a bitch roof to come down" (89). He comes to uneasy terms with the mountain.

Huw Morgan, like Rondal Lloyd, learns to deal with his fear of the mine, but he never forgets the sense of menace he feels when underground, and he shares Rondal's conception of the mountain as a creature violated. Watching his father die under tons of coal and rock, Huw feels a keen awareness of the earth as an entity exploited by men,

> ... The Earth bore down in mightiness. ... There is patience in the Earth to allow us to go into her, and dig, and hurt with tunnels and shafts, and if we put back the flesh we have torn from her and make good what we have weakened, she is content to let us blood her. But when we take, and leave her weak where we have taken, she has a soreness, and anger that we should be so cruel to her and so thoughtless of her comfort. So she waits for us, and finding us, bears down, and bearing down, makes us a part of her, flesh of her flesh, with our clay in place of the clay we thoughtlessly have shovelled away. (49)

Although Llewellyn does not emphasize as Giardina does the role of mine owners and operators in mandating irresponsible and unsafe mining practices, both authors deal at length in their works with the dangerous nature of a miner's work and the various ways people have of coping with their fear.

Another reality of life in a coal community is pollution, the damage done to the earth, air, and water by mine owners whose only concern is profit. The slag that eventually swallows up the Morgan house first shows its destructive nature down in the Valley. Surveying the site after some time away, Huw notices first of all the advance of the slag heap,

> Big it had grown, and long, and black ... on both sides of the river. The green grass, and the reeds and the flowers, all had gone, crushed beneath it. ... The river ... banks were stained, and the reeds of their dirtiness, ready to die of shame,

they seemed, and of sorrow for their dear friend, the river. (103–04)

The waste products of the local mining operations, carelessly discarded in order to save time and money for the owners, slowly but relentlessly destroy the once beautiful Welsh Valley.

In the hills of West Virginia, the same process of destruction takes place. The child Rondal has never known the creek any different from the way it is now, "black with mine drainage and raw sewage," but his Daddy recalls an earlier time when "The creek was clear as glass, and we used to git trout outen it, and bullfrogs. ... Now the creek won't run clear til kingdom come, I reckon" (24). Contamination of water in the coal camps, where the operators have built the privies too close to the water supply, results in an epidemic of typhoid. As the local nurse, Carrie Bishop treats the victims and presses for new sanitary facilities at the camp. According to the absentee owners, however, there is "no money in the budget for such frills," so the people continue to sicken and die. The condition of the air, too, is deplorable. When Carrie first comes to Vulcan coal camp, she comments on the quality of the air: "Clouds of black bug dust whipped through the streets, and when the wind was right, the sulphurous fumes from the burning slag heap above Hunkie Holler choked the air in the narrow bottom" (102). A coal operation wherever it is located invariably means pollution of the environment.

A coal operation also seems to mean dissatisfaction with working conditions and wages, and all too often violence is the result. Both Giardina's and Llewellyn's books focus on the causes of the miners' discontent, the efforts made to resolve differences peacefully, and the strikes and violence that occur when these efforts fail. In *How Green Was My Valley*, most of the mine owners are Londoners; in *Storming Heaven*, the owners live in New York or Boston. In both cases the absentee owners thrive while the miners struggle to survive.

Interestingly, in both books the community leader who encourages miners to fight for better wages and safer conditions is a minister. When reminded that his business as a man of God is the *spiritual* welfare of his congregation, the Reverend Mr. Gruffydd justifies his involvement in mining politics: "My business,' shouted Mr. Gruffydd, 'is anything that comes between man and the spirit of God. ... Let it not be forgotten that the Lord Jesus drove the money-changers from the Temple" (154). We see Mr. Gruffydd as a man who respects authority and teaches his parishioners to do likewise—until authority is proven to be unjust; then he counsels the formation of an orderly society, a union, to negotiate for justice. Mr. Gruffydd encourages the men to state their grievances boldly and to fight for their rights, and he helps them to keep up their spirits through the desperate days of hardship and strike, foregoing his own meager salary, collecting clothes and food for the families most in need, and presiding over the funerals of those who starve to death.

The Reverend Gruffydd has his counterpart in West Virginia in Albion Freeman, who goes into the mines in order to carry his message as a preacher to the men. Albion persuades the operators to allow him to hold Bible study meetings during dinner breaks in the mine, and prayer meetings at his coal camp home in the evenings. The superintendent recognizes the importance of religion in the peoples' lives and thinks that a minister will encourage the miners to accept their lot. Instead, Albion reads to them from the books of Exodus and Deuteronomy, preaching that the children of Israel should be delivered from their oppressors, that the first shall be last and the last shall be first. Albion and his flock study the United Mineworkers along with the Bible. Albion, like the Reverend Gruffydd, suffers along with the strikers, as hungry and cold as they. He preaches faithfulness to a just cause and faith in a God who will one day see his people to the Promised Land.

The goal of both Albion Freeman and Merddyn Gruffydd is to inspire their congregations to believe in themselves, as well as in God. The gospel they preach is not patience and submission, but battle for the glory of God. Even coal miners, they dare to claim, are entitled as children of the Lord to a decent life, which can be made possible only by humane working conditions and a fair share of the profits which the owners would prefer to hoard.

The owners and operators who would deny these rights to their employees are certainly motivated by avarice, but perhaps by something else as well—prejudice against the very people whose work has made them wealthy. In the first place, miners perform physical labor, which immediately lowers them in the eyes of the "upper" classes. After all, how much respect can be due a bluecollar—in this case, black-collar—worker? Also, the nature and setting of the work itself is hardly likely to lend the miners status. Coal miners spend their working lives underground in holes, like rats or moles, and even when they emerge into the light, they carry blackness with them. If cleanliness is next to godliness, then the miners and their families who live in the coal camps spend a large proportion of their time far from God. The work which makes their employers rich lowers the status of the miners, enabling the Boston owners of a West Virginia coal camp to refuse to improve sanitary conditions there, claiming that the typhoid is "caused by the filthy habits of the miners and their families" (105). A teacher at the National School in Wales can tell Huw Morgan, "Your dirty coal mining ways are not wanted here" (189), and a jealous housekeeper can refer to Huw's sister as a "slut" who is "fouling" her husband's home because she is a coal miner's daughter.

Not only by virtue of their association with coal mining, however, are the people in South Wales and Appalachia scorned by outsiders. The natives of both regions have been victims of stereotyping in their respective countries, and both novels illustrate the damage that such stereotyping can do. To the teachers brought from the city to educate the children in the West Virginia coal camps and to the mine owners from Boston, the people of Appalachia are hillbillies—dirty, backward, and stupid. To the Londoners who own the collieries in South Wales and to the teachers in the school across the mountain from Huw Morgan's home, the Welsh people are savages—dirty, backward, and stupid.

Criticism of a regional group often focuses on its dialect, and we see in *Storming Heaven* and *How Green Was My Valley* how the distinctive speech of a region earns its people contempt. The voices that we hear in both books are rich in regional accents, colorful with slang expressions and vivid figures of speech, so that we as readers are all the more dismayed to see how the speakers are made to suffer for their speech. Carrie Bishop is an amazingly feisty woman, but even she is defensive about her Appalachian dialect. When she must ask the help of two New York reporters in moving Rondal over Blair Mountain following his serious injury, one of the reporters mimics Carrie's accent. Although Carrie needs his help too much to show resentment, his mockery makes her self-conscious and defensive about her speech, even in a life-and-death situation.

In *How Green Was My Valley*, dialect becomes a crucial issue when Huw Morgan enrolls in the National School established by the English. The Welsh language is considered "jargon" by the teachers there, and as such it is forbidden. Being an older student, Huw usually remembers to speak only in English, but some of the younger children at the school who cannot remember are at the mercy of a cruel teacher who claims that "Welsh was never a language, but only a crude means of communication between tribes of Barbarians" (356). In order to impress upon his students the superiority of English over Welsh, Mr. Jonas uses a device known as a cribban,

> A small girl came through the door . . . with sobs to rend the heavens and shake her little bit of ribbon off.
> About her neck a piece of new cord, and from the cord, a board that hung to her shins and cut her as she walked. Chalked on the board, in the fist of Mr. Elijah Jonas-Sessions, "I must not speak Welsh in school." (348–49)

Huw flies at Mr. Jonas in a rage and beats him soundly, with the result that he is expelled from school. We see that anti-Welsh prejudice has been institutionalized in Wales, where the people are taught that their language and culture are inferior to those of the British, just as people in Appalachia have been taught to be ashamed of the dialect and culture that set them apart from the American mainstream.

A final similarity between the two books is a tone of regret, of sorrow over irrevocable loss. Huw Morgan mourns the destruction of his valley and the Welsh community that had once prospered there in peace and harmony. Although he takes some comfort in the thought that the people and land he loved will live in his memory, the fact is that the once beautiful Valley and a way of life have been destroyed. Nothing can restore them.

In Appalachia, too, Carrie Bishop learns the hard lesson "that there are forces in this world, principalities and powers, that wrench away the things that are loved, people and land, and return only exile" (61). Loss is natural, of course, and inevitable in a changing and imperfect world, but the kind and degree of loss suffered by the people in these mining regions after the coming of the coal industry is neither natural nor inevitable. As Rondal Lloyd remarks, "Progress is always at somebody's expense" (118). Giardina's and Llewellyn's novels about coal mining communities make us aware of the cost of progress—and lead us to conclude that the price paid in human suffering and wasted resources is certainly too high.

These novels are only "regional" works, but they speak to people everywhere of what it means to be human. The characters in *Storming Heaven* and *How Green Was My Valley* struggle against enormous odds, suffer grievous pain and loss, and in spite of everything maintain a measure of dignity and pride. Giardina's and Llewellyn's books are "regional" books that make a universal statement.

References Cited

Giardina, Denise. *Storming Heaven*. New York, W.W. Norton, 1987.

Holman, C. Hugh. *A Handbook to Literature*. Indianapolis: Bobbs-Merrill, 1980.

Llewellyn, Richard. *How Green Was My Valley*. New York: Macmillan, 1940.

Traditional Appalachian Culture and Traditional Scottish Highland Culture Compared: A Personal Perspective

by
Clyde H. Ray

Traditional Appalachian culture and traditional Scottish Highland culture have many similarities, shaped by a similar mountain geography which has determined their respective social systems, their folklore and poetry, and their isolation from and relationship to an outside world.

It must be granted that defining such similarities between two traditional cultures 3000 miles and over two centuries apart is a delicate and challenging exercise. Certainly, no one would confuse the McGregors of Dark Hollow in Haywood County with the 18th-century tacksmen of a Scottish chieftain, nor is there a likelihood that the spirit of the Bonnie Prince will step lightly from a laurel thicket on Roan Mountain. History is the art of alteration, as well as preservation. People, both as social units and as individuals, are made up of many contradictions, illusions, deceptions, and misconceptions. Political, religious, and social differences between the Highlanders of Scotland and America are too numerous to delineate. And to translate a Burns poem into Appalachian dialect is as major a transition and challenge as it would be to translate it into standard English, with the same deplorable results.

Nor is it impossible that a hypothetically equally good case could probably be made for comparing Sioux tribal society with the Basques of Spain, or Scotch-Irish history with the national experience of the Zulu. But the truth has many forms: the commonality of experience, geography, society, and economics, wherever it is to be found, does not negate, but rather confirms a common human experience. This confrontation of a common bond, a common experience, perhaps even a common fate between the two traditional highland cultures of Appalachia and Scotland is the focus here.

Keeping these restrictions well in mind, some common similarities between the two cultures nevertheless are definable. In both the traditional Highland and the Appalachian experience, territorial control revolved around a dominant extended family unit. Historically, the clan chief and the Appalachian patriarch both had similar responsibilities for the people. Both had an almost mystical right to their position by right of inheritance or tradition. Among their people, blood relationship and custom took precedence over other social or political ties. A noted European anthropologist expressed the idea succinctly: "for to be of the same blood is to possess the same vital principle and in this sense all who are of like blood make one single living being. It is in this that the clan relationship really consists."[1]

A rich oral history and tradition provided a basis of continuity with both peoples. Both cultures placed importance on genealogy and family tradition. Directed to meeting the social and economic needs of a predominantly rural people, family institutions and allegiances were stronger in the absence of the larger social, political, and corporate institutions of a more industrial world. Both have been affected by similar elements of change—roads and transportation, media, education, relocation of population, and economic development. And both provided a rich military resource for their respective nations.

It must never be forgotten that the Appalachian and the Highland extended family unit comprised the basic social unit of their respective peoples. Indeed, many Appalachian families are at least in part descendants of Highland families, and the family was the one vitally important avenue by which accustomed traditions and patterns of human behavior were conveyed from the old world to the new. A closer inspection of both social units demonstrates the same wide relationship of the individual members. For example, most Highland clans had (and still have) subsidiary branches of membership called "septs"—families related to the clan either by residing in the same territory or by blood connection along maternal lines. The MacDonalds had well over 100 septs not bearing the name of MacDonald but considered to be an integral part of the clan. Conversely, many extended Appalachian families also contain many members not bearing the family name but considered to be part of it, referring to those members as cousins or as relatives, rather than septs. It was through the family and not through any social program or restoration project that the culture was preserved. And it is through the family that even when relocated, whether to Nova Scotia or the Over-the-Rhine community of Cincinnati, that both cultures retain their Highland or Appalachian identity

It is obvious enough, even to the most casual observer, that both cultures developed a distinctive attire, music, dance, dialect, and folklore. It will not be the purpose of this paper to examine the many similarities or derivations in these areas, each of which is deserving of a separate paper of its own. But it should be noted that both cultures have also experienced a somewhat similar fate from the intrusion of a curious, but not always understanding or sympathetic outside world. Both have been stereotyped, caricatured, and over-romanticized. Both have been exploited for economic gain from both within and without. Both have been directly affected by an alien culture: the Highlanders by the English, the Appalachians by the mainstream American. Today, the most public display of both cultures is in similar types of social gatherings directed in part toward the outside observer: the Appalachian Folk Festivals on the one hand and the Highland Games and Ceileahs on the other.

And we would be less than honest if we did not also note that some of the most destructive elements of cultural exploitation resided within both cultures, and some of the most effective preservers of its traditions were found outside its limits. Perhaps the worst enemy of the traditional Highland culture was not to be found among the troopers of the Duke of Cumberland, but rather among the Highland chiefs themselves, who aided and abetted the worst excesses of the enclosure movement. And many an informed admirer of the most intricate and delicate modulations of Appalachian art and music has never climbed a ridge steeper than Beacon Hill in Boston. In both cultures, the enemy was found to be within as well as without.

The forces of rapid and irreversible change have operated in similar fashion on both the Scottish and the Appalachian highlander. The improvement of transportation—whether it was the building of Marshal Wades roads over the central Highlands in the 18th century or the improvement of major interstates in the Appalachia of the 20th century—has had the same mixed effect on the traditional culture of both regions. It is not only that traditionalism thrives in an isolated and parochial environment. Transportation provides rapid accessibility to social and cultural elements from the outside world as well as encouraging outmigration of the native people. Education, when it assumes a national perspective, tends to replace traditional values with those of a more rapidly changing world. Expanding media tends to impose a more standard, if wider, perception of an individual's place in the greater society. Any utilization for its own ends. It would be rash to place any value judgment on the universal end result of both trends, equally rash to determine whether improved social service is adequate compensation for a loss of identity and a sense of place. In the absence of final definitive judgment, there must remain only perception of what can be perceived: depressed economy, farmland rapidly reverting to wilderness, a proliferation of lodges and second-home development for vacationers from London or Atlanta. John Prebble, who is an Englishman, states that by the 19th century, the lowlander had inherited the hills and the tartan is a shroud.[2] To a disturbing extent, the Appalachian quilt serves much the same purpose.

For these reasons, the future for both the Highland and Appalachian traditional cultures appears to be a mixed one. Both will have to endure continued exploitation as entertainment resources for an audience increasingly middle-class, cosmopolitan, economically powerful, and indiscriminately the same. In this role, the man behind the bib overalls or in the tartan is less noticed for what he is than for what he seems to be—someone to be entertaining, to be observed, certainly to be photographed, but not really to be taken too seriously and to be kept somewhat separate from the greater mainstream or national society about him. The past collective efforts of society to eradicate or to civilize the Appalachian and the Highlander have been largely replaced by one of curious paternalism which, however subtle in application, can be yet insensitive and injurious to the fierce pride of a people with strong ties to land and identity. As we have seen, the people, the land, and the identity are all alike imperiled by undirected, even misdirected social and economic change.

But on the other hand, both traditional cultures—where they exist—continue to value their respective and common heritage. Both resist any connotation that their culture is inferior to economic concerns or to the more cosmopolitan and urban culture of the nation at large. Perhaps both will ultimately continue to value tradition more than innovation, knowing that there is something there, behind the sad, defiant cry of the pipes and the mountain fiddles that the family of man needs, knowing that, without it, there is the vague, lingering disquietude of incompleteness perceived.

Notes

1. Lucien Levy-Bruhl, *Primitives and the Supernatural.*

2. John Prebble, *The Highland Clearances.*

Subscription Form

Detach and mail to: Appalachian Consortium, University Hall, Boone, NC 28608. Please make checks payable to the Appalachian Consortium.

Subscriptions for the <u>Journal of the Appalachian Studies Association</u> are available through the Appalachian Consortium. The cost is $13.95 per copy with shipping and handling included. Orders will be kept on file with automatic shipping and billing occurring once each year unless cancelled by written correspondence.

Please enter my subscription for _____ copy(s) of the <u>Journal of the Appalachian Studies Association</u>. I understand that orders are on a bill-only basis with shipment and billing occurring annually for the number of copies indicated above unless cancelled by written notice.

Name _____

Address _____

City _____

State _____ Zip _____

Phone _____

Order Form
Past Issues of Applachian Studies Conference Proceedings

Detach and mail to: Apppalachian Consortium, University Hall, Boone, North Carolina 28606. Please make checks payable to the Appalachian Consortium.

Number of copies		Price
	Appalachia/America (2nd ASC)	$
	Critical Essays (5th ASC)	$
	The Appalachian Experience (6th ASC)	$
	The Many Faces of Appalachia (7th ASC)	$
	The Impact of Institutions in Appalachia (8th ASC)	$
	Contemporary Appalachia (9th ASC)	$
	Remembrance, Reunion, Revival (10th ASC)	$
	Subtotal	$
	5% N.C. Sales Tax	$
	Handling	$ 2.00
	Shipping is $1.00 per copy	$
	Total Enclosed	$

All Proceedings are $10.95 each.

Name_____

Address_____

City_____ State_____

Zip_____ Phone_____

ABBOTT, SUSAN
UNIVERSITY OF KENTUCKY
ANTHROPOLOGY
LEXINTON, KY 40506
606-257-2793

ADAMS, MICHAEL
NATIONAL PARK SERVICE
150 HWY 441 N
CHEROKEE, NC 28719
704-497-9146

ALLEY, LINDA
PIKEVILLE COLLEGE
CRUM, WV 25669
393-3000

ALLEY, MYRTLE
PIKEVILLE COLLEGE
CRUM, WV 25669

ALTIZER, ANNA
UNIVERSITY OF KENTUCKY
S-205 AG SCIENCE CTR
LEXINGTON, KY 40546
606-258-5989

ANDERSON, BILL
WESTERN CAROLINA UNIVERSITY
HISTORY DEPARTMENT
CULLOWHEE, NC 28723
704-227-7243

ANGLIN, MARY K.
LENOIR-RHYNE COLLEGE
PENLAND, NC 28765
704-765-4294

ARCURY, THOMAS A.
UNIVERSITY OF KENTUCKY
CTR. FOR DEV. CHANGE
LEXINGTON, KY 40506

ARNOW, PAT
EAST TENNESSEE STATE UNIVERSITY
BOX 19180A
JOHNSON CITY, TN 37614
615-929-5348

ASBURY, JO ANN
RADFORD UNIVERSITY
515 NEWBERN ROAD
PULASKI, VA 24301
703-980-5036

ASKINS, JUSTIN
RADFORD UNIVERSITY
DEPT. OF ENGLISH
RADFORD, VA 24142

ATHEY, JEAN
FRANKLIN AND MARSHALL COLLEGE
922 VIRGINIA AVENUE
LANCASTER, PA 17604
717-291-4231

ATHEY, LOU
FRANKLIN AND MARCSHALL COLLEGE
922 VIRGINIA AVENUE
LANCASTER, PA 17604
717-291-4231ry

AUSTIN, SONYA
RADFORD UNIVERSITY
COPPER HILL, VA 24079
703-651-3522

BABER, BOB HENRY
APPALSHOP, INC.
306 MADISON STREET
WHITESBURG, KY 41858

BADGETT, KENNETH
ROUTE 4 BOX 491
DOBSON, NC 27017
704-262-3633

BAGBY, JANE
UNIVERSITY OF KENTUCKY
APPALACHIAN CENTER
LEXINGTON, KY 40506
606-257-4851

BANKER, MARK T.
P.O. BOX 70
KINGSTON, TN 37763

BARBER, ELIZABETH
CITY SALEM SCHOOLS
SALEM, VA 24153
703-389-8523

BEAMER, EVELYN
GALAX HIGH SCHOOL
ROUTE 2 BOX 219A
WOODLAWN, VA 24381
703-728-2688

BEST, BILLY
BEREA COLLEGE
C P O 42
BEREA, KY 40404
606-986-3204

BIAGI, CAROLYN
W V WRITERS
249 PINE CIRLE
DUNBAR, WV 25064
304-766-8418

BICKERS, PHYLLIS
WEST GEORGIA COLLEGE
147 GRIFFEN DRIVE
CARROLLTON, GA 30117
404-836-6582

BLAKENEY, ANNE
EAST KENTUCKY UNIVERISTY
1221 DEE DEE DRIVE
RICHMOND, KY 40475
622-3300

BAKER, MOIRA P.
RADFORD UNIVERSITY
DEPT. OF ENGLISH
RADFORD, VA 24142

BANKS, JEANETTE
RADFORD UNIVERSITY
1020 GROVE AVENUE
RADFORD, VA 24141
703-639-4767

BARKER, GARRY
BEREA COLLEGE
C P O 2347
BEREA, KY 40404
606-986-9341

BELL, JOHN
WESTERN CAROLINA UNIVERSITY
MT. HERITAGE CENTER
CULLOWHEE, NC 28723

BEST, IRMGARD
BEREA COLLEGE
CPO 42
BEREA, KY 40404
606-986-3204

BICKERS, DOYLE
WEST GEORGIA COLLEGE
147 GRIFFEN DRIVE
CARROLLTON, GA 30117
836-6416

BLACK, KATE
UNIVERSITY OF KENTUCKY
APP COLLECTION
LEXINGTON, KY 40506
606-257-8634

BLAUSTEIN, RICHARD
EAST TENNESSEE STATE UNIVERSITY
BOX 19180A
JOHNSON CITY, TN 37614
615-929-5348

BLETHEN, TYLER
WESTERN CAROLINA UNIVERSITY
CULLOWHEE, NC 28723
704-227-7129

BLOSE, VIRGINIA
GALAX, VA 24333
236-2325

BOYD, CLIFF
RADFORD UNIVERSITY
ANTHROPOLOGY DEPT
RADFORD, VA 24142
703-831-5159

BREWIN, DAVID
WESTERN CAROLINA UNIVERSITY
MT. HERITAGE CENTER
CULLOWHEE, NC 28723
704-227-7129

BROSI, GEORGE
APPALACHIAN MOUNTAIN BOOKS
123 WALNUT STREET
BEREA, KY 40403
606-986-1663

BROWN, HARRY
EAST TENNESSEE STATE UNIVERISTY
WALLACE 217
RICHMOND, VA 40475
606-622-2102

BROWN, WILLIAM
HUME-FOGG ACADEMIE
GOODLETTSVILLE, TN 37072
615-876-4069

BURTON, THOMAS G
EAST TENNESSEE STATE UNIVERSITY
BOX 22, 990A
JOHNSON CITY, TN 37614
615-929-6668

BLEVINS, MARGO
318 HARPERTOWN ROAD
ELKINS, WV 26241
304-636-0068

BOUSQUET, WOODWARD
WARREN WILSON COLLEGE
701 WARREN WILSON RD
SWANNANOA, NC 28778
704-298-3325

BOYD, TOM
BEREA COLLEGE
C P O 65
BEREA, KY 40404
606-986-9341

BROGAN, MARY
WHITTIER, NC 28789
497-9452

BROWN, ALICE
UNIVERSITY OF KENTUCKY
641 S LIMESTONE
LEXINGTON, KY 40506
606-287-8269

BROWN, TRACY
WAKE FOREST UNIVERSITY
P O BOX 6363
WINSTON-SALEM, NC 27109
919-723-0593

BURNETT, KIMBERLY
RADFORD UNIVERSITY
ROUTE 2 BOX 66
MEADOWS OF DAN, VA 24120
703-952-2787

BUXTON, BARRY
APPALACHIAN CONSORTIUM
A S U
BOONE, NC 28608
704-262-2064

BYER, JAMES
WESTERN CAROLINA UNIVERSITY
CULLOWHEE, NC 28723
227-7264

BYERS, JUDY P.
FAIRMONT STATE COLLEGE
ENGLISH & FOLKLORE
FAIRMONT, WV 26554

CAGLE, STEPHEN
P.O. BOX 7244
RADFORD, VA 24142

CAHAPE, BETH A.
WEST VIRGINIA UNIVERSITY
MORGANTOWN, WV 26505

CAMPBELL, ANNE
UNIVERSITY OF KENTUCKY
KING LIBRARY
LEXINGTON, KY 40506
606-257-9386

CANTRELL, PAT VANCE
RADFORD UNIVERSITY
RADFORD, VA 24142
703-831-5630

CARDEN, GARY N.
CHEROKEE MUSEUM
118 CHERRY STREET
SYLVA, NC 28779
704-497-3481

CARPENTER, CLAIRE
APPALACHIAN CENTER
UNIV OF KENTUCKY
LEXINGTON, KY 40506
606-257-4852

CARR, MARGARET
EAST TENNESSEE STATE UNIVERSITY
BOX 22, 300A
JOHNSON CITY, TN 37614
615-929-4283

CASON, AJENA L.
BLUE RIDGE PARKWAY
ROANOKE, VA 24017
345-6214

CATRON, RHONDA
RADFORD UNIVERSITY
603 MADISON STREET
RADFORD, VA 24141
703-639-3528

CHADWICK, THOMAS
AUGUSTA COLLEGE
2333 CENTRAL AVENUE
AUGUSTA, GA 30904
404-738-6256

CHEEK, EDWIN R
MARS HILL COLLEGE
P O BOX 502
MARS HILL, NC 28754
704-689-2172

CHEEK, PAULINE
P O BOX 502
MARS HILL, NC 28754
704-689-2172

CLASEN, JONNIE
P O BOX 2405
CULLOWHEE, NC 28723
704-293-3998

COMPHER, KELLEY
RADFORD UNIVERSITY
RADFORD, VA 24141

COOK, WILLIAM H
EAST TENNESSEE STATE UNIVERSITY
BOX 19180A
JOHNSON CITY, TN 37614
615-929-5348

COX, L.J.
UNION COLLEGE
BARBOURVILLE, KY 40905
606-546-4151

COX, RICKY
RT. 2, BOX 135
WILLIS, VA 24380
703-382-8698

CROUCH, JEROME
UNIVERSITY PRESS OF KENTUCKY
201 CASSIDY AVENUE
LEXINGTON, KY 40502
606-257-8434

CULLEY, JOSH
EARLHAM COLLEGE
905 WINSTON PLACE
NASHVILLE, TN 37204
615-298-1476

CLELLAND, DONALD
UNIVERSITY OF TENNESSEE
SOCIOLOGY DEPARTMENT
KNOXVILLE, TN 37996

CONWAY, CECELIA
APPALACHIAN STATE UNIVERSITY
BOONE, NC 28608
704-262-2350

COX, JAMES
NEW RIVER COMMUNITY COLLEGE
ROUTE 1
ALLISONIA, VA 24345
980-1967

COX, PAUL
RADFORD UNIVERSITY
HILLSVILLE, VA 24343
703-766-3329

CRISSMAN, JAMES
ILLINOIS BENEDICTINE COLLEGE
LISLE, IL 60532
312-960-1500

CROUCH, KAY
CALDWELL COMMUNITY COLLEGE
1000 HICKORY BLVD
HUDSON, NC 28638
704-728-4323

CUNNINGHAM, RODGER
SUE BENNETT COLLEGE
LONDON, KY 40741
606-864-4178

DAVIDSON, JAN
WESTERN CAROLINA UNIVERSITY
MT. HERITAGE CENTER
CULLOWHEE, NC 28723

DAVIS, BETTYE
ROUTE 6 BOX 785
BLUFF CITY, TN 37618
615-538-7888

DAVIS, PEGGY E.
PIKEVILLE COLLEGE
PIKEVILLE, KY 41501
606-432-5013

DEAN, HARRY
920 HAYWOOD DR. NW
CLEVELAND, TN 37312

DEFOE, MARK
WEST VIRGINIA WESLEYAN COLLEGE
BUCKHANNON, WV 26201

DETITTA, THOMAS M
203 BOULDER BLUFF TR
CHAPEL HILL, NC 27514
404-536-3431

DEYOUNG, ALAN J.
UNIVERSITY OF KENTUCKY
ED. POLICY STUDIES
LEXINGTON, KY 40506

DICKERSON, LYNN
UNIVERSITY OF RICHMOND
518 GARDINER ROAD
RICHMOND, VA 23229
804-285-2270

DICKSTEIN, CARLA
WEST VIRGINIA UNIVERSITY
REG. RESEARCH INST.
MORGANTOWN, WV 26506

DORGAN, HOWARD
APPALACHIAN STATE UNIVERSITY
COMMUNICATION ARTS
BOONE, NC 28608
704-262-2403

DRAKE, JULIA
BEREA COLLEGE
100 VAN WINKLE GROVE
BEREA, KY 40403
986-4716

DRAKE, RICHARD
BEREA COLLEGE
BOX 2283
BEREA, KY 40404
606-986-9341

DUFFY, TIM
FRIENDS WORLD COLLEGE
#1242 ROUTE 8
ASHEVILLE, NC 28806
669-5693

DUNN, DURWOOD
TENNESSEE WESLEYAN COLLEGE
HISTORY DEPARTMENT
ATHENS, TN 37303
615-745-7504

DeYOUNG, ALAN
UNIVERSITY OF KENTUCKY
COLLEGE OF EDUCATION
LEXINGTON, KY 40506

ECKERD, STEPHEN T.
HEDGESVILLE, WV 25427

EDWARDS, CAROL L.
APPALACHIAN WRITER'S ASSOCIATION
SALEM, VA 24153
703-389-1604

EDWARDS, GRACE
RADFORD UNIVERSITY
P O BOX 5917
RADFORD, VA 24142
703-831-5366

EDWARDS, MICHAEL
RADFORD UNIVERSITY
603 MADISON STREET
RADFORD, VA 24141
731-1875

ELLEDGE, BARRY
APPALACHIAN STATE UNIVERSITY
ECONOMICS DEPARTMENT
BOONE, NC 28608
704-262-6121

ELLINGTON, LUKE
WAKE FOREST UNIVERSITY
P O BOX 8031
WINSTON-SALEM, NC 27109
919-722-3061

ENGLAND, RHONDA G.
UNIVERSITY OF KENTUCKY
ED. POLICY STUDIES
LEXINGTON, KY 40506

EVANS, DR DAVID
WAKE FOREST UNIVERSITY
ANTHROPOLOGY DEPT
WINSTON-SALEM, NC 27109
919-761-5276

FARLEY, YVONNE
RALEIGH COUNTY PUBLIC LIBRARY
P O BOX 1876
BECKLEY, WV 25801

FARR, SIDNEY
BEREA COLLEGE
BEREA, KY 40404
986-9341

FARWELL, HAROLD
WESTERN CAROLINA UNIVERSITY
P O BOX 528
CULLOWHEE, NC 28723
704-227-7264

FAULKNER, GAVIN
ROWAN MOUNTAIN PRESS
BLACKSBURG, VA 24060

FERGUSON, PATRICIA
PIKEVILLE COLLEGE
MATEWAN, WV 25678

FISCHER, SUZANNAH
RADFORD UNIVERSITY
RADFORD, VA 24141
731-3184

FISHER, STEVE
EMORY & HENRY COLLEGE
P O BOX BBB
EMORY, VA 24237

FITZPATRICK, LAURA
459 HAMPTON COURT
FALLS CHURCH, VA 22046
703-241-2218

FITZSIMONS, SHARON
1594 ARLINGTON AVE.
COLUMBUS, OH 43212

FLEMING, DAN
VIRGINIA TECH
306 WAR MEMORIAL GYM
BLACKSBURG, VA 24061
961-5121

FRIZZELL, GEORGE
WESTERN CAROLINA UNIVERSITY
SPECIAL COLLECTIONS
CULLOWHEE, NC 28723
704-227-7474

FULP-PARKER, GLORIA
APPALACHIAN STATE UNIVERSITY
SOCIOLOGY DEPT
BOONE, NC 28607
704-262-8724

GAVENTA, JOHN
THE UNIVERSITY OF TENNESSEE-KNOX.
DEPT. OF SOCIOLOGY
KNOXVILLE, TN 37996

GENTRY, JIM
SOUTHERN HIGHLANDS HANDICRAFT GUILD
P O BOX 9545
ASHEVILLE, NC 28815
704-298-7928

GIARDINA, DENISE
P O BOX 216
DAVID, KY 41616
606-886-6499

GIPPERT, JODY M.
RADFORD UNIVERSITY
RADFORD, VA 24142
703-731-7148

GLASS, MALCOLM
A P S U
CLARKSVILLE, TN 37044
615-648-7882

GLEN, JOHN
BALL STATE UNIVERSITY
HISTORY DEPARTMENT
MUNCIE, IN 47306
317-285-8729

GODFREY, THERESE
WESTERN CAROLINA UNIVERSITY
P O BOX 2439
CULLOWHEE, NC 28723
704-293-3044

GOODWIN, SARA
THE RIVER FOUNDATION
101 S JEFFERSON ST
ROANOKE, VA 24011
703-345-1295

GOSS, ROSEMARY
V P I & S U
204 HUMAN RESOURCE
BLACKSBURG, VA 24061
703-961-4784

GRAVES, GLENNA
UNIVERSITY OF KENTUCKY
3515 DANADA DRIVE
LEXINGTON, KY 40502
606-271-0886

GREENWELL, BETH
609A FAIRFAX STREET
RADFORD, VA 24141
731-1682

GUNTER, CHARLES
8 OKEECHOBEE DR
JOHNSON CITY, TN 37604
615-926-6788

HALL, KRISTI
APPALKIDS
68 PIFER DRIVE
DUBLIN, VA 24084
703-674-5411

HANCOCK, REBECCA
APPALKIDS
78 VEST DRIVE
DUBLIN, VA 24084
703-674-0179

HARDIN, SONYA
APPALACHIAN STATE UNIVERSITY
ROUTE 4 BOX 109
CONOVER, NC 28613
704-256-8087

HARRILL, ANNABEL
118 BLANWOOD DRIVE
BOONE, NC 28607
704-262-4507

GREENE, MARY
APPALACHIAN STATE UNIVERSITY
ROUTE 2 BOX 951
BOONE, NC 28607
704-262-5995

GROSE, SHIRLEY
SUMMERVILLE, WV 26651
308-872-6962

HAGA, NANCY K.
V.P.I & S.U.
418 MARLINGTON ST.
BLACKSBURG, VA 24061
961-4500

HALLAM, HALLIE LU
ROLLINS COLLEGE
WINTERPARK, FL 32789
305-646-2818

HANNAH, PEGGY
PIKEVILLE COLLEGE
DELBARTON, WV 25670
475-2450

HARMS, LOUISE
TENNESSEE WESLEYAN COLLEGE
112 HICKORY LANE
SWEETWATER, TN 37874
615-337-6150

HARRILL, EDWARD
APPALACHIAN STATE UNIVERSITY
118 BLANWOOD DRIVE
BOONE, NC 28607
704-264-4507

HARRIS-WOODSIDE, JANE
EAST TENNESSEE STATE UNIVERSITY
BOX 19180A
JOHNSON CITY, TN 37614
615-929-5348

HART, W A
P O BOX 752
ARDEN, NC 28704
704-684-7976

HATCHER, WILMA
2312 SPRING GARDEN
BLUEFIED, WV 24701
327-6626

HAYDEN, JR, WILBURN
WESTERN CAROLINA UNIVERSITY
CULLOWHEE, NC 28723
704-227-7112

HEDGSPETT, JOYCE
PIKEVILLE COLLEGE
ROBINSON, KY 41560

HELPER, MONA KAY
10108 TRINITY LANE
MANASSAS, VA 22110
703-335-1770

HINES, PERCY
ARCHIVES AND HISTORY
13 VETERANS DRIVE
ASHEVILLE, NC 28805
704-298-5024

HART, ALICE
P O BOX 752
ARDEN, NC 28704
704-684-7976

HASKELL SPEER, JEAN
VIRGINIA TECH
APPALACHIAN STUDIES
BLACKSBRUG, VA 24061
703-961-5874

HAWKINS, NYOKA
UNIVERSITY OF KENETUCKY
LEXINGTON, KY 40502
606-266-6374

HAYS, DIANA
APPALACHIAN MUSEUM
C P O 995
BEREA, KY 40404
606-986-9341

HELLER, SHARON
RADFORD UNIVERSITY
285 TANGLEWOOD DRIVE
CHRISTIANSBURG, VA 24073
382-1180

HERRIN, ROBERTA
EAST TENNESSEE STATE UNIVERSITY
BOX 22, 990A
JOHNSON CITY, TN 37614
615-929-6682

HOLLIMAN, MARY C
POCAHONTAS PRESS
2805 WELLESLEY COURT
BLACKSBURG, VA 24060
703-951-0467

HOOPER, ROSE
WESTERN NORTH CAROLINA TOMORROW
CULLOWHEE, NC 28723
704-227-7492

HORN, ROBERT W.
ALEXANDRA, VA 22314

HORTON, JAMES H.
WESTERN CAROLINA UNIVERSITY
CULLOWHEE, NC 28723
704-293-5448

HORTON, JANE S.
WESTERN CAROLINA UNIVERSITY
CULLOWHEE, NC 28723
704-293-5448

HOWE, BARBARA J.
WEST VIRGINIA UNIVERSITY
DEPT. OF HISTORY
MORGANTOWN, WV 26506

HOWELL, BENITA
7225 WELLSWOOD LANE
KNOXVILLE, TN 37909
615-974-4408

HOWELL, THOMAS
7225 WELLSWOOD LANE
KNOXVILLE, TN 37909
615-974-4408

HSIUNG, DAVID C.
UNIVERSITY OF MICHIGAN
ANN ARBOR, MI 48105
313-747-1545

HUNTER, HELEN R
3167 VENTNOR ROAD SE
ROANOKE, VA 24014
703-344-5093

HUNTLEY, JOY
157 MORRIS AVENUE
ATHENS, OH 45701
614-593-7524

HYDE, WILLIAM
CENTER FOR APPALACHIAN STUDIES
UNIVERSITY HALL
BOONE, NC 28608
704-262-4089

HYLTON, CAROLYN
PIKEVILLE COLLEGE
BELFRY, KY 41514
353-8123

HYMES, VIRGINIA
UNIV OF VIRGINIA-CHARLOTTESVILLE
ANTHROPOLOGY DEPT
CHARLOTTESVILLE, VA 22903
804-979-5381

INSCOE, JOHN
UNIVERSITY OF GEORGIA
250 WEYMANDA CIRCLE
ATHENS, GA 30606
404-542-2053

JELEN, TED G.
ILLINOIS BENEDICTINE COLLEGE
POLITICAL SCIENCE
LISLE, IL 60532

JOHNSON, BETH
MAXMEADOWS, VA 24360
699-6365

JOHNSON, JR, CHARLES
UNIVERSITY OF RICHMOND
MODLIN FINE ARTS
RICHMOND, VA 23173
804-289-8272

JOHNSON, TAMMY
PIKEVILLE COLLEGE
PIKEVILLE, KY 41501

JONES, ANN
CARSON-NEWMAN COLLEGE
1886 CARSON NEWMAN
JEFFERSON CITY, TN 37760
475-3166

JONES, LOYAL
BEREA COLLEGE
APPALACHIAN CENTER
BEREA, KY 40404
606-986-9341

JONES, PEGGY
PIKEVILLE COLLEGE
PIKEVILLE, KY 41501

JOYNER, NANCY L.
WESTERN CAROLINA UNIVERSITY
CULLOWHEE, NC 28723
704-227-7264

JUDKINS, BENNETT
BELMONT ABBEY COLLEGE
DEPT OF SOCIOLOGY
BELMONT, NC 28012
704-825-3711

KARNES, SHERRY
BEREA COLLEGE
C P O 1315
BEREA, KY 40404
606-986-9341

KEEFE, SUSAN
APPALACHIAN STATE UNIVERSITY
ANTHROPOLOGY DEPT
BOONE, NC 28608
704-262-6384

KEGLEY, GEORGE
TINKER CREEK LANE
ROANOKE, VA 24019
703-366-4607

KESSLER, CLYDE
A S A
106 P T TRAVIS AVE
RADFORD, VA 24141
639-5076

KING, KATHERINE
RADFORD UNIVERSITY
524 CALHOUN
RADFORD, VA 24141
731-3228

KIRBY, CHARLIE O
924 W OUTER DRIVE
OAK RIDGE, TN 37830
483-6005

KLINE, MICHAEL
MT HERITAGE CENTER
W C U
CULLOWHEE, NC 28723
704-227-7129

LANCASTER, PAUL
VIRGINIA TECH.
BLACKSBURG, VA 24060
703-961-5861

LANG, JOHN
EMORY & HENRY COLLEGE
EMORY, VA 24327
703-944-3121

LANIER, PARKS
RADFORD UNIVERSITY
BOX 5917
RADFORD, VA 24142
703-831-5269

LAPRESTO, BRIGITTE
PIKEVILLE COLLEGE
399 HAMBLEY BLVD
PIKEVILLE, KY 41501
606-432-5970

LAPRESTO, CRAIG
PIKEVILLE COLLEGE
399 HAMBLEY BLVD
PIKEVILLE, KY 41501
606-432-5970

LAWSON, GARLENE
PIKEVILLE COLELGE
PIKEVILLE, KY 41501

LEADBETTER, JENNY
RADFORD UNIVERSITY
WILLOW WOODS APTS.
RADFORD, VA 24141
731-0316

LEARY, SAM
APPALKIDS
ROUTE 1 BOX 373
RADFORD, VA 24141
703-639-0656

LEFLER, LISA
WESTERN CAROLINA UNIVERSITY
P O BOX 179A
CULLOWHEE, NC 28723
704-293-3100

LEFTWICH, CHRISTI
RADFORD UNIVERSITY
RADFORD, VA 24141
731-4845

LEWIS, HELEN
HIGHLANDER CENTER
ROUTE 1 BOX 270
DUNGANNON, VA 24245
703-467-2240

LEWIS, JOHN
BEREA COLLEGE
CPO 2298
BEREA, KY 40404
986-9341

LEWIS, RONALD
WEST VIRGINIA UNIVERSITY
HISTORY DEPARTMENT
MORGANTOWN, WV 26506
293-2421

LINDBERG, LAURIE K.
PIKEVILLE COLLEGE
PIKEVILLE, KY 41501
432-9379/2342

LITTLE, PAT
SOUTH MAYO TRAIL
PIKEVILLE, KY 41501

LLOYD, JAMES B.
UNIVERSITY OF TENNESSEE
KNOXVILLE, TN 37916
615-974-4480

LOHR, KAREN
APPALACHIAN CONSORTIUM
A S U
BOONE, NC 28608
704-262-2064

LUSHKO, RENE
WESTERN CAROLINA UNIVERSITY
P O BOX 1794
CULLOWHEE, NC 28723
704-293-3100

MACDONALD, FREDERICK
WESTERN MICHIGAN UNIVERSITY
SCHOOL OF SOCIAL WRK
KALAMAZOO, MI 49008

LIGHTFOOT, W E
APPALACHIAN STATE UNIVERSITY
ENGLICH DEPARTMENT
BOONE, NC 28608
704-262-2337

LINEWEAVER, DEBBIE
NEW RIVER COMMUNITY COLLEGE
DRAWER 1127
DUBLIN, VA 24084
674-3600

LITTRELL, ROBERT A.
LINCOLN MEMORIAL UNIVERSITY
EWING, VA 24248
703-445-4595

LOHMANN, ROGER A.
WEST VIRGINIA UNIVERSITY
SCHOOL OF SOCIAL WRK
MORGANTOWN, WV 26506

LOOPE, GLYNN
CENTER FOR PUBLIC SERVICE
COLLEGE AVENUE
WISE, VA 24293

MABBS, DENNY
ROUTE 1 BOX 332
OCOEE, TN 37361
615-338-2200

MALONEY, MICHAEL
APPALACHIAN PEOPLES SERVICE ORGANIZ
4139 KIRBY AVENUE
CINCINNATI, OH 45223
513-541-0064

MANN, RALPH
UNIVERSITY OF COLORADO, BOULDER
2814-16TH STREET
BOULDER, CO 80302
443-5435

MARSHALL, GANELL
ROUTE 1 BOX 228
ST PAUL, VA 24283
703-395-2582

MARTIN, LEAH
APPALKIDS
306 TWIN OAKS
PULASKI, VA 24084
703-980-7486

MARTIN-PERDUE, NANCY J
UNIV OF VIRGINIA-CHARLOTTESVILLE
CHARLOTTESVILLE, VA 22904
804-924-3855

MAXEY, DEREK
VIRGINIA WESTERN COMMUNITY COLLEGE
VINTON, VA 24179
929-4744

MCCLURE, PAUL
NORTH GEORGIA COLLEGE
ENGLISH DEPARTMENT
DAHLONEGA, GA 30597
404-864-3391

MCCRUMB, SHARYN
V P I
ROUTE 1 BOX 109
NEW CASTLE, VA 24127
961-7528

MARSHALL, DARVIN
ROUTE 1 BOX 228
ST PAUL, VA 24283
703-395-2582

MARTIN, E LEWIS
NEW RIVER COMMUNITY COLLEGE
SOCIOLOGY DEPARTMENT
DUBLIN, VA 24084
703-674-3600

MARTIN, MILES
S U N Y
1 BLAIR AVENUE
PLATTSBURGH, NY 12901
518-561-0844

MAUDE-GEMBLER, CYNTHIA
SYRACUSE UNIVERSITY PRESS
ACQUISITIONS EDITOR
SYRACUSE, NY 13244

MCCLANAHAN, HUD
WAKE FOREST UNIVERSITY
BOX 6191
WINSTON-SALEM, NC 27109
919-724-5550

MCCOMBS, DOROTHY
V P I & S U
UNIVERSITY LIBRARIES
BLACKSBURG, VA 24060
961-5069

MCCULLOH, JUDITH
UNIV OF ILLINOIS PRESS
54 EAST GREGORY DR
CHAMPAIGN, IL 61820
217-244-4681

MCCUTCHEN, GENE
UNIVERSITY OF TENNESSEE
1914 ANDY HOLT AVE.
KNOXVILLE, TN 37996

MCHONE, CHRISTIE
WESTERN CAROLINA UNIVERSITY
401 B HELDER
CULLOWHEE, NC 28723
704-227-4235

MCKENZIE, ROBERTA
UNIVERSITY OF KENTUCKY
424 LINDEN WALK #1
LEXINGTON, KY 40508
606-252-8676

MCNUTT, JOHN
JAMES MADISON UNIVERSITY
SOCIOLOGY DEPARTMENT
HARRISONBURG, VA 22807
568-6974

MELTON, SARA E.
RADFORD UNIVERSITY
DUBLIN, VA 24084
703-674-5863

MILLER, DANNY
NORTHERN KENTUCKY UNIVERSITY
2624 JEFFERSON AVE
CINCINNATI, OH 45219
606-572-5619

MILLER, JUDY K.
ABINDON, VA 24210
703-628-3760

MCGRIFF, JAMES H.
UNION COLLEGE
POLITICAL SCIENCE
BARBOURVILLE, KY 40906

MCKEE, GENIA
BEREA COLLEGE
C P O 1315
BEREA, KY 40404
606-986-9341

MCKINNEY, GORDON
WESTERN CAROLINA UNIVERSITY
HISTORY DEPARTMENT
CULLOWHEE, NC 28723
704-227-7243

MEADOWS, RICK
WAKE FOREST UNIVERSITY
P O BOX 7870
WINSTON-SALEM, NC 27109
919-723-5607

MILES, CELIA H
ASHEVILLE-BUNCOMBE TECH
3 CELIA PLACE
ASHEVILLE, NC 28801
704-254-1921

MILLER, JIM WAYNE
WESTERN KENTUCKY UNIVERSITY
IWFAC 272
BOWLING GREEN, KY 42101
502-745-5904

MILLER, SALLIE M
APPALACHIAN STATE UNIVERSITY
APPALACHIAN STUDIES
BOONE, NC 28608
704-262-2550

MILLER, WILBUR R.
STATE UNIVERSITY OF NEW YORK
AT STONY BROOK
STONY BROOK, NY 11794

MOBBS, REBECCA
ROUTE 1 BOX 332
OCOEE, TN 37361
615-338-2200

MOREFIELD, JOHN
EAST TENNESSEE STATE UNIVERSITY
ROUTE 2 BOX 303
ERVIN, TN 37650
615-743-8143

MOSER, ANN
RADFORD UNIVERSITY
ROUTE 2 BOX 251
BLUE RIDGE, VA 24064
703-977-1579

MOSER, MABEL
311 WILSON COVE ROAD
SWANNANOA, NC 28778
704-298-7640

MOSSER, REVONDA
712 JOAN CIRCLE
SALEM, VA 24153
703-389-0560

MULCAHY, RICHARD
WEST VIRGINIA UNIVERSITY
DEPT. OF HISTORY
MORGANTOWN, WV 26506

MITCHELL, GLENN
WARREN WILSON COLLEGE
701 WARREN WILSON RD
SWANNANOA, NC 28778
704-298-3325

MOORE, DALE
JAMES AGEE FILM PROJECT
316.5 E MAIN STREET
JOHNSON CITY, TN 37601
615-926-8637

MORETZ, RAY
UNC-CHAPEL HILL
ROUTE 2 BOX 514
BOONE, NC 28607
704-264-1989

MOSER, JOAN
WARREN WILSON COLLEGE
312 WILSON COVE ROAD
SWANNANOA, NC 28778
298-8971

MOSIER, PAUL
RADFORD UNIVERSITY
502 TYLER APT F
RADFORD, VA 24141
731-4204

MUENINGHOFF, ELAINE
UNIVERSITY OF CINCINNATI
CINCINNATI, OH 45255
513-732-5262

MURRAY, CHARLES M
UNION CHURCH
C P O 2332
BERA, KY 40404
606-986-3725

MURRAY, MARY ANN
BEREA COLLEGE
C P O 2268
BEREA, KY 40404
606-986-9341

McGRIFF, JOHN
UNION COLLEGE
BARBOURVILLE, KY 40906
606-423-2469

NEWELL, MARTY
UNIVERSITY OF KENTUCKY
NORTH FORK UNIT
WHITESBURG, KY 41858
606-633-0108

NORDEEN, ELIZABETH
MARSHALL UNIVERSITY
ROUTE 1 BOX 422
CHESAPEAKE, OH 45619
304-696-2357

O'DELL, JAMES
GREEN RIVER WRITERS
ROUTE 3, BOX 2
HODGENVILLE, KY 42748
802-358-9970

OBERMILLER, PHILLIP
NORTHERN KENTUCKY UNIVERSITY
5137 SALEM HILLS LN
CINCINNATI, OH 45230
513-232-2669

OGLE, VIOLET
PIKEVILLE COLLEGE
PHELPS, KY 41553

McGOWAN, THOMAS
APPALACHIAN STATE UNIVERSITY
NC FOLKLORE SOCIETY
BOONE, NC 28608
704-262-2323

NELSON, KEN
MAYLAND COMMUNITY COLLEGE
P O BOX 547
SPRUCE PINE, NC 28777
704-765-7735

NOE, KENNETH
BEREA COLLEGE
BEREA, KY 40404
606-986-7854

NORRIS, MONICA
APPALACHIAN CONSORTIUM
A S U
BOONE, NC 28608
704-262-2064

O'DELL, MARY
GREEN RIVER WRITERS
ROUTE 3, BOX 2
HODGENVILLE, KY 42748
502-358-9970

ODUM, SALLIE
BEREA COLLEGE
BEREA, KY 40404
616-986-9341

OLIVER, SCOTT
UNIVERSITY OF KENTUCKY
NORTH FORK UNIT
WHITESBURG, KY 41858
606-633-0108

OLSON, ERIC
APPALACHIAN STATE UNIVERSITY
APP COLLECTION
BOONE, NC 28608
704-262-4041

PABON, ALBERTA
P O BOX 1272
CULLOWHEE, NC 28723
704-293-9066

PARKER, AUDREY
ROUTE 5 BOX 658
BOONE, NC 28607
704-262-1844

PECK, THELMA
CUMBERLAND MT COMMUNITY SERVICE
ROUTE 2 BOX 541
HONAKER, VA 24260
873-7313

PERRON, JAMES
UNC-CHARLOTTE
333 S EASTWAY DRIVE
TROUTMAN, NC 28166
528-9847

PEYTON, BILLY JOE
WSWP-TV
BECKLEY, WV 25802

PLUMLEE, STEPHEN W.
MICHAEL BLACKWOOD PRODUCTIONS
251 W. 57TH STREET
NEW YORK, NY 10017

ORR, JOAN
MUSEUM OF THE CHEROKEE INDIAN
PINEY GROVE APT C
CHEROKEE, NC 28719
704-497-4447

PALMER, LOUIS H.
TRYON, NC 28782
704-863-2129

PARKER, CLINTON
APPALACHIAN CONSORTIUM
A.S.U.
BOONE, NC 28608
704-262-2070

PERDUE, JR, CHARLES
UNIV OF VIRGINIA-CHARLOTTESVILLE
CHARLOTTESVILLE, VA 22904
804-924-3855

PETERSON, THOMAS
ROLLINS COLLEGE
WINTERPARK, FL 32789
305-646-2818

PHILLIBER, WILLIAM
ROUTE 2 BOX 145
ACCORD, NY 12404
914-687-7175

PORTER, JULIA D.
1601 SPRING GARDEN, #516
PHILADELPHIA, PA 19130

POTEAT, JOEL R
APPALACHIAN STATE UNIVERSITY
A V SERVICES
BOONE, NC 28608
704-262-4080

PREECE, ANNA
PIKEVILLE COLLEGE
PILGRAM, KY 41250
395-5679

PURDY, RITA S
VIRGINIA TECH
211 WALLACE HALL
BLACKSBURG, VA 24061
703-961-6770

QUINN, CAROLYN
RADFORD UNIVERSITY
1090 CHESTNUT DRIVE
CHRISTIANSBURG, VA 24073
382-0091

QUINNETT, JOHN
ROUTE 3 BOX 13W
BRYSON CITY, NC 28713
488-3724

RANDOLPH, JOHN H.
FORT NEW SALEM/SALEM COLLEGE
SALEM, WV 26426
304-782-5245

RASMUSSEN, BARBARA
WEST VIRGINIA UNIVERSITY
224 WILSON AVENUE
MORGANTOWN, WV 26505
304-293-2421

PRATT, ELLIOTT
WESTERN CAROLINA UNIVERSITY
P O BOX 1508
CULLOWHEE, NC 28723
704-586-2827

PUDUP, MARY BETH
WEST VIRGINIA UNIVERISTY
REGIONAL RESEARCH
MORGANTOWN, WV 26506
304-293-2896

QUESENBERRY, RANDALL
APPALKIDS
P O BOX 212
HIWASEE, VA 24347
703-980-5854

QUINN-CARO, EDIE
WHITE PLAINS, KY 10605
914-949-7170

RAINEY, HARLAN H.
6026 WESTCHESTER DR
COLLEGE PARK, MD 20740

RANKIN, TOM
EMORY UNIVERSITY
556 GRANT STREET S E
ATLANTA, GA 30312
404-523-4931

RAY, CLYDE
WESTERN CAROLINA UNIVERSITY
CULLOWHEE, NC 28723
704-227-7492

READY, MILTON
UNIVERSITY OF NORTH CAROLINA
DEPT OF HISTORY
ASHEVILLE, NC 28804

REID, MOSIE
BLUE RIDGE PARKWAY
VINTON, VA 24179
890-6926

REIMAN, ROBERT E
APPALACHIAN STATE UNIVERSITY
GEOGRAPHY & PLANNING
BOONE, NC 38608
704-262-2651

RILEY, JAMES A.
PIKEVILLE COLLEGE
HUMANITIES DEPT.
PIKEVILLE, KY 41501

ROBERTSON, DOT J.
SIX MILE, SC 29682
803-868-2591

ROGERS, ANNE
WESTERN CAROLINA UNIVERSITY
ANTHROPOLOGY DEPT.
CULLOWHEE, NC 28723
704-227-7268

ROSEBERRY, HELEN
EAST TENNESSEE STATE UNIVERSITY
BOX 22, 300A
JOHNSON CITY, TN 37614
615-929-4392

REID, HERBERT
UNIVERSITY OF KENTUCKY
LEXINGTON, KY 40506
606-257-2709

REIHMAN, ANN
EMORY & HENRY COLLEGE
247 PLEASANT VIEW DR
EMORY, VA 24327
628-2651

RICHMAN, L K
VA HIGHLANDS COMMUNITY COLLEGE
247 PLEASANTVIEW DR
ABINGDON, VA 24210
703-628-6094

ROBERTS, SAM
TENNESSEE WESLEYAN COLLEGE
DEPT. OF RELIGION
ATHENS, TN 37303

ROBINSON, BETH
WAKE FOREST UNIVERSITY
P O BOX 6865
WINSTON-SALEM, NC 27109
919-761-5695

ROGOSIN, DONN
WSWP-TV
111 WHITE AVENUE
BECKLEY, WV 25801
304-255-1501

ROSS, CARL A
APPALACHIAN STATE UNIVERSITY
APPALACHIAN STUDIES
BOONE, NC 28608
704-262-4089

ROSS CHARLOTTE
APPALACHIAN STATE UNIVERSITY
410 PINNACLE DRIVE
BOONE, NC 28607
704-264-8989

SALSTROM, PAUL
BRANDEIS UNIVERSITY
HISTORY DEPARTMENT
WALTHAM, MA 02154
617-891-8496

SAWN, PATRICIA
426 E 12TH STRET
BLOOMINGTON, IN 47401
812-333-6276

SELLERS, BETTIE
YOUNG HARRIS COLLEGE
YOUN HARRIS, GA 30582
404-379-3111

SHARP, GEORGE W.
RADFORD UNIVERSITY
RADFORD, VA 24142
703-731-6903

SHEEPPARD, GWEN
WESTERN NORTH CAROLINA TOMORROW
WAYNESVILLE, NC 28723
704-227-7492

SHIFFLETT, PEGGY
RADFORD UNIVERSITY
SOCIOLOGY DEPARTMENT
RADFORD, VA 24142
703-831-5857

RUDOLPH, DEBORAH
APPALACHIAN STATE UNIVERSITY
805 EAST KING STREET
BOONE, NC 28607
704-262-1440

SAUNDERS, CYNTHIA
ROUTE 1 BOX 185
WILLIA, VA 24380
703-789-7278

SCANCARELLI, JANINE
UNIVERSITY OF KENTUCKY
ENGLISH DEPARTMENT
LEXINGTON, KY 40506
606-257-6987

SEMONES, KARON
HOLLINS COLLEGE
ROANOKE, VA 24019
703-563-1466

SHARP, SHARON
FREELANCE EDITOR & WRITER
P O BOX 3345
BOONE, NC 28607
704-264-6870

SHEPPARD, TRACIE
PIKEVILLE COLLEGE
DELBARTON, WV 25670

SHIRLEY, PATRICIA
1431 CHEROKEE TRAIL
KNOXVILLE, TN 37920
615-573-5081

SHOOK, JANE
APPALACHIAN CONSORTIUM
A S U
BOONE, NC 28608
704-262-2064

SIMMONS, KIM
WAKE FOREST UNIVERSITY
REY STREET
WINSTON-SALEM, NC 27109
919-724-5039

SIMPKINS, KAREN LI
MARSHALL UNIVERSITY
DEPT. OF SOCIOLOGY/
HUNTINGTON, WV 25701
304-696-2793

SLUSHER, ALICE
ROUTE 2 BOX 613
FLOYD, VA 24091
703-789-7311

SMITH, BETTY N
475 BLUFF ROAD
HOT SPRINGS, NC 28743
704-622-3381

SMITH, JEFF
UNIVERSITY OF MICHIGAN
ANN ARBOR, MI 48104
313-763-1460

SPEER, ALLEN
LEES-MCRAE COLLEGE
BOX 128
BANNER ELK, NC 28604
704-898-5241

SHORT, EVA
APPALKIDS
ROUTE 1 BOX 122-D
DUBLIN, VA 24084
703-674-1260

SIMPKINS, CHRIS
NEW RIVER CC
DUBLIN, VA 24084
674-3607

SINCLAIR, BENNIE LEE
CLEVELAND, SC 29635
803-836-8489

SMALLEY, LORRAINE
WESTERN CAROLINA UNIVERSITY
P O BOX 1174
CULLOWHEE, NC 28723
704-293-3498

SMITH, DIXIE
W V WRITER'S
1025 GREENLAND
CHARLESTON, WV 25309
304-766-8002

SPALDING, SUSAN
EAST TENNESSEE STATE UNIVERSITY
BOX 19180A
JOHNSON CITY, TN 37614
615-929-5348

SPENCER, DEBORAH
1223 HANEY
SOUTH BEND, IN 46613
219-232-3330

SPRAGUE, STUART
MOREHEAD STATE UNIVERSITY
U P O 846
MOREHEAD, KY 40351
606-784-7416

STANWITZ, SANDRA
RADFORD UNIVERSITY
MAXMEADOWS, VA 24360
699-6365

STEELE, PAUL
P O BOX 3485
RADFORD, VA 24143
703-639-6383

STEVENS, BERNICE A
ROUTE 3 BOX 963
GATLINBURG, TN 37738
615-436-4512

STINGEL, RENATE
PIKEVILLE COLLEGE
PIKEVILLE, KY 41501

STIPES, KAREN
BLACKSBURG HIGH SCHOOL
BLACKSBURG, VA 24060

STONE, CONSTANCE
1549 WANAGA WAY
SALEM, VA 24153
703-389-1923

STAMM, HENRY E
APPALACHIAN STATE UNIVERSITY
ROUTE 1 BOX 196-A
BANNER ELK, NC 28604
704-898-9265

STARNES, BOBBY
HARVARD EDUCATIONAL
13 APPIAN WAY
CAMBRIDGE, MA 02138
617-495-3432

STEELE, ROBERTA
P O BOX 3485 FSS
RADFORD, VA 24143
703-639-6383

STEVENS, ELIZABETH
APPALACHIAN STATE UNIVERSITY
BOX 747
VALLE CRUCIS, NC 28691
704-264-7986

STINTON-GLEN, KATHY LEA
BALL STATE UNIVERSITY
1409 W WASHINGTON
MUNCIE, IN 47303
317-282-0976

STITZEL, JUDITH
WEST VIRGINIA UNIVERSITY
CTR. FOR WOMEN'S ST.
MORGANTOWN, WV 26505

STONE, JAMES W.
DAVIS & ELKINS COLLEGE
SOCIOLOGY DEPT.
ELKINS, WV 26241

STRAW, RICHARD
RADFORD UNIVERSITY
BOX 5764
RADFORD, VA 24142
703-831-5873

STURGILL, CAROLYN H.
APPALSHOP, INC.
WHITESBURG, KY 41858
606-633-0108

SULLIVAN, KEN
W.V. DEPT. OF CULTURE AND HISTORY
CHARLESTON, WV 25314
304-348-0220

SUTTON, DAVID
APPALACHIAN STATE UNIVERSITY
CTR. FOR APPALACHIAN
BOONE, NC 28608

SUTTON CAHOON, JAME
QUINN PUBLISHING COMPANY
231 UPPER HERRON RD
WEAVERVILLE, NC 28787
704-645-5770

SWART, SHEILA
RADFORD UNIVERSITY
1207C CLEMENT ST.
RADFORD, VA 24141

TAUL, GLEN E.
UNIVERSITY OF KENTUCKY
CHRISTIAN APPALACHIA
LANCASTER, KY 40446
606-792-3051

TAYLOR, JOHN C
UNION COLLEGE
BOX 463
BARBOURVILLE, KY 40906
606-546-4151

TAYLOR, JOHN C .
UNIONCOLLEGE
DEPT. OF HISTORY
BARBOURVILLE, KY 40906

TENNEY, NOEL W.
FORT NEW SALEM/SALEM COLLEGE
SALEM, WV 26426
304-782-5245

THOMAS, NORMA
EAST TENNESSEE STATE UNIVERSITY
BOX 22, 450A
JOHNSON CITY, TN 37614
615-929-6690

THOMPSON, DEBORAH
APPALACHIAN STATE UNIVERSITY
P O BOX 566 DT5
BOONE, NC 28607
704-262-4089

THOMPSON, EDGAR H
EMORY & HENRY COLLEGE
NEFF EDUCATION CTR
EMORY, VA 24327
703-944-3121

THOMPSON, JIM
RADFORD UNIVERSITY
P O BOX 2545
CHRISTIANSBURG, VA 24073
382-8450

THOMPSON, NANCY
335 ELLISON AVENUE
BECKLEY, WV 25801
252-7679

THOMPSON, RENIA
RADFORD UNIVERSITY
CHRISTIANSBURG, VA 24073
382-8450

TIMM, PAT
UNIVERSITY OF CINCINNATI
4450 ERIC AVENUE
CINCINNATI, OH 45227
271-9539

TITON, JEFF
BROWN UNIVERSITY
MUSIC DEPARTMENT
PROVIDENCE, RI 02912

TREVINO, DIANA
7304 SCOTTWOOD AVE
CINCINNATI, OH 45237
513-761-9195

TRIBE, IVAN M.
RIO GRANDE COLLEGE
McARTHUR, OH 45651
614-596-4201

TUCKER, JOHN
WALSWORTH PUBLISHING CO.
MARCELINE, MO 64658
816-376-3543

THOMPSON, PAULINE
APPALACHIAN CONSORTIUM
100 ORCHARD DRIVE
BOONE, NC 28607
704-262-1979

THORN, WILLIAM
UNIVERSITY OF RICHMOND
1601 WILMINGTON AVE
RICHMOND, VA 23227
804-353-9363

TIPTON GRAY, AMY
CALDWELL COMMUNITY COLLEGE
1000 HICKORY BLVD
HUDSON, NC 28638
704-728-4323

TRESTAIN, CHARLENE
APPALACHIAN STATE UNIVERSITY
305.5 GRAND BLVD
BOONE, NC 28607
704-264-0247

TRIBE, DEANNA L.
OHIO COOPERATIVE EXTENSION SERVICE
017 STANDPIPE ROAD
JACKSON, OH 45640

TRIGGS, KATHLEEN
HARPERS FERRY, WV 25425
304-876-3641

UNDERWOOD, SHIRLEY
KNOX COUNTY SCHOOLS
ROUTE 12
KNOXVILLE, TN 37918
615-521-2413

WAGMAN, GENA D.
WEST VIRGINIA UNIVERSITY
DEPT. OF ENGLISH
MORGANTOWN, WV 26506

WAGNER, MELINDA
RADFORD UNIVERSITY
APP STUDIES PROGRAM
RADFORD, VA 24142
703-831-5159

WALLENSTEIN, PETE
V P I & S U
HISTORY DEPARTMENT
BLACKSBURG, VA 24061
703-961-5331

WALLER, ALTINA
STATE UNIVERSITY OF NEW YORK
DEPT. OF HISTORY
PLATTSBURGH, NY 12901
518-564-5220

WALPOLE, MATTHEW
APPALACHIAN STUDIES
A S U
BOONE, NC 28608
704-262-4089

WARN, SUEANNE
WESTERN CAROLINA UNIVERSITY
P O BOX 1174
CULLOWHEE, NC 28723
704-293-3498

WATSON, STEVE
P O BOX 753
RADFORD, VA 24141
831-5349

WAUGH, LILLIAM J.
WOMEN'S CENTENARY RESEARCH
200 CLARK HALL
MORGANTOWN, WV 26506

WEAVER, HANK
CTR. FOR APPALACHIAN STUDIES
A.S.U.
BOONE, NC 28608
704-262-4041

WEAVER, JOSEPH
ALLEGHANY COMMUNITY COLLEGE
CUMBERLAND, MD 21502
301-724-7700

WEBB, JEANETTE
APPALKIDS
ROUTE 1 BOX 53
PULASKI, VA 24301
703-980-1348

WEBB, JIM
UNIVERSITY OF KENTUCKY
NORTH FORK UNIT
WHITESBURG, KY 41858
606-633-0108

WEBB, VAUGHN
BLUE RIDGE INSTITUTE OF FERRUM COLL
FERRUM, VA 24088
703-365-4417

WEDDINGTON, MERETTA
PIKEVILLE COLLEGE
PIKEVILLE, KY 41501

WEINGARTNER, PAUL J.
UNIVERSITY OF KENTUCKY
LEXINGTON, KY 40508

WEINSTEIN, SHARON
NORFOLK STATE UNIVERSITY
ENGLISH & FOR. LANG.
NORFOLK, VA 23504

WELCH, ROB
EASTERN KENTUCKY UNIVERSITY
BOX 332A RR 2
BEREA, KY 40403
606-986-1042

WESLEY, CHARLES
SAVE THE CHILDREN
BOX 319
BEREA, KY 40403
606-986-3901

WESSINGER, CARROLL L.
LUTHERAN CHURCH IN AMERICA
WYTHEVILLE, VA 24382
703-228-4861

WEST, MARK
P O BOX 325
CHAPEL HILL, NC 27514
919-929-7436

WHEELING, THERESA
RADFORD UNIVERSITY
ROUTE 2 APT 88
RADFORD, VA 24141
703-731-1519

WHITE, BLAIR
EAST TENNESSEE STATE UNIVERSITY
BOX 22, 300A
JOHNSON CITY, TN 37614
615-929-4392

WHITE, DENNIS
APPALSHOP, INC.
WHITESBURG, KY 41858
606-633-0108

WIGGINS, EUGENE
103 JONES CIRCLE
DAHLONEGA, GA 30533
404-864-6439

WIGGINS, GENEVIEVE
TENNESSEE WESLEYAN COLLEGE
ENGLISH DEPARTMENT
ATHENS, TN 37303
615-745-7504

WIGGINS, JEAN
103 JONES CIRCLE
DAHLONEGA, GA 30533
404-864-6439

WILLIAMS, DAVID
AUBURN UNIVERSITY
1318 WRIGHT'S MILL
AUBURN, AL 36830
821-9864

WILLIAMS, DEAN
CENTER FOR APPALACHIAN STUDIES
P O BOX 9
TODD, NC 28684
919-877-5803

WILLIAMS, MAX
WESTERN CAROLINA UNIVERSITY
MT. HERITAGE CENTER
CULLOWHEE, NC 28723

WILLIS, JENNIFER
WAKE FOREST UNIVERSITY
P O BOX 7854
WINSTON-SALEM, NC 27109
919-724-2571

WINGFIELD, PATSY
CITY OF SALEM SCHOOLS
ROANOKE, VA 24015
387-2503

WOOD, SHARON
FLOYD HIGH SCHOOL
ROUTE 1
COPPER HILL, VA 24079
651-8353

WORKMAN, MICHAEL E.
WEST VIRGINIA UNIVERSITY
MORGANTOWN, VA 26505
293-3867

YARROW, MIKE
ITHACA COLLEGE
407 HANCOCK STREET
ITHACA, NY 14850
607-272-4943

YOST, GREG
WAKE FOREST UNIVERSITY
BOX 7683
WINSTON-SALEM, NC 27109
919-722-7654

WILLIAMSON, J W
APPALACHIAN JOURNAL
UNIVERSITY HALL
BOONE, NC 28608
704-262-4072

WILLOUGHBY, J. RONALD
RADFORD UNIVERSITY
RADFORD, VA 24141
703-831-5441

WOOD, CURTIS
WESTERN CAROLINA UNIVERSITY
MOUNTAIN HERITAGE
CULLOWHEE, NC 28723
704-293-7129

WORKMAN, JERRY
SAVE THE CHILDREN
BOX 319
BEREA, KY 40403
606-986-3901

WRIGHT, TONYA
PIKEVILLE COLLEGE
JENKINS, KY 41537
639-8407

YORK, J T
STONEVILLE HIGH SCHOOL
2600 DUCK CLUB ROAD
GREENSBORO, NC 27410
919-288-7285

YOUNG, RHONDA
APPALKIDS
ROUTE 1 BOX 302-A
DUBLIN, VA 24084
703-674-8754

ZAHORIK, PAMELA
EAST TENNESSEE STATE UNIVERSITY
P O BOX 21130A
JOHNSON CITY, TN 37614
615-929-6738

ZIPSER, ANDY
ROANOKE TIMES
P.O. BOX 2491
ROANOKE, VA 24010

ZIPSER, ANDREW
ROANOKE TIMES
ROANOKE, VA 24010
983-3352

www.ingramcontent.com/pod-product-compliance
Lightning Source LLC
Chambersburg PA
CBHW051059160426
43193CB00010B/1244